"This book is an essential tool for all professionals who apply evidence-based psychotherapies. It goes straight to the core of the ACT and all other evidence-based models: helping the patient to move in the chosen valued direction. It describes how to build flexible patterns of committed actions by creating and working inside a meaningful therapeutic relationship. As the therapist's actions are the quintessential element of the therapeutic relationship, it also carefully addresses the obstacles in his or her own committed patterns to ease the process with the clients. A must-have, -read, and -practice for every ACT and non-ACT therapist."

> —**Giovambattista Presti, MD, PhD**, psychotherapist, associate professor
> in the department of general psychology at Kore University (Enna, Italy),
> and president of the Association for Contextual Behavioral Science

"A must-read for ACT practitioners! The crucial importance of committed action is evident, yet it is rarely illuminated how this core process is interwoven into the entire model. Considering how committed action functions within the context of one's life can make the difference between intent and action, and Moran, Bach, and Batten give us the tools to do just that."

> —**M. Joann Wright, PhD,** peer-reviewed ACT trainer, and coauthor of
> *Learning ACT for Group Treatment*

"What a breath of fresh air! I highly recommend this original and much-needed book, which truly fleshes out the ACT model in a myriad of ways. If you think committed action is just goals, action plans, and problem-solving, think again. Committed action is an exciting and ever-expanding part of ACT, and the authors do a fantastic job of explaining the vast range of different interventions and strategies it covers, and teaching you how to quickly and effectively implement them. No two ways about it: if you've got stuck clients (and hey, who doesn't?), you need this book!"

> —**Russ Harris**, author of *ACT Made Simple* and *The Happiness Trap*

## *The Mastering ACT Series*

Acceptance and commitment therapy (ACT) is a powerful, evidence-based model that has been used successfully in treating an array of disorders such as addiction, depression, anxiety, self-harm, post-traumatic stress, and eating disorders. Written by renowned leaders and researchers in the field of ACT, the *Mastering ACT* series explores each of the six processes of the ACT hexaflex: acceptance, cognitive defusion, being present, self-as-context, values, and committed action.

Based in the latest ACT research, this series is designed to take complex theories and translate them into easy-to-apply skills clinicians can utilize in treatment sessions. Each book examines the theoretical aspects of a core ACT process, details how each process can be seamlessly and effectively introduced into therapy, and offers multiple techniques to enhance treatment outcomes and increase client psychological flexibility—the backbone of ACT. These books are essential tools for clinicians, researchers, students, and anyone interested in ACT.

*Visit www.newharbinger.com for more books in this series.*

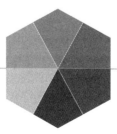

# Committed Action
# IN PRACTICE

### A CLINICIAN'S GUIDE TO
### ASSESSING, PLANNING & SUPPORTING CHANGE IN YOUR CLIENT

DANIEL J. MORAN, PhD
PATRICIA A. BACH, PhD
SONJA V. BATTEN, PhD

CONTEXT PRESS
An Imprint of New Harbinger Publications, Inc.

## Publisher's Note

Distributed in Canada by Raincoast Books

Copyright © 2018 by Daniel J. Moran, Patricia A. Bach, and Sonja V. Batten
        Context Press
        An imprint of New Harbinger Publications, Inc.
        5674 Shattuck Avenue
        Oakland, CA 94609
        www.newharbinger.com

Cover design by Amy Shoup

Acquired by Catharine Meyers

Edited by Susan LaCroix

Indexed by James Minkin

All Rights Reserved

Library of Congress Cataloging-in-Publication Data on file

20    19    18

10   9   8   7   6   5   4   3   2   1           First Printing

# Contents

CHAPTER 1

# What Is Committed Action?

Sofia complains to her clinician that therapy isn't helping her become the person she wants to be. After three months, she still doesn't have a job, she still lives with her parents, she hasn't lost any weight, and her English skills haven't improved. In addition, she is still depressed and anxious most of the time, and isn't sure she can change anything else in her life while feeling so depressed and anxious. At a casual glance, Sofia appears to be a dedicated therapy client, always arriving early to her sessions, completing detailed and neatly written behavioral logs between sessions, and able to articulate goals. However, when it comes to action, she frequently makes plans to do things, and rarely carries them out.

Sofia wants to move out of her parents' house and live independently, and she's acknowledged that she needs to earn an income in order to do so, yet she's been unemployed since she completed training as a dental hygienist two years ago. At times, she says that she really wants to earn money, and at other times she says that her parents owe it to her to take care of her. Further, she recently stated that because she's an immigrant from Mexico and speaks English with a heavy accent, she can't apply for jobs until she improves her English. However, when her therapist invites her to brainstorm about opportunities to practice her English, Sofia balks at most of the suggestions because she doesn't want to look stupid to others. She also reports that she believes she'll have more success finding a job if she loses weight. Every few weeks she announces that she has a new diet plan and describes in detail why she thinks this one will work. She successfully follows each diet for five to ten days, then abandons it, giving reasons such as "It's unbearable feeling hungry all the time," "This week was really stressful, and I just can't diet when I'm stressed out," or "It was my mother's birthday, and I had to eat the birthday cake my *tía* made for my mom. Since I broke my diet, I just gave up."

Sofia is like many clients in therapy. She wants her life to be different, yet she isn't entirely clear about how she wants it to be different. Perhaps more importantly, she's convinced that she must feel better before she can take action and that she can't behave effectively when she feels distressing emotions. She gives up easily when obstacles arise, and she isn't very open to exploring the multiple courses of action available to her. Sofia can sometimes describe what she wants in vague terms or articulate specific goals, such as getting a job; however, those statements don't serve as commitments with which she follows through. And although she can come up with actions she might take that are consistent with her stated goals, that isn't committed action either.

*Committed action* means engaging in behavior guided by personal values, even in the presence of unwanted thoughts or feelings and external hindrances that can impede such behaviors. Committed action is one of the six core processes in acceptance and commitment therapy (ACT). It is also both a process and an outcome of the therapy specifically, and of psychological flexibility more generally. The aims of this book are to aid clinicians in three key ways: developing and increasing a repertoire of interventions that build commitment; working with other core ACT processes to assist clients with committed action; and promoting values-consistent client behaviors in the service of psychological flexibility.

Take a moment to analyze the behavior you're engaged in right now: reading this book. You might be reading this book as a committed action in the service of learning, perfecting, or expanding your understanding of ACT to improve your ability to increase committed actions of your clients, or you might be reading the book because you're completing an assignment in a graduate course in psychotherapy. Maybe you're reading this book because a friend gave it a stellar review and you want to see what your friend was excited about. Alternatively, reading this volume might merely be an action in the service of passing idle time on a long flight or avoiding a more aversive task, such as washing the dishes. Your behavior, and the behavior of all people, is influenced by lots of different variables. Human behavior has many different functions, and we will explore that concept throughout the book. We hope you find that the time you spend reading this volume increases your clinical repertoire and flexibility in regard to applying ACT, no matter what the endeavor is in the service of.

# About This Book

We approached writing this book with an assumption that readers may have differing levels of familiarity with ACT. In order to minimize redundancy with content that's available in many other excellent books on ACT and its clinical application, and because the principal topic of this book is committed action, we've worked to balance adequate scope with sufficient depth. On the one hand, because ACT's six core processes are related, we must give considerable attention to all of them. On the other hand, in order to minimize repetition and stay focused on committed action, we've chosen to keep general discussion of the ACT model brief, summarizing or referring readers to other sources of information. Of course, in regard to committed action, we dive in deep and explore working with this process in ACT, as well as other evidence-based psychotherapies, and consider applications of committed action work to both clients and clinicians. We also provide brief case examples throughout the book, as well as detailed case descriptions as an aid in applying ACT and committed action techniques to specific problems and presenting complaints. We hope that, by the end of reading this book, the reader will have both a bird's-eye view of the importance of commitment throughout the therapy process and a close-up, detailed understanding of how to apply committed action interventions at discrete moments in session.

## What Are You Committed To?

Now we'll return to the issues raised earlier in regard to reading this book: "What is that in the service of?" We invite you to briefly consider what goals and values bring you to this book. Perhaps you hope to become a better ACT therapist, or learn new techniques to promote client behavior change; maybe you're reading this for a class, or maybe you have a large deadline looming and reading this book is nothing more than an avoidance strategy. Whatever brings you to this book, welcome!—and read on. If, by the time you reach the end of this volume, you have a better understanding of committed action, we will have successfully executed at least one of our commitments toward a valued direction.

## The ACT Model and Core ACT Processes

Before we delve further into committed action, we'll review all of the core ACT processes and consider each as it relates to committed action. The desired outcome of ACT is increased *psychological flexibility*, defined as "contacting the present moment as a conscious human being, fully and without needless defense—as it is and not as what it says it is—and persisting with or changing behavior in the service of chosen values" (Hayes, Strosahl, & Wilson, 2012, pp. 96–97). To put it another way, "individuals with greater psychological flexibility are focused on the 'here-and-now,' agile when dealing with emotions, and personally motivated to achieve significant objectives" (Moran, 2015, p. 26). The ultimate goal of most psychotherapies is behavior change. These definitions of psychological flexibility are all about action, and psychological flexibility is only apparent in actions in context. In other words, the behavior of the individual is understood when considered in the context in which it occurs.

Behavior change is hard. It does not matter whether a person is committed to losing ten pounds, learning a second language, reducing anxious avoidance, or learning to cope with chronic pain—all worthy goals require effort. Effort can be experienced as aversive. Losing ten pounds often requires effortful exercise and adopting a restrictive diet. Many people do not like those efforts and restrictions, so there are many people who continue to be overweight. Making a commitment to lose weight is difficult. The same can be said for the other aforementioned behavior changes. They require aversive effort, and some people are unwilling to have those experiences. The committed action piece of the ACT model helps to deal with those obstacles while building psychological flexibility. While committed action refers to specific behaviors in specific contexts, psychological flexibility is more general. The psychologically flexible person is able to use the core ACT processes to support the identification of committed actions and opportunities to engage in them, and increase willingness to sustain and overcome obstacles to behavior change in the service of values.

ACT is based on the assumption that experiential avoidance is a core problem in much of what is considered to be psychopathology. *Experiential avoidance* is a process that involves avoiding unwanted thoughts, emotions, sensations, and other private events, such as memories or negative judgments about oneself. In the short term, avoidance of these events often seems like a means to feeling good. However, there is considerable evidence indicating that attempts to suppress unwanted private events usually fail, and can paradoxically increase, rather than decrease, negative private experiences (Wenzlaff & Wegner, 2000). Thus, within the ACT model, attempting to control private experience is seen as a core part of the problem, rather than a solution. A detailed review of the ACT model is beyond the scope of this volume, so for in-depth information, please refer to the suggested readings at the end of this chapter. This volume offers a brief description of the core ACT processes to help you understand how committed action fits the context of the full ACT model. The six core ACT processes are acceptance, defusion, contact with the present moment, self-as-context, values, and committed action. The ACT model is often represented using a hexagonal diagram, as in figure 1.

Each core ACT process is represented by a point on the hexagon, and psychological flexibility—the desired outcome—is placed at the center. Because the hexagon model represents an attempt to build psychological flexibility, it has been nicknamed "the hexaflex." The lines connecting all of the processes with each other illustrate that they are all interrelated. Specifically, each process entails and facilitates the other processes. We may talk about them at times as if they are distinct processes, and specific ACT interventions might highlight one or more processes over the others, but multiple processes are almost always involved in any given behavior or intervention (Hayes, 2006). Now let's talk about the six processes.

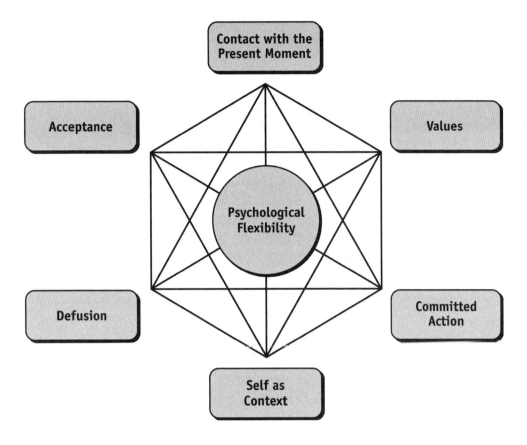

**Figure 1.** The ACT hexaflex.

## Committed Action

Jean-Paul Sartre (1963) famously observed that "Commitment is an act, not a word." Commitment is a fundamental aspect of ACT. In psychological treatments, committed action occurs when clients engage in clinically relevant behaviors that reflect improvement. The new or altered behavior is engaged in the service of the person's values and without entanglement with the person's problematic thoughts, unhelpful rules, or other verbal events. The committed action happens while the client is in contact with the present moment, and the person is accepting of the physiological and emotional responses elicited in that context. In such situations, clients have a better platform from which to take steps toward clinical improvement. Countless behaviors can constitute committed action: A client with social anxiety disorder might interact with others more often. A client who values spending time with his family might commit to a regular date night with his wife, attending his daughter's soccer games, and helping his son with his homework. A client with obsessive-compulsive disorder might engage in exposure and response prevention (also known as exposure and *ritual* prevention—the terms will be used interchangeably in this text) therapy. A recovering heroin user might attend regular meetings of Narcotics Anonymous, take the opioid agonist drug naltrexone, and identify and engage in activities she enjoys that support her sobriety.

Because committed actions are always tied to individual values, they are always selected by the client. The clinician's role is to work with clients to brainstorm and identify achievable committed actions while also identifying the potential barriers and ways to overcome those barriers. As alluded to just above, committed action is aided by and involves the other core ACT processes. We will touch upon these relationships in the descriptions of the other core ACT processes that follow, and we will explore these interrelationships more deeply throughout the book.

As you review the descriptions of the other processes that follow, we invite you to be mindful that although the word "action" appears only in the term "committed action," all six of the ACT processes are demonstrated through action. Westrup (2014) cautions clinicians that it can be easy to regard the core ACT processes as six separate things, rather than more accurately seeing them as interrelated abilities that ACT therapists work to cultivate in clients over time. At any time in session, one process or another might be especially apt for addressing a behavior in the moment. It is worth revisiting the idea that work on any one of the processes necessarily entails or facilitates work on the others, and promotes the overarching process of psychological flexibility. Now that we've discussed the committed action process directly, let's look at the other five processes as they relate to commitment.

## Acceptance

*Acceptance* means being willing to experience all the thoughts and feelings that show up in the course of living fully (Hayes, 1994), whether they are experienced as positive or negative, desirable or undesirable. Experiential avoidance is the opposite of acceptance. Trying to control or regulate private experiences such as thoughts and feelings reduces people's capacity to respond effectively. For example, clients with an anxiety disorder might avoid or escape situations that elicit anxiety in order to stave off unwanted thoughts and feelings. For such clients, acceptance might mean increased willingness to feel anxious when anxiety accompanies behavior that moves them toward desired outcomes. In order to facilitate acceptance, ACT therapists help clients explore their history, assess the potential or actual costs of unwillingness, and consider when acceptance might be a beneficial alternative. Acceptance is not the same as wanting or liking the feelings; rather, it reflects willingness to experience all thoughts, feelings, bodily sensations, and other private experiences, when avoiding them has negative consequences.

Attempts to avoid, control, or regulate thoughts and feelings can be costly. Focusing on unwanted experiences and attempting to regulate them takes time and draws upon limited attentional resources and stamina (Kashdan, Morina, & Priebe, 2009). For example, someone with social anxiety who's attempting to control her nervousness while giving a speech has a diminished ability to effectively give her speech. Avoiding unwanted feelings through inaction is also costly. For instance, a depressed client who has committed to go for a walk and contact one friend each day may find that he has thoughts that tell him, *There's no point in doing this*, or *Go back to bed*, accompanied by feelings of despair. He might avoid such feelings of despair by going back to bed. This creates a downward spiral, because when he gets out of bed, he's likely to have more self-denigrating thoughts, because he didn't follow through on his action plan. In contrast, if he's willing to have unwanted thoughts and feelings of despair and doesn't try to fight or avoid them, he'll be in a better position to successfully execute his plan. Thus, experiential avoidance hinders committed action, whereas acceptance facilitates it.

# Defusion

*Defusion* means noticing our thoughts as a natural private experience rather than being controlled by the thoughts as if they were literal truths or required guidelines for action. Conversely, *cognitive fusion* involves taking thoughts literally and relating to them as if they capture reality. When we're fused with inner content, we don't notice that the mind produces all kinds of thoughts, such as judgments, evaluations, memories about the past, and plans about the future. Rather, we actually let those experiences have an impact on our actions. When we are fused to certain thoughts that have little or no bearing on what's happening in the moment, we might miss out on important cues for valued action in the present moment.

In ACT, defusion techniques help clients see their thoughts as mere mind chatter. For example, a person fused with the thought *I am unlovable* might avoid spending time with others, have a negative take on neutral or positive experiences, minimize emotional risks, and behave in ways that keep others at a distance. In contrast, a person engaging in defusion might notice negative thoughts and self-judgments, see them as products of his own mind, and move on without taking any overt action to change the content of those thoughts. Defusion increases one's flexibility to act in the moment based on the events that are actually unfolding, rather than based primarily on what's going on in the mind. In this way, defusion frees clients to act on the basis of their values and their current environmental contingencies. However, defusion might be described as "simple, but not easy." Fusion is actually a by-product of language, and it isn't possible to remain defused from language at all times (Hayes, Strosahl, et al., 2012).

ACT therapists facilitate defusion through experiential exercises that aim to make clients more aware of how automatically most language processes occur, and by having clients practice noticing their thoughts as thoughts in the moment. Defusion facilitates committed action, because a defused stance allows clients to keep their focus on engaging in valued behavior rather than buying into judgments, evaluations, and other mind chatter.

## Contact with the Present Moment

Contact with the present moment can be fostered by mindful behavior. When people are behaving mindfully, their attention is fully in the present moment, and they are nonjudgmental and accepting of their experience (Baer, Smith, Hopkins, Kreitemeyer, & Toney, 2006). As seen through an ACT lens, contact with the present moment entails acceptance and defusion. It also facilitates committed action, as it increases people's capacity to see opportunities to act effectively and frees cognitive resources that might otherwise be fixated on the future or past, making those resources available for effective action in the moment. In many approaches to the practice of mindfulness, the person chooses a behavior (breathing, sensing the body, gazing at a candle, and so on), and then makes a commitment to continue focusing on that behavior. When the person gets distracted by thoughts or sensations or other private events unrelated to the commitment to pay attention to that chosen behavior, the person practices re-attending to that commitment by gently letting the distracting stimuli go, and reorienting attention to the chosen behavior. Mindfulness exercises are at their very core a skills building approach for engaging in committed action: you choose a behavior, you do the behavior, and when you stop doing the behavior because of external or internal stimuli, you practice changing how you related to the distractions, and come back to doing the chosen behavior.

This is an important skill for people to have, and even more importantly, this skill will hopefully generalize to other situations beyond when the person is sitting on a meditation cushion. From a behavioral science point of view, the skills learned during a mindfulness exercise can help a person to commit to attending to other things besides just the breath or a candle flame. For example, when a client begins to have a regular mindfulness practice, she might build the skills to be more attentive at the workplace, and if her occupational values influence her to choose to increase her productivity at work, her mindfulness exercise outcomes might help her notice an opportunity to take the lead on a project. If, on the other hand, her mind is occupied with the future or past, such as worrying about whether or not she'll still have her job in six months or mentally criticizing a comment she made in a staff meeting several minutes earlier, she may not fully apprehend opportunities for committed action as they arise in the moment.

Our minds are often focused on the past and the future, and this isn't necessarily problematic. In fact, it can be quite helpful to make plans for a trip to the grocery store later in the day, for a vacation that's months away, or for retirement potentially decades in the future. Likewise, reminiscing about the past may be enjoyable, and analyzing past behavior might reduce the chances of repeating a mistake. Still, because we can only carry out committed actions *now*—in the present moment—excessive focus on a feared future or a verbally constructed and evaluated past can interfere with attention to environmental contingencies in the present moment. For example, the chronic worry about the future typical of generalized anxiety disorder is associated with increased nervous activity and procrastination, and decreased problem solving and engagement in activities that are goal-directed or otherwise desirable (Roemer & Orsillo, 2002).

## Self-as-Context

*Self-as-context*, also sometimes called *self-as-perspective* or the *observing self*, refers to a sense of the self as being the locus from which events are experienced and observations are made. Put another way, the self is a context for verbal knowing, rather than the content of what is known (Hayes, Luoma, Bond, Masuda, & Lillis, 2006). The idea that language leads to a sense of self as a locus or perspective is central to ACT, and there is evidence that this sense of self is important to understanding others and cultivating empathy.

The word "context" refers to circumstances that form a setting for an event, or a place where things occur. A context holds content, while not actually being the content. When you look at a bowl of oatmeal, the bowl is the context for what it contains. The bowl is not the oatmeal. The term "self-as-context" implies that the self can be viewed as a place where events and things happen, such as feelings and sensations. Being able to come into contact with the self-as-context helps you view your own feelings and sensations as things, and to *not* identify those private events as who you are. This characteristic of being separate from your content helps prevent you from identifying with thoughts and emotions that might impede committed actions.

Contacting this sense of self is more likely to come from experiential learning rather than verbal learning because as soon as you start to label the self, it is just more content. It also accounts for why self-as-context is immensely difficult to talk about! This explains why self-as-context is often described as a transcendent sense of self: it transcends verbal discussion. Self-as-context is an important component of the ACT model because from this perspective, we can be aware of our ongoing experiences without attachment to them, and this awareness facilitates acceptance and defusion. ACT therapists build this sense of self through metaphors, mindfulness practices, and guided experiential exercises in which clients are invited to observe memories, feelings, sensations, and thoughts, and then to notice who is noticing those experiences. For instance, a client might notice a feeling of anger during a session. The ACT therapist could then invite the client to notice who is having that feeling of anger. This kind of noticing sets up a bit of distance between the self and the emotion, and can depotentiate problematic behavior that is provoked by anger.

In ACT, self-as-context is contrasted with two other senses of self: *self-as-content* and *self-as-process*. The *self-as-content* (also known as the *conceptualized self*) comprises verbal content and encompasses many of the labels we use to talk about ourselves, such as "I have two sisters," "I am a therapist," and "I come from California." Self-as-content does have some utility, particularly for allowing us to communicate with others. When you tell someone that you come from California, you might be about to generate interesting conversation or explain why you have certain habits or attitudes. The content of your life experiences can help you connect with other people, and it can lead to other important outcomes. For instance, when a person says, "I am a therapist" in certain situations, another person might offer him paid employment in her clinic. Describing your self-as-content is an important social skill. However, it can also be harmful, as when people become fused with negative self-evaluations such as "I'm a loser" or "No one likes me" and equate themselves with that content. When this occurs, an ACT therapist would help clients distance themselves from such evaluations, and can do so by having a client experience a self-as-context exercise.

The third key sense of self in ACT is the *self-as-process*. The word *process* refers to a series of actions or changes over time. *Self-as-process* refers to the series of actions the person is engaged in and the changing experiences the person is having. Self-as-process is similar to ongoing self-awareness, or noticing what you are experiencing in the moment. For example, being able to say "I am sitting in this chair," or "I am reading this book," demonstrates contact with the self-as-process. The clinically relevant issue comes up with the self-as-process when the client says, "I feel anxious," or "I'm stressing out about these compulsive urges." Teaching the client to contact the self-as-context through mindfulness or experiential exercises can help the client gain some perspective about the ongoing emotional processes he is having. This could reduce the influence of such self-as-process language, and help the client engage in valued behavior even in the presence of his anxiety, stress, or urges.

Self-as-context facilitates committed action because it increases awareness of ongoing experiences without attachment to accompanying verbal content, such as judgments and evaluations about the self. Contacting the self-as-context also promotes acceptance and defusion. For another example, consider an alcoholic client who's flooded with negative thoughts about herself and her ability to remain abstinent from alcohol whenever she attempts to stop drinking. If she can develop a stronger sense of self-as-context, she can more effectively manage urges to drink by noticing that although she has urges to drink and negative judgments about herself, a more fundamental part of herself isn't defined by her urges or self-judgments.

# Values

Values are often described as chosen life directions. Hayes and colleagues describe values as "chosen qualities of purposive action that can never be obtained as an object but can be instantiated moment by moment" (2006, p. 8). As part of values clarification, ACT therapists ask clients questions such as "What do you want your life to be about?" or "What is important to you?"

Values help set up the motivation to accomplish certain goals. Once you have articulated what makes life meaningful, you can develop objectives to accomplish to make sure you are living in a valued direction. For instance, when a person clarifies that he cares about making the world more beautiful, then these aesthetic values might influence him to plant a flower garden. He can actually complete the goal of growing daffodils in his front yard. When that goal is finished, he can continue to engage in other behaviors related to the value of making the world a more beautiful place. Values do not get "completed." To consider the distinction in a clinical context, a value might be "extending compassion toward others," whereas goals that instantiate this value might be "acting with forgiveness toward my son next week at Thanksgiving dinner," "volunteering at my temple," or "practicing loving-kindness meditation."

The distinction between goals and values is important clinically because although goals can be set and attained in the service of values, goals often highlight something that's considered to be missing from one's life. By their very definition, goals represent what we don't yet have and want to attain. In contrast, values are linked to larger patterns of action, and we can always act in the service of a value even while we haven't yet achieved related goals. In other words, although a goal of losing ten pounds, making more friends, or raising $5,000 for a charity may or may not be attainable in the near future, behaviors in the service of related values (such as taking care of one's physical health, being a good friend, or helping others) are always possible in the present moment. For example, the person with the goal of losing ten pounds can choose to eat a salad instead of pizza, or opt to go for a walk instead of watching television. These behaviors won't instantly result in substantial weight loss, but they are immediately actionable choices in the service of taking care of one's health.

Importantly, values are personal and freely chosen by the individual. Therefore, ACT clinicians help clients clarify their values without insinuating what those values should be. However, therapists may sometimes point out that all behavior is in the service of something; whether doing so with or without self-awareness, clients are always metaphorically moving in a direction.

Here's an example. Consider a client who's enrolled in college and *says* she values learning, but she belies that with her actions. She set a goal of earning good grades, yet is dismayed by her poor performance. The problem is that on a near-daily basis, she smokes marijuana within an hour of waking up and gets high again in the evening after her classes. She seldom studies, and she spends most evenings watching television or playing video games with her boyfriend. An ACT therapist might ask question such as, "What is smoking marijuana in the service of?" and "What meaning are you getting from playing video games?" The clinician may ask, "What are you valuing in your actions?" When it comes to values, the old adage that actions speak louder than words is apt, and the client's behavior isn't consistent with valuing learning.

At this juncture, the clinician might engage the client in values clarification. The client might come to realize that perhaps she doesn't value learning, but she just said that because the people in her life have been pushing her to go to college. Maybe pleasing others, such as her boyfriend, is a more important value to her than learning. Alternatively, the clinician might consider this client's behavior in terms of other ACT processes. For example, perhaps she's fused with thoughts such as *I'm stupid* or *I can't do this*, which show up whenever she starts to study, or she might be avoiding an aversive state, such as boredom or anxiety, when faced with reading a dense textbook. The therapist might also explore the client's substance use with her to see whether smoking marijuana is interfering with learning or presents a barrier to committed action.

In values work, the aim of ACT therapists is to help clients articulate their own values in order to identify behaviors that are consistent with what they care about. In other words, clarifying values leads to more committed action. This work also involves helping clients identify barriers to valued action—circumstances and behaviors that are inconsistent with their stated values or that hinder living in accordance with their values. Clearly, values are related to committed action, and we'll discuss this further throughout the book. For now, we'll simply say that committed actions are an important and observable component of values, given that they are the demonstrable execution of values.

# Context Influences Committed Action

After discussing all six of the ACT processes in the hexagon model, let's return to committed action. At first glance, committed action can appear to be the simplest of ACT's core processes to understand and apply, since it's usually more easily quantifiable and observable than the other processes. This is true in the sense that committed actions are often overt behaviors that are easily counted, tracked, or otherwise measured. However, although the task of measuring the frequency or intensity of a behavior may be simple, the ACT therapist is not simply focused on the form or occurrence of a person's behavior. The ACT therapist really wants to investigate the *function* of the behavior. ACT is a functional intervention and therefore is looking not just at what the person is doing, but why he is doing it. Committed action is not just about the presence of behavior, but it is about the function of that behavior in the current context for that individual. ACT is a functional contextual approach, and therefore the function of behaviors, rather than their form, is what's most important. We'll discuss functional contextualism in the next chapter, but for now, keep in mind that any committed action should be considered in the context of all of the other processes.

Let's take a look at a concrete example of how committed action is influenced by many different functions given the context of the behavior. Taylor has committed to run 30 minutes per day and reports that this behavior is in the service of her value of improving and maintaining her health. It's a relatively easy matter to ask her to record her running behavior. She could even use video documentation, a wearable device, or reports from an accountability partner to create a more objective record of her adherence. However, in the ACT model, the clinician needs to do more than merely measure behavior. Although measurement is important, it often doesn't tell the whole story. The clinician needs to see how this commitment will function given the context of the client's life. As a thought exercise, consider how workable or effective Taylor's committed action would be in each of these scenarios:

- She often reports that she wants to improve her health, and she is also overweight, abuses alcohol, and smokes half a pack of cigarettes per day.

- She's morbidly obese.

- She's in treatment because she's had frequent panic attacks ever since she lost her job three months ago, and her primary treatment goals are to improve her ability to cope with anxiety, improve her social skills, and gain occupational skills that will aid her in finding a new job.

- She's a triathlete and typically runs 50 miles a week.

- She's 62 years old and hasn't walked more than a mile at a time in over five years.

- She made the commitment a few days after her sister and chief rival made the same commitment.

- She says she's upset because her husband told her that she looks fat and she believes runners are skinny.

- She has a history of setting goals she can't achieve.

- She also recently committed to studying 60 minutes per day and attending tutoring sessions twice a week in the service of getting past academic probation.

Committed action must be considered in the context of the client's history, presenting complaint, and goals and values. And in addition to considering this context when clients make a commitment or set a goal, therapists must also consider the context when evaluating the outcome, while keeping in mind that increased psychological flexibility is an overarching goal. So now, to extend this exercise, consider how you would evaluate Taylor's actions during the first week in each of the following contexts:

- Her academic advisor told her that she must make several revisions to her thesis before defending it at the end of the week, and she told her advisor she didn't have time because she committed to run every day.

- She didn't run after her physician advised her that she should have a complete physical examination before beginning an exercise program.

- She ran 30 minutes on one day, skipped the next five days, and ran for three hours on the seventh day.

- She reports that meeting her goal was easy, because before making the commitment, she usually ran for 60 minutes per day.

- She tells you she didn't run 30 minutes the day after she came down with the flu.

- She tells you that she didn't run 30 minutes per day because she felt too depressed.

- She says that even though she was late to work three times because of her early-morning running schedule, she's pleased to report that she did indeed keep her commitment to run 30 minutes each day of the week.

- She's confused about whether or not she kept her commitment, because she wasn't sure if it was okay that she didn't run one day, after she unexpectedly had to work late, and she made up for it by running for 45 minutes the next two days.

There are no easy right or wrong answers to the question "Did Taylor fail in executing her committed action?" On the one hand, the material in the preceding list might provide enough information to make it easy to answer the question. On the other hand, because we must always consider committed actions in context, there can be multiple ways of looking at the same behavior. Committed action is not quite so simple when considered in the context of the full ACT model and the full lives, competing values, and multiple committed actions most people have.

# Summary

In this chapter, we've provided an introduction to committed action, a core ACT process when clients engage in clinically relevant behavior change. The other five ACT processes—acceptance, defusion, contact with the present moment, self-as-context, and values—were briefly described, and their relationship to committed action explored. In chapter 2, we will explore the definition of committed action, explain why ACT focuses on behavior, and begin to explore how values and committed action are related.

# Suggested Readings

Bach, P. A., & Moran, D. J. (2008). *ACT in practice: Case conceptualization in acceptance and commitment therapy.* Oakland, CA: New Harbinger.

Batten, S. V. (2011). *Essentials of acceptance and commitment therapy.* London: Sage.

Harris, R. (2009). *ACT made simple: An easy-to-read primer on acceptance and commitment therapy.* Oakland, CA: New Harbinger.

Hayes, S. C., Strosahl, K. D., & Wilson, K. G. (1999). *Acceptance and commitment therapy: An experiential approach to behavior change.* NY: Guilford.

Luoma, J., Hayes, S. C., & Walser, R. D. (2007). *Learning ACT: An acceptance and commitment therapy skills-training manual for therapists.* Oakland, CA: New Harbinger.

# CHAPTER 2

# Perspectives on Commitment

I n this chapter, we dive deep into the definition of "commitment," then turn to why committed action is so important in the ACT model. Indeed, as mentioned in chapter 1, behavior change is central to ACT, in large part because of the ways in which values and committed action are inextricably intertwined, so we discuss that connection at length in this chapter. Another facet of committed action that makes it central to ACT, and many other therapies, is that behavior is an overt and measurable indicator of psychological processes, so in this chapter we also discuss how to measure behavioral change, in part by zeroing in on specific aspects of behavior.

## General Perspectives on Commitment

The word *commit* comes from the Latin roots *com* and *mittere*, which mean "with" and "send or give over." So, from an etymological point of view, "committing" in an applied behavioral science context means giving oneself over to a goal or a plan. The word "commit" has many connotations. For example, graduate students in the behavioral sciences might have to commit to memory the diagnostic criteria for many mental health disorders, and then when they start working with clients, they might work to prevent people who are antisocial from committing a crime. The same graduate student might diagnose someone with a serious mental illness, in which case the client may be committed to a psychiatric ward.

In some usages of the word, "commit" simply means "to pledge or promise," and in others it means "to do." Colloquially (and regrettably), the word "commit" subsumes both of these disparate meanings. Of course, promising to act a certain way and measurably doing the action are two different things, and ACT therapists often have to highlight this distinction for clients. In this chapter, we'll sharpen the definition of the phrase "committed action" to ensure that it's used in therapy and case conceptualization with precision and to target measurable behavior.

Elucidating the difference between talking and doing is an ancient endeavor. *Facta non verba*, or "actions not words," is a Latin motto that's been handed down through the centuries—and adopted by many organizations dedicated to doing what they say they're going to do. Going much further back, with the advent of language it became necessary to guide people to discriminate between what they say and what they do. Often, such guidance includes the suggestion that people should take care to do what they say they will, and to only say what they will actually do.

Take a moment to imagine prehistoric times when our ancestors didn't yet engage in complex symbolic language. They acquired important consequences related to survival (such as food and shelter) from direct contingencies in their social group as a result of competition and cooperation responses. With the advent of verbal behavior (the ability to engage in relational responses), our ancestors could say things (probably in the form of monosyllabic grunts) that would lead to acquisition of food and shelter. As that repertoire developed over time, humans could pledge to do something, get reinforcers from other members of the social group for their pledge, but then not follow through on the action they pledged to do. For instance, a beta male in a tribe might pledge to protect the community if invaders attacked. Because of his verbal pledge, he would be well taken care of by the tribe. The immediate reinforcers for pledging might include food, shelter, camaraderie, and sex, among other things. In this way, the verbal behavior of promising to do something was immediately reinforced. The relations the beta male engaged in, "I" in relation with "will protect," led others to give him important appetitive, or naturally desired, stimuli. However, when invaders actually attack, the direct contingencies related to anxiety and the threat of harm or death might lead the beta male to run away or otherwise avoid the situation and *not* protect the group. Given this kind of scenario, we can imagine that early language, while abundantly useful, also had a downside, at least for those who didn't receive the pledged benefits. For this reason, since the dawn of language human communities have tended to be watchful about the correspondence between words and actions. Indeed, some of the earliest human literature, such as the Maxims of Ptahhotep (circa 2400 BCE), and the Code of Hammurabi (circa 1754 BCE) provided advice on how to use language prudently and responsibly.

Throughout the ages, scholars and visionaries have talked about the problem of saying one thing and doing another, observing that individuals perform better for their community and support their own reputation when they keep their word. Even today, entire branches of law (contract law, for example) are dedicated to codifying and regulating verbal commitments, enforcing them, and punishing failures to adhere to them. This ongoing context underscores the need to identify ways of facilitating commitment. Even now, in the twenty-first century, people continue to struggle to do what they say they're going to do. Sometimes people purposefully lie or make promises they don't adhere to. They create verbal relations that have the potential to govern behavior through the transformation of stimulus functions, but these relations don't always have that effect.

The way we discuss commitment in ACT helps enlighten people about the connections between words and deeds, or between relational responding and overt responding. (We will discuss more about relational responding in the relational frame theory section in the next chapter.) Acceptance and commitment therapy aims to illuminate the tricky relationship between indirect contingencies that arise from verbal behavior, such as the social consequences of making a pledge, and direct contingencies that come from the natural environment as people execute the pledged behavior. Understanding this relationship can help people engage in committed action that's both more effective and more contextually sensitive.

# The ACT Perspective on Committed Action

Acceptance and commitment therapy is an empirically supported cognitive behavioral psychotherapy designed to increase psychological flexibility through mindfulness and behavior change strategies. ACT's core process of committed action is somewhat unusual because it relies on evidence-based behavior change strategies, including strategies from other treatment models, with the rest of the ACT model contributing to making such changes in a mindful manner. Therefore, ACT can be used as a stand-alone treatment or to supplement other psychotherapeutic approaches, creating a context for viewing treatment plans as committed actions supported by acceptance, defusion, self-as-context, values, and contacting the present moment.

Acceptance and commitment therapy was developed as an outgrowth of the science of behavior analysis and was nurtured in the behavior therapy community, so ACT has a deep dedication to influencing people's behavior in functional ways. The allegiance to behavior change in therapy isn't simply born out of adherence to scientific tradition; rather, it is key, because psychotherapy literature demonstrates that behavioral interventions help clients reach important clinical goals. ACT therapists aim to help clients engage in committed actions in order to reduce suffering and improve quality of living, and this necessarily entails changing behavior in measurable ways.

## Why Focus on Behavior?

In ACT, the process of committed action is the lens used for focusing on clinically relevant behaviors. ACT was founded within contextual behavioral science, which "seeks the development of basic and applied scientific concepts and methods that are useful in predicting-and-influencing the contextually embedded *actions* of whole organisms…with precision, scope, and depth…to create a *behavioral* science more adequate to the challenges of the human condition" (Hayes, Barnes-Holmes, & Wilson, 2012, p. 2, italics added). This entire contextual behavioral science approach is brought to bear on working with clients to increase their engagement in functional behaviors through committed action.

Because we are discussing ACT as an applied science, let's take a closer look at what, specifically, the science analyzes. Any time you engage in a scientific endeavor, you should be able to articulate exactly what you're studying. In other words, you should be able to declare your unit of analysis. For instance, in the science of microbiology, a scientist might declare that she's studying the cell. Her unit of analysis is the cell, and she therefore focuses her efforts, time, and grant money on studying certain aspects of the cell. That doesn't mean it's the "right" thing to study, the better scientific endeavor, or the only appropriate unit of analysis. She's simply choosing to study that particular facet of the known universe.

Within contextual behavioral science, the unit of analysis is the act-in-context. ACT therapists and contextual behavioral scientists choose to focus their efforts on this specific aspect of the known universe: "the behavior of organisms interacting in and with a context, considered both historically and situationally" (Hayes, Barnes-Holmes, et al., 2012, p. 3). Again, this is not to say that behavior or the act-in-context is the "right" thing to study or the most meaningful scientific endeavor. Other psychological scientists might study the brain, neurochemicals, or the ego. However, when using ACT, which is based in contextual behavioral science, we choose to study the act-in-context.

Before moving forward, please realize that in the term "act-in-context," the hyphens are actually very important. The hyphens make clear that contextual behavioral scientists don't separate human actions from the contexts in which they occur. So, while reading this book, keep in mind that committed action always happens in a context. ACT doesn't simply influence people to change their behavior; it aims to help them engage in certain behaviors in the appropriate environments and in the service of chosen values. We'll discuss this further in chapter 3, but for now, please realize that in ACT, the application of behavioral science is always done with contextual support and for a purpose.

In general, mental health practitioners see the benefit of behavior change as an aim and outcome of therapy. The World Health Organization defines mental health as "a state of well-being in which every individual realizes his or her own potential, can cope with the normal stresses of life, can work productively and fruitfully, and is able to make a contribution to her or his community" (World Health Organization, 2014). Although that definition is less precise than typical behavioral science fare, it highlights that people's actions contribute to their state of mental health (as in "work productively," and "make a contribution").

Another important reason ACT therapists focus on behavior change is simply due to practical issues. Clients and third-party payers (especially in the economy of the early twenty-first century) want to see measurable, objective change in behavior. After a few sessions of psychotherapy, consumers and payers would like evidence that the client's experience is changing, for example, that a person diagnosed with social anxiety talks to more people, or a person diagnosed with depression engages in valued actions instead of staying in bed for twenty hours per day. Within the ACT model, the process of committed action is crucial to this aspect of mental health treatment. And no matter how interested ACT therapists might be in the other five core processes, insurance companies are unlikely to be satisfied with treatment goals stating that clients will be in more frequent contact with the present moment, defuse from unhelpful verbal events, or get in touch with the self-as-context perspective. So, through an emphasis on committed action, ACT can provide solid objective and behavioral treatment goals that are more likely to be acceptable to third-party payers and clients, as these goals provide for measurable, observable outcomes.

# The Most Measurable Hexaflex Process

As noted in chapter 1, committed action is the most measurable process in the ACT model because it typically involves overt behavior. After a psychological and behavioral assessment, therapist and client collaborate on a treatment plan, which will be most useful if it includes an operational definition of the clinically relevant behavior the therapy will target. An *operational definition* precisely identifies the client's specific observable or measurable behaviors as they relate to the clinical concern that brought that person to treatment. Therapist, client, and the therapy itself all benefit from discussing what the behavior looks like, the function of the behavior, and in what environments it can be a problem for the client. For some clients (and clinicians, for that matter), the phrase "operational definition" might not resonate in regard to their clinical issues. In those cases, therapists can use a more colloquial synonym, such as "pinpoint" or "target behavior."

Incidentally, committed action need not be publicly observable. For instance, a client with social anxiety can commit to engaging in the action of privately rehearsing her social skills prior to entering a room of coworkers, and also to privately reviewing the names and hobbies of each person before going into that context so she'll be better prepared for socializing. However, clinical work generally benefits from choosing observable or measurable target behaviors.

One benefit of targeting observable behaviors in the treatment plan is that doing so allows clients to more easily track if and when they are engaging in committed actions. In addition, an accountability partner, whether the clinician or confidant of the client, will also be able to witness whether the problematic behavior is diminishing or the desired behavior is increasing, and provide feedback about the change. In more technical terms, when therapist and client work together to operationalize what improved, healthier behavior will look like, they can leverage behavioral assessment techniques to measure change in the target behavior, and capitalize on applied behavioral science methods to encourage ongoing success. (We will discuss applied behavioral science in the next chapter.)

After the committed action is operationally defined and a way to observe it is established, therapist and client work together to choose what dimensions of the behavior will be measured. The dimensions of human behavior typically used in psychotherapy are its rate, duration, latency, intensity, and perseverance.

## Rate

*Rate* is the measure of the number of instances of a target behavior in a given period of time. This characteristic of human behavior is widely used in clinical work. Therapists typically want to count how many times a clinically relevant action happens and then attempt to accelerate or decelerate its occurrence using behavior therapy methods. B. F. Skinner argued extensively that rate of response was a crucial measure in the field of psychology and believed that highlighting this topic was one of his most important contributions to the field.

It's fairly simple to give examples of measuring rate in clinical work. Suppose a client is working on living a healthier lifestyle. He can track his own behavior or have someone else observe it to ascertain how many times he goes to the gym in one week, for example, or how many cigarettes he smokes each day. As that example illustrates, it's necessary to count behaviors in the context of a specific period of time.

## Duration

*Duration* measures the time between the onset of a behavior and the end of that behavior. Essentially, it's a measure of how long a person is doing a particular action. When doing a behavioral assessment for someone diagnosed with depression, the therapist might initially request that the client monitor how many hours she stays in bed per day to establish a benchmark. Then the therapist could use behavioral activation methods, activity scheduling, and mindfulness training to help the client stay out of bed for longer periods of time each day while engaging in valued actions. Conversely, duration can be used to measure increases in healthy behaviors, such as practicing mindfulness for two minutes per day the first week and increasing to 12 minutes per day by the end of the month.

## Latency

*Latency* is also a measure of time, but it assesses how much time passes before the person engages in the committed action. More specifically, when a cue for action shows up in the environment, latency measures how long it takes for the person to respond to that cue. Suppose a man would like to ask a woman out on a date and is dealing with nervousness about doing so. If he declares, "I'll call her on the phone at 7:30 p.m. tonight," and then, when the time comes, ruminates, worries, and rehearses what he's going to say so that he doesn't get around to calling until 7:47 p.m., he has a 17-minute latency of response. In this case, his therapist can help him contact the positive natural contingencies for actually engaging in the action, and in therapy they could consider what private events impeded him from acting when his self-imposed deadline arose.

Sometimes latency and duration are opposite sides of the same coin. Continuing with this same example, it could also be said that there was a 17-minute duration of nervous rumination. For another example, consider working with a family in which the parents want to increase their child's behavior of following instructions. If there's a 20-minute interval between the time when the child was requested to start doing her homework and the time she actually began doing it, it could be said either that there was a 20-minute latency period, or that there was a 20-minute duration of playing video games (or some other activity) that interfered with following the instruction.

## Intensity

*Intensity* is a measure of the force or magnitude of a behavior. Generally, intensity assesses how strong a behavior is, such as how loudly a person yells at his children or how much heroin a person uses. This measure might also be used in clinical work when helping people who engage in self-injury. For instance, a pressure sensor could be mounted on a wall where a person with developmental delays typically bangs her head. With such an instrument, we can measure the intensity of the head-banging behavior. Given that intensity is a measure of physical strength or power, and instruments for measuring such a dimension for much of clinical work are typically unconventional, ACT therapists can use subjective scales of intensity. The subjective units of distress scale (SUDS) is a commonly used measurement of intensity. For example, asking a client, "On a scale of 1 to 10, how angry were you?" is a measure of intensity.

## Perseverance

*Perseverance* is somewhat different from the previous characteristics of behavior. Sometimes ACT clinicians are interested in the number of different environments that set a client up to engage in a particular action throughout the day. Because ACT is a contextual science, therapists are often interested in determining whether clinically relevant behavior perseveres all day or is only evoked under certain circumstances.

For example, consider a boy provisionally diagnosed with oppositional defiant disorder. His therapist could send a behavioral assessment tool with him in his backpack so that people he interacts with during the day can rate whether or not he acted in a problematic manner during the period of observation. His caregivers and teachers—along with bus drivers, lunchroom staff, playground attendants, coaches, and other relevant adults—could then fill out this assessment. After collecting two weeks' worth of data, the therapist can determine whether the diagnosis is appropriate. If the boy acts in a recalcitrant way in many different environments throughout the day (on the bus, in gym, in science class, at lunch, on the playground), then his defiant behaviors are persevering. In other words, his problematic repertoire is evoked in different contexts. On the other hand, the therapist might find that the boy's target behavior is happening only in his social studies class but happens there almost every day. In that case, the target behavior isn't persevering across contexts, and perhaps the diagnosis is unwarranted. Perhaps he simply dislikes social studies, or maybe the teacher needs to learn better classroom management skills. The extent of perseverance of a problematic response is an important piece of data for ACT therapists because they can better target the behavior if they know what provokes it and how pervasive it is. Put another way, in what contexts does the behavior occur?

All of these measurable dimensions of behavior can provide valuable perspectives on clients' psychological flexibility. To reiterate, psychological flexibility is the capacity to contact the present moment while also being aware of thoughts and emotions—without trying to change those private experiences and without being adversely controlled by them—and then, depending upon the situation, persisting in or changing behavior in the pursuit of values and goals. The measurable characteristics of behavior we just reviewed—rate, duration, latency, intensity, and perseverance—let therapists know whether clients' responses are persisting or changing over time.

## ACT Therapists' Perspectives on the Importance of Committed Action and Its Measurability

Committed action is obviously important to ACT therapists, and a survey of members of the Association for Contextual Behavioral Science, an international organization affiliated with ACT work, supports this notion (Moran, 2014). The answers of a sample of members to the following two questions demonstrate the importance they invest in committed action and their belief that it's highly measurable.

The first question was "The hexagon model in acceptance and commitment therapy suggests that there are six different constructs that comprise psychological flexibility: acceptance, contact with the present moment, values, committed action, self-as-context, and defusion. These six constructs are generally regarded as creating a unitary whole, but we can differentiate them for practical reasons. In your opinion and in general, which one of these six domains would you most want to see change after delivering ACT?"

Committed action was endorsed by 50 percent of respondents (n = 98), with the other five processes sharing the remaining 50 percent of the votes. Here's a breakdown of the percentages:

Committed action: 50.0%

Acceptance: 13.3%

Defusion: 8.2%

Values: 4.1%

Contact with the present moment: 8.2%

Self-as-context: 16.3%

The second question was "In your opinion, which construct can be most objectively measured? Please choose only one:"

Committed action won by a landslide, taking over 85 percent of the votes while the other five processes shared the remaining 15 percent of the vote. Here's a breakdown of the percentages:

Committed action: 85.7%

Acceptance: 6.1%

Defusion: 5.1%

Values: 2.0%

Contact with the present moment: 1.0%

Self-as-context: 0.0%

Overall, this poll showed a strong tendency for ACT therapists to focus on committed action as the primary target for change in ACT and also indicated that therapists firmly believe that committed action is the most observably measurable of the six core ACT processes.

# Goal Setting for Committed Action

Because committed action focuses on measurable and clinically relevant behavior change, the ACT clinician will prudently use *goal setting* as part of the therapeutic endeavor. The client and clinician collaborate on defining some type of new or different behavior, and work at building the skills and opportunities for such behaviors to occur in appropriate contexts. Research on goal setting (Locke & Latham, 2006) suggests that "specific, high (hard) goals lead to a higher level of task performance… [and] there is a positive, linear relationship between goal difficulty and task performance" (p. 265). ACT therapists can maximize behavioral change with prudent use of goal setting.

One traditional approach to developing goals is using SMART criteria, and this conventional mnemonic certainly has a place in ACT for creating committed actions. There are several variations for what the letters in SMART can stand for (Locke & Latham, 2006; O'Neil & Conzemius, 2006; Frey & Osterloh, 2002), and ACT therapists can say that "SMART goals" are Specific, Measurable, Attainable, Relevant, and Time-bound. *Specific* suggests that the clinical dyad will operationally define or pinpoint what action is going to be done so that they know if it has been executed correctly. *Measurable* means that the behavior is observable, is countable, and can be assessed with rate, duration, latency, intensity, and/or perseverance. *Attainable* is an important criterion, because the ACT clinician would like the client to be able to achieve the goal so it will garner reinforcement, and thereby have a greater likelihood to continue and become a more generalized commitment strategy. If it is not an attainable goal, then the consequences of failure at reaching this goal could make the person quit her goal-directed behavior. *Relevant* suggests that these goals are related to the client's values, and as we will see later in the chapter, the more a committed action is related to values, the more tenacious the behavior will be, even in the face of obstacles and lack of immediate gratification. *Time-bound* is an important criterion for a goal, because having a deadline motivates regular action (Ariely, 2010) and allows the clinical dyad to set a date to review the progress on the committed action, which will allow for the clinician to provide social reinforcement, and an opportunity to evaluate how to improve the goal-directed behavior.

ACT aims to support greater committed actions leading to psychological flexibility, and SMART goals support committed action. Therapists can successfully use goal setting while creating a treatment plan incorporating evidence-based behavior therapy, and such an approach can be supplemented when the therapist understands committed action from the ACT perspective.

# Exploring Committed Action in the ACT Literature

While discussing very early pilot investigations of ACT (way back when it was still called "comprehensive distancing"), Zettle and Hayes suggested that after receiving such treatment, "it becomes possible for patients to behave more effectively" (1986, p. 32). In the first book-length explanation of ACT (Hayes, Strosahl, & Wilson, 1999), the authors state that "behavioral commitments involve actively engaging in actions that may invite the presence of negatively evaluated thoughts, emotions, and bodily states" (p. 236). In ACT, the concept of committed action has always held a measurable, behavioral connotation, but also goes beyond simply engaging in quantifiable responses. The main thrust of commitment is taking action even if doing so is difficult, and while developing a meaningful life by engaging in those behaviors. It's an overt response that's influenced by direct contingencies and verbally construed indirect contingencies, and it is maintained in the presence of aversive and distracting stimuli. More colloquially, committing means working toward a goal that's meaningful enough to propel a person forward even if problems or barriers arise, including barriers that come in the form of emotions and other private events. For clients, this means engaging in behaviors that lead to personally relevant, long-term consequences even when aversive stimuli are present.

In their book *Learning ACT*, which is part of the training canon for ACT practitioners, Luoma, Hayes, and Walser (2007) provide a broad view of commitment: "Committed action is a step-by-step process of acting to create a whole life, a life of integrity, true to one's deepest wishes and longings. Commitment involves both persistence and change—whichever is called for in living one's value. Commitment also includes engaging in a range of behaviors. This is important because sometimes sustaining a valued direction means being flexible, rather than being rigidly committed to and persevering in unworkable actions" (158).

Committed action occurs in treatment when clients engage in clinically relevant behaviors suggestive of improvement. When clients engage in committed action, their behavior is in the service of values, defused from unhelpful rules and verbal events, and executed in contact with the present moment—while accepting all physiological and cognitive responses elicited during that situation—and then they have a better platform on which to take their first steps toward clinical improvement.

Based on the preceding discussion, the core elements of commitment can be set forth very succinctly: "Commitment means acting in the direction of what you care about even in the presence of obstacles" (Moran, 2013). There are three major parts to this definition that we will unpack.

**Acting**: As you can see in the first word of that definition, committing requires action. Just talking about doing something is not committing. When it comes to chosen actions, people often say that they're committed to certain outcomes but don't consistently act to achieve their objectives. Action is a definite requirement for commitment, and ACT can provide the skills to help people achieve their goals.

**In the direction of what you care about:** This part of the definition suggests that commitments are personal and based on values. Long-term dedication to a certain direction is more likely when people have a reason to care about the process and the outcomes of their efforts. Linking goals and objectives to values increases optimal performance. Acting on a goal that's personally important strengthens commitment.

**Even in the presence of obstacles:** This last part of the definition suggests that accomplishing important tasks is neither simple nor easy. When people set out to achieve a goal, it's important to devise a plan for dealing with complications, because barriers inevitably arise. Committed action persists even when obstacles present themselves. The process of commitment provides the tools needed to handle difficult private events and obstacles in the external world that might impede engaging in target behaviors. Acknowledging the presence of potential or actual stumbling blocks and then working to plan for or solve them is a hallmark of committed actions.

# Values and Commitments

As set forth in the simple definition just above, commitment involves "acting in the direction of what you care about." This aspect of commitment requires that people elucidate what is truly vital for them in their life on this planet. When people can articulate what they find to be meaningful in their lives, and they can link that purpose to their actions, they're getting closer to building a stronger commitment.

From a contextual behavioral science perspective, engaging in language about how certain behavioral choices lead to living a life of meaning can have a beneficial impact on making difficult choices. For example, if a mother makes a values statement, such as "I care for children," this would probably support playing with her kids during their free time because doing so is meaningful to her. Such a values declaration clarifies that the choice to play would likely be rewarding. But more importantly, this way of talking would also encourage her to pull her car over to the side of the street and get out when she sees two children in a fistfight on a playground. The choice to get between the two combatants might not lead to an immediate reinforcer; in fact, it could lead to inadvertently getting struck, or it might cause the woman to be late for work. Both of these are aversive events, and such potential outcomes could lead many people to avoid such a stimulus event. However, a person who affirms, "I care for children" is more likely to accept the aversiveness and follow through with committed action. Because the woman in this example has developed a values statement that influences her caring for children's well-being, intervening in the fistfight is a committed action and is rewarding because she's engaged in the process of caring, even if the act of breaking up the fight isn't immediately reinforced. We will talk about how language has that kind of effect on human behavior when we discuss relational frame theory in the next chapter.

# Unpacking an ACT Definition of Values

In acceptance and commitment therapy, authorship of values is essential when attempting to influence clinically relevant change. The clinician explores the client's way of talking about a life well-lived and sets the context for making a statement about personal values. In ACT parlance, "values are verbally construed global desired life consequences" (Hayes et al., 1999, p. 206). That's a pretty dense definition, so let's unpack it.

## Verbally Construed

For much of this chapter, we've discussed how words can be an obstacle to engaging in action or, at a minimum, that words may be divorced from committed action, highlighting that committing requires engaging in the intended behavior, not just making a promise to do so. Making a pledge to do something is simply a verbalization, and though pledges can lead to positive outcomes, people can fail to follow through on their pledges. That's an example of one of the negative aspects of language: words can be confused, at least temporarily, for the actions they represent.

Of course, language and words have a positive side, especially in regard to values. Starting in early childhood, parents, teachers, family members, and spiritual leaders talk with children in ways that provide guidance on how to access meaningful experiences and develop a behavioral repertoire that aims their behavior in the direction of continuing to contact outcomes and processes that sustain a vital life. Engaging with books, movies, plays, and conversations with peers can produce similar results. As all of this is happening, verbal behavior is occurring. This dynamic continues throughout life. For example, when interacting with a social group, people may engage in conversations and discussions about how to experience the good things that life has to offer. In these ways, people *construe*, or interpret, meaning from social interactions that are anchored in verbal communication. So verbal behavior certainly has a significant positive side in regard to committed action: it metes out which actions a person will choose to do and why.

## Global

Values are large-scale, comprehensive, and inclusive characteristics of behavior. Including the word "global" in the dense definition of values above doesn't mean they involve worldwide, Earth-based events and issues; rather, it means that individuals, in the great, grand scheme of their lives, deeply care about the consequences implied by their values across contexts. In therapy, a discussion of values might start by highlighting a specific goal the person has in mind, with the ACT therapist seeking the meaning or purpose behind choosing a specific goal. As a reminder, values are not something that can ever be fully accomplished, but they do direct people to aim toward certain accomplishments.

ACT therapists consider values as directions for behavior. An oft-used metaphor in ACT suggests that "Life is a journey," and a person should choose the direction of that journey. When we discussed scientific values earlier in the chapter, we made sure to clarify that there are no "right" values. In this journey metaphor, there are no "right" directions. You could go north, south, east, or west, and none of them would be "right," but they would be chosen by you, and the evidence would be seen by what direction your behavior takes. Suppose you choose west as your valued direction. You can then establish goals in a westward direction. Imagine that you're starting in New York with the value "I care about moving west with my life!" You can then set a course of behavior to drive a car to Chicago. Making it to Chicago means that you've engaged in committed action that was successful in achieving a goal and also values-based. Once you're in Chicago, you've achieved a goal, but haven't achieved your value, because you can still travel in a westward direction. You can always set another goal to engage in behavioral actions that head in your valued direction.

So, suppose you choose San Francisco as your next goal, but your car breaks down. You would be required to use your psychological flexibility to choose another action plan that would help you continue traveling in your valued direction; sometimes it's necessary to change behaviors that were successful in the past in order to get to a valued destination. So, you might choose to take a train to San Francisco instead. Once you've arrived in San Francisco, you've once again achieved a values-based goal, and you can still choose to continue west—the direction that's meaningful for you—by setting a goal to get to Tokyo. Although that will require a different set of behaviors than what got you to San Francisco, if you've made a commitment to act in the *direction* of what you care about, you'll flexibly change your behavior to help you achieve this next measurable goal.

A key point illuminated by this metaphor is that goals are specific, whereas values are global. An additional important point to consider is that sometimes you might not make it to a particular destination on your westerly journey, but it is still a worthwhile journey as long as you keep heading west. If your car breaks down in San Francisco, for example, the world may not offer the opportunity to take a train, or it may require you to backtrack in a northeast direction for a while to get to the next mode of transportation. In this case, you might have to walk in a westerly direction instead of driving, or you might have to meander around in a way that looks like it's going the opposite way for a bit. You may never make it to San Francisco, but every slow step you take is still meaningful. Life can be vital even if goals are not met.

## Desired

Values are *appetitive*, a behavioral science term for something desired that could be reinforcing of behavior. When people choose their values, they're articulating what they find interesting, attractive, or important about the consequences of living life a certain way and committing to a long-term behavioral repertoire. Values-based actions are responses that are worthwhile just through doing them. There might be external rewards for engaging in a values-based action, but the action in itself is rewarding by its very nature. For example, someone who values helping others might be paid for his services, and he also might find volunteering rewarding because he values helping in and of itself, as a process, even if it doesn't lead to the outcome of payment.

Valuing is a choice. Given everything offered by the world around us, individuals are presented with the opportunity to interpret, or construe, what's worthwhile and vital to them and can leverage that verbal ability to shape their responses to the world at large. How people ultimately behave, not how they talk about their values, is how their values are demonstrated and subsequently assessed.

## Life Consequences

Values are both an outcome of living and a process of living. In ACT, the term *values* clearly does not refer to achieving a goal, though goals certainly support valued commitments. For instance, if you make a commitment to lifelong learning, perhaps you'll choose to take an adult education class in art history. There are consequences that are inextricably tied to your commitment to lifelong learning during this course. You can aim for the goal of getting an A in the course, and that will be a consequence of your hard work and diligence, yet there are other outcomes beyond the grade you receive. You will also be engaged in the processes of learning more about art, devoting your time to a new task, challenging yourself to learn new facts and skills, visiting museums, writing about concepts related to aestheticism that you've never considered before, and acting on your desire to broaden your experiences in this lifetime—and these are just some of the many processes that are also consequences of this values-based committed action. Both the outcomes of your behavior and the process of behavior are consequences. In the next chapter, we'll explore how important consequences are for maintaining committed action.

# A Practical Matter: Committed Action Is Doing the Therapy

Of course, committed action isn't just for clients to engage in; it's also central for therapists in their work. In the words of Luoma, Hayes, and Walser, "Committed action is the core process through which the therapist can best incorporate traditional behavioral methods into the ACT model" (Luoma et al., 2007, p. 158). In other words, delivery of empirically supported treatments during ACT therapy is conceptualized as committed action on the part of the therapist. The other five core ACT processes are also present; however, they are more of a supplement to the treatment plan and are engaged to support clients during the committed actions related to the therapeutic endeavor.

Let's look at how the main thrust of ACT's committed action process is meted out by the evidence-based treatment plan. Say you're treating someone with obsessive-compulsive disorder (OCD) with an ACT approach. You wouldn't ignore the treatment literature and just teach the client about acceptance, defusion, and mindfulness. The treatment plan would embrace exposure and response prevention, the gold standard approach for treating OCD. The same goes for all other diagnoses that can be targeted with empirically supported treatments. (The American Psychological Association's Division 12, the Society of Clinical Psychology, has a robust list of treatments shown to be effective for many diagnoses, and using these in ACT-consistent ways will be the focus of chapters 8 and 9.) ACT therapists often use these approaches in order to be consistent with their clinical dedication to evidence-based practice.

A core issue in the practical application of ACT as a clinical treatment model is inviting clients to commit to the treatment plan in order to address the target behavior in a measurable manner. In other words, ACT sets the occasion for clients to engage in evidence-based, planned actions in the direction of what they care about (because it's personally meaningful, not just to "get better," but to develop more psychological flexibility and live their values)—even in the presence of obstacles such as negative thoughts, feelings, and bodily sensations, which are addressed by the other five core ACT processes. Having clients commit to treatment is generally a prerequisite for success, and helping them follow through on that commitment is the ACT therapist's challenge.

## Summary

To summarize, a commitment is action in the direction of what a person cares about even in the presence of obstacles. In this chapter, we discussed how crucial it is to define behavior in order to create a commitment. We also described how values support motivation for chosen actions. In chapter 3, we'll discuss the basics of applied behavioral science, and how to utilize context to change behavior and maintain committed action.

# The Fundamentals of Contextual Behavioral Science for Supporting Committed Action

The purpose of this chapter is to survey the basic principles and assumptions of applied behavioral science as they are relevant to the topic of commitment in contextual behavioral therapy. Understanding these fundamentals will assist clinicians in delivering effective psychotherapy to support each client's values-based committed actions. Behavior change is one of acceptance and commitment therapy's therapeutic endeavors, and that is especially true when talking about the committed action domain of the traditional hexaflex model. ACT therapists leverage the power of these scientific concepts to help assess the clinically relevant concern and apply them for measurable results.

In chapter 2, we introduced the idea that ACT is built on contextual behavioral science, which is a paradigm founded on specified scientific values, coherent philosophical assumptions, and detailed methodological approaches aiming to influence the development of theory and technology to help humankind. In the broadest sense, the goal of most ACT interventions is predicting and influencing psychological events with precision, scope, and depth. This is a pragmatic goal, meaning that the practitioner or scientist chooses *practical and measurable* methods of behavioral change strategies to ascertain whether the intervention was successful and the defined goal was met. While working with an individual to increase committed actions in ACT, the therapeutic dyad develops a treatment goal of behavior change that can be objectively monitored and is in line with the client's values. ACT targets values-based committed action, and leverages applied behavioral science interventions that traditionally aim to alter the characteristics of behavior in a quantifiable way. (See chapter 2 for a discussion on the characteristics of behavior that can be regularly measured.)

The ACT approach invites practitioners to develop measurable and useful treatment goals of behavior change. This is *not necessarily the right way to do therapy*, but rather the way contextual behavioral practitioners value doing therapy. The ACT therapist is aware that other schools of thought exist, and those approaches have other goals and values. While respecting the diverse nature of psychological theories, the ACT practitioner promotes the contextual behavioral science approach, because it is practical, with appreciable behavior change results. ACT aims to precisely, broadly, and fully analyze human actions, and influence those actions according to the values of the client, through empirically supported behavior change interventions in order to reduce suffering and improve quality of living.

For example, Miguel is a client who exhibited an obsessive-compulsive repertoire by washing his hands approximately 60 times a day. He was beleaguered by obsessive thoughts of contamination, and compulsively washing his hands with antibacterial soap to take away the contamination and reduce the worries about being contaminated, negatively reinforced that high rate of scrubbing his hands with detergent. (If you are unfamiliar with the term "negative reinforcement," the basic behavioral terminology will be defined later in this chapter.) Miguel's repetitive daily action resulted in lesions on his hands, which made him worry even more about contamination.

The research-supported psychological treatment for OCD is exposure and response prevention (E/RP), and an ACT therapist will integrate empirically supported treatment protocols into the therapeutic endeavor, not just because of a rule-governed adherence to scientific pursuits, but because most clients want practical, appreciable behavior change results. However, applying E/RP to Miguel's concern is not just behavior change for behavior change's sake. The ACT therapist also asks what Miguel cares about in life, and discusses his values. Miguel reports caring about his social and family relationships, but his fears keep him isolated in his house because he thinks it is germ-free. He doesn't go to parties or social gatherings, so that he can avoid the anxiety-provoking situations of interacting with others. He doesn't shake hands with people he meets or hug the people he loves. The ACT therapist precisely, broadly, and fully analyzes Miguel's actions, and operationally defines a clinically relevant behavior as "having skin coming into physical contact with another human being in public environments." Once that behavior is defined, the ACT therapist has Miguel expose himself to anxiety-provoking stimuli by shaking hands with people, not simply for the purpose of reducing the anxiety, but for expanding his psychological flexibility to have that anxiety while following through on commitments to behaviors that are in line with caring about social relationships. The committed actions performed as part of an empirically supported behavior change intervention are not just for symptom reduction, but for living a life of meaning and purpose.

# Assumptions in Contextual Behavioral Science as Related to Committed Action

Because ACT is a science aiming to achieve quantifiable objectives with specific methodologies, it is important to discuss the *assumptions* that the scientists make during this goal-directed work. All scientific endeavors make assumptions regarding how the work will be done; however, not all scientists actually declare their assumptions. The development of acceptance and commitment therapy occurred with the assumptions explicitly articulated through a philosophy of science called *functional contextualism*.

According to Merriam-Webster Online Dictionary (m-w.com), there are several definitions of *assumption*, and the definitions all hint at what is meant by the contextual behavioral science use of the word *assumption*: 1) "a taking to or upon oneself," 2) "the act of laying claim to or taking possession of something," and 3) "an assuming that something is true." The combination of these definitions alludes to scientists taking it upon themselves to articulate their goals, measures, and methods, and consider if those are the most workable and effective (not necessarily "true") ways of performing a particular endeavor. An assumption is decidedly not *true* in the way that it cannot be considered wrong. An assumption is simply a firmly held supposition that a particular way of behaving will achieve certain chosen goals.

Assumptions help generate a systematic approach to achieving goals. When a person endeavors to do something, he should be able to declare what the goal will be, how he will measure success, and what methods can be used to achieve that success. The goal, measurement, and methods are not correct or right; they are simply chosen. Let's take an example outside psychology. Suppose a person values bringing beauty into the world, and then has a goal to write music to do so. It's not that aestheticism is the right value to have; it is simply chosen. (Some people live meaningful lives without purposefully bringing beauty into the world.) It's not that writing music is the correct goal to have, given that value (some artists choose painting, dance, or sculpture), but the musician *assumes* that it will meet her chosen goal (especially given her personal history and current environment). The person can then choose to measure success by achieving a particular goal. For instance, she might choose to write a 15-minute string quartet piece. Whether that is the *right* type of music is not the question—the artist can simply choose that goal. The pragmatic approach to this endeavor does not debate about which is the right or wrong approach—it merely lays out the goal explicitly. The goal, measure, and method *cannot be evaluated* as right or wrong; they are just *assumed* to be workable for the person's chosen values. And, here is an important point: once the assumptions are declared, one *can evaluate* the artist's success. If she writes a piece that lasts three minutes and includes only one violin along with four brass instruments, then the artist did not meet the goal. Once the assumptions are declared, only then can one evaluate whether the artist successfully achieved the behavioral goal. If the artist's creation did not reach 15 minutes and did not include a full string quartet, then one would say the person failed to meet her goal.

Before moving forward, think about how all of this relates to conducting therapy with a client, especially regarding the ACT component of committed action. In order to use this applied contextual behavioral science with clients, values need to be assessed and then authored, goals chosen (which are not right or wrong in the pragmatic sense), and measurement approaches for the committed actions declared. Only then will one see the successful working of acceptance and commitment therapy.

Going back to the example of Miguel's treatment protocol, the exposure aspect of the treatment might request that Miguel practice shaking hands with strangers. That is not because it's the "right" thing to do in treatment; rather, the ACT therapist can make the assumption that following replicated empirically supported treatment protocols will help reinforce hand-shaking with other people so there is an increased likelihood of that behavior, and that it might generalize to encourage Miguel to be more in contact with his family members and friends. The ACT therapist collaborates with Miguel and they agree to go to an automobile expo where there will be many salespeople who will be willing to shake Miguel's hand. As a therapeutic exercise, Miguel commits to the action of shaking hands with strangers 25 times during his visit to the car show, and also agrees to prevent himself from his ritualistic hand washing. The committed actions he is doing might countercondition the anxiety he feels when exposed to such provocative events, yet the ACT therapist is also interested in the fact that he is practicing values-based behavior. The ACT therapist makes the assumption that evidence-based therapy such as E/RP is a workable approach for achieving operationally defined goals, such as handshaking, and engaging in such committed actions because they are related to living life in a meaningful manner. In clinical behavior analysis, the therapist assists the client in authoring his values, collaborates on developing goals, and sets up empirical measures to assess the client's successful working on the values-based committed action toward those goals. Functional contextualism sets the stage for this approach.

# Functional Contextualism

ACT is based on the philosophy of science called *functional contextualism*, which specifically analyzes "the act-in-context." You might recall from chapter 2 that the hyphens between words stress the unitary nature of the relationship between the act and the context. The *unit* investigated in functional contextualism is the interaction between the whole organism and the environment defined situationally (such as current antecedents and consequences) and historically (such as the organism's learning history). To reiterate that sentence, the unit—or the "one thing"—that functional contextualism investigates is the combination of what came before a behavior (the antecedent), the measured response (the behavior), and what comes after the behavior (the consequence). Functional contextualism looks at that chain of events as unitary, and contextual behavioral science analyzes the environment-behavior relationship. To put it simply (but loosely), an ACT therapist looks at the whole integrated interaction between the client's actions, the client's history, and the world around him. When speaking of "the world around" the behavior, sometimes it is useful to divide the act-in-context unit into the antecedent-behavior-consequence demarcations. Keep in mind, contextualism assumes that they are not three distinct events, but one unitary event.

The reason why functional contextualism stresses the unitary perspective with the environment is not purely academic. It is practical and related to influencing committed action. A behavior cannot be effectively and pragmatically analyzed as an isolated unit. The client's responses do not occur in a vacuum. For instance, if we analyze the behavior of "running," the analysis is meaningless without knowing the purpose of the running response. Is the rapid bipedal motion occurring because a ferocious dog is chasing the person (an aversive antecedent event is being avoided), or because the person desires a runner's high (an immediate physical consequence), or in the service of spending some time with a few pals in a running club (an immediate social consequence), or for better health (a distant, verbally-constructed consequence)? When you did the thought exercise in chapter 1 about how Taylor made a commitment to start running 30 minutes a day, you probably realized just how impactful context is when talking about behavior. Doing a robust clinical behavioral assessment with an eye on being practical and helpful to the client requires looking at the unitary nature of the act-in-context. ACT benefits from looking not just at the clinically relevant behavior, but also what comes before it and after it.

Now here is where it can get tricky. Functional contextualism aims to be practical and useful, and if it is practical and useful to scientifically discuss antecedents, consequences, and behaviors as distinct from each other, then doing so can still be consistent with the functional contextual approach. After all, ACT does champion "flexibility," so an ACT therapist wouldn't rigidly hold onto her philosophical language if it were not helpful to the goals. Sometimes, discriminating between the consequences, behaviors, and antecedents can help the scientific analysis.

For instance, Miguel's ACT therapist would functionally analyze his clinically relevant act-in-context. During assessment, Miguel reports that if he touches a doorknob in a public place, he'll feel uncomfortable and go wash his hands to reduce the discomfort. From a functional contextual point of view, there are not three different things happening there; rather it is *one* act-in-context. Mechanistically, the therapist could parse out the antecedent as the touching of the doorknob and the feelings of discomfort, the behavior as washing, and the negatively reinforcing consequence of having the discomfort reduced. When trying to change obsessive-compulsive behaviors to more values-based committed actions, it can be helpful to talk this way. A functional contextualist will be flexible enough to use that mechanistic analysis, not because it is a "true" depiction, but because it helps with communication. In addition, the flexible scientist-practitioner also views the act-in-context as a single clinically relevant issue, and applies the same approach to the committed actions.

ACT therapists can utilize the traditional methods of functional analysis and behavior therapy from the past several decades of psychological science, even though much of the earlier work was rooted in the philosophical approach of mechanism rather than contextualism. Functional assessment and prior behavior therapy theories discussed the antecedent-behavior-consequence approach as if there were three separate events, and the behavioral science theory talked about them as if the antecedents, behaviors, and consequences interacted much like cogs, wheels, and gears in a machine. The ACT application of behavior therapy and functional assessment methods would simply eschew the mechanistic perspective by observing consequences, behaviors, and antecedents as part of a whole functional unit. Functional contextualism allows flexibility in the language of analysis while maintaining the core assumption that the whole environment-behavior relationship is the unit of analysis, because that is the way to perceive purpose in the behavior. Let's now turn to the fundamental elements of a functional analysis by talking about the how antecedents, behaviors, and consequences relate, and in chapter 4, we will explain how to assess clinically relevant behaviors with these basic elements.

## The Elements of the ABC Model

ACT grew from the behavior therapy community and philosophy, and behavior therapy grew from Skinner's basic work on principles of operant psychology. The three-term contingency from operant psychology describes how antecedents precede behavior and that consequences follow. In an analysis of behavior, the stimuli occurring just before and just after the response (in other words, temporally contiguous stimuli) are crucial to the analysis. A simple behavior analysis of eating unhealthy food might look similar to this table.

| Antecedent | Behavior | Consequence |
| --- | --- | --- |
| *The presence of unhealthy food* | *Eating the unhealthy food* | *Feeling satisfied* |

Antecedents serve as a signal that if the person engages in a particular behavior, a consequence will occur. Consequences have a significant impact on whether that behavior happens again in the presence of that antecedent. If the consequence is reinforcing, the behavior is more likely to occur again. If the consequence is punishing, the behavior is less likely to occur again. (We will talk about reinforcement and punishment later in this chapter). This approach is typically described as the "ABC" model in behavior therapy and applied behavior analysis. In this example, the presence of the unhealthy food is a cue for an action that would lead to satisfaction for the person. If the person engages in the behavior of eating, and the consequence is satisfying, then that behavior will likely occur again if the unhealthy food is in the environment.

If ACT therapists want a more a robust analysis about clinically relevant behavior, especially if they want to use an evidence-based approach for increasing values-based committed actions, they will need to look at the environmental influences of the consequences and antecedents with greater precision, scope, and depth. We spent much of chapter 2 discussing behavior—the B, in the ABC model—especially that it needs to be operationally defined and that there are several characteristics that can be measured for behavior. Now let's talk about what surrounds behavior in the act-in-context.

## CONSEQUENCES

One might assume when talking about an ABC model, the "C" would be the last part talked about. Conventionally, it would make sense to go in alphabetical order or in the order of time. However, consequences are so critical to analyzing behavior, they have a more powerful impact on behavior than antecedents, and it is simpler to understand the influence of antecedents once consequences have been introduced, so we will talk about them first.

In general, the term "consequence" simply means an event produced after another event. In behavioral science, a consequence is a stimulus event produced by a response. After a person engages in a particular behavior, an environmental event follows. There are two dimensions to consequences that we will discuss in this chapter. The first one is the effect consequences have on the likelihood of behavior. Sometimes, a consequence of behavior *increases* the likelihood of the behavior to happen again under similar conditions, and this is considered a reinforcing consequence. Other times, a consequence *decreases* the probability of the behavior occurring again under similar conditions, and this is considered a punishing consequence. Understanding how to alter the environment to increase and decrease the probability of behavior assists in helping clients engage in committed action.

Applied behavioral scientists also look at a different dimension of the consequence, as well. Some consequences of the behavior might lead to the *addition* of environmental stimuli, and this is called a *positive* consequence. When an environmental stimulus is removed, this is called a negative consequence. *Nota bene*, this is often easily confused in colloquial speech. In behavioral science, a positive consequence does not mean that it is good or wanted; it simply means that a stimulus event was added or presented in that situation. Likewise, a negative consequence—in behavioral science—is not bad or unwanted; it simply means that a stimulus event was removed or subtracted from the situation. Now let's look at what happens when behavioral science combines these two dimensions.

**Positive reinforcement.** When something is *added to* the environment by a person's actions, and the person is *more likely* to do that behavior again in the future because of that consequence, the behavioral scientist would say that behavior was positively reinforced. A popular example of positive reinforcement is giving a child a lollipop for making her bed, and then seeing an increase in the probability of her making the bed the next time it is messy. For a clinical example, consider A.J., who has a significant substance use concern, and is struggling with making a commitment to stop using. Despite the fact that his life is in shambles, he goes to a crack house every day to buy drugs. His behaviors of walking to the crack den and purchasing the substance are positively reinforced. In other words, his responses are followed by something being added to his world (a bag of crack in his hand) and being able to obtain that substance makes it more likely that he will go again to that drug dealer's building and hand over money. When he smokes the drug, he is presented with a feeling of euphoria, which is also a positive reinforcer that increases the likelihood he will buy and consume drugs again. Acquiring illegal drugs can be viewed as positively reinforcing, and competes with making a commitment to live a drug-free life. It is incumbent on ACT therapists to analyze which positively reinforcing consequences for clinically relevant behavior compete with committing to a more functional, values-based life. In turn, they should also identify how the likelihood of changing behavior to be more values-directed and healthful can be increased with creating or increasing the availability of positive reinforcers.

**Negative reinforcement.** When something is *removed from* the environment by a person's actions, and the person is *more likely* to do that behavior again in the future because of that consequence, the ACT therapist would say that behavior was negatively reinforced. A typical example is scratching an itch. When a person takes his fingernails and drags them across an irritated area on the skin, and that removes the feeling of irritation, then the next time the skin is irritated and the person scratches that area, a behavioral scientist would say that the original behavior was negatively reinforced. We can continue with A.J. for our clinical example. Engaging in the behavior of smoking the crack cocaine might actually remove feelings of tension, withdrawal symptoms, and private verbalizations (cognitions) about how crummy his life is for a period of time. The next time he is telling himself his life is no good, is feeling stressed, and has cravings associated with withdrawal, he might have an increased likelihood of smoking crack to remove those aversive events, because they were previously removed or lessened upon using crack. The negatively reinforcing consequences of drug use thwart keeping a commitment to live drug-free. In this way, his crack smoking is under the influence of both negative reinforcement and positive reinforcement (as is the case with many behaviors). For this reason, the responsible ACT therapist also analyzes the negatively reinforcing consequences for clinically relevant behavior competing with healthier committed actions.

**Positive punishment.** When something is *added to* the environment by a person's actions, and the person is *less likely* to do that behavior again in the future because of that consequence, the behavioral scientist would say that the effect on the behavior comes from positive punishment. The typical theoretical example is corporal punishment. Suppose a child talks back to his mother and she responds to the recalcitrant behavior with a spanking. If the "talking back to mother" behavior has a reduced likelihood of happening again, then adding the swats on his rear end was a positive punisher. In a clinical example, an ACT therapist might have to look out for positive punishers from the environment when a client is make solid gains. For instance, a client with dependent personality disorder might be responding well to the therapist's assertiveness training in the counseling sessions, but when she tries to be assertive with her mother, her mom presents very critical comments and insults. Under those conditions, there is a reduced likelihood that the assertive behaviors are going to happen in the context with her mother because the insults are positively punishing.

**Negative punishment.** When something is *removed from* the environment by a person's actions, and the person is *less likely* to do that behavior again in the future because of that consequence, the behavioral scientist would say that the effect on the behavior comes from negative punishment. The oft-cited example is grounding a teenager. When a 17-year-old girl walks in the door after her curfew has passed, her father tells her she cannot go out with her friends for a week. When she is finally allowed out again after the week is over, she has a decreased probability of coming in the door after curfew because the access to her friends was contingently removed by the punishment. Clinically, an ACT therapist should assess for negatively punishing events that reduce the likelihood of improvement. For instance, a husband might aim to commit to making more intimate comments and gestures to his spouse, but every time he does, the spouse turns away or leaves the situation. The spouse's removal from the context would present negatively punishing consequences to the intimacy attempts, if indeed the husband's behaviors reduce in probability.

**Extinction.** Sometimes, previously reinforced behaviors will not lead to a reinforcer, and when this happens, the applied behavioral scientist cannot say that the behavior is being reinforced *or* punished. When this happens, the suspension of reinforcement over time is called *extinction* and leads to special behavioral phenomena. Initially, when the previously reinforced behavior no longer has access to a reinforcer, there is typically an increase in the response rate, which is followed by a decrease in response rate. When we look at extinction in a research laboratory, we can observe a pigeon in an operant chamber where it reliably pecks a key for food pellets. If the food hopper stops delivering the pellets, the pigeon does not stop pecking; in fact, we will likely observe the rate of pecking increasing. This is called the "extinction burst." If the responses during the extinction burst continue not to be reinforced, the pigeon will likely cease the pecking behavior after a period of attempts.

The extinction burst phenomenon is important for clinicians to understand for two reasons. First, when extinction bursts happen, there is also an exacerbation of conditioned emotional responses (such as adrenal reflex response, increased heart rate, or heightened muscle tension). Put simply, if the client is used to getting good stuff for certain actions, but then the good stuff stops, she will likely get irritated or angry. Second, extinction bursts can be affiliated with a client's escalation in clinically relevant behaviors. When previously reinforced behavior change strategies do not work like they used to (are no longer reinforced), the clinically relevant behaviors can increase in measurable characteristics, such as rate and intensity. For instance, let's turn and look at A.J.'s drug use. If previous consequences do not happen from the clinically relevant behaviors of smoking crack, because a tolerance has built up, the drug addict might take more puffs from the pipe to get the same sensations. Consider how Miguel struggles with his obsessive-compulsive repertoire due to thoughts of contamination. Miguel might experience that after weeks of washing regularly, he has to scrub harder to feel comfortable. The significant problem with this is that if the extinction burst *does* get reinforced, that tends to be the new baseline for the clinically relevant behavior. When A.J. is attempting to get high, he will just start at that increased dose. When Miguel starts to wash, he will immediately begin with the heightened vigor.

Consequences to behavior are powerful in terms of making it less or more likely to occur. Behavior therapists attempt to assess what consequences might be maintaining a clinically relevant behavior, and build a functional intervention to remove or change that environment-behavior relationship, so that the clinically relevant behavior is less likely to occur. Further, the ACT therapist utilizes these principles to increase the likelihood of the committed actions that are important to the client. This approach can be done in many different ways, and we will discuss those codified treatments in future chapters. Another approach to intervening with clinically relevant behaviors is assessing and altering the antecedents to such behaviors, and also changing antecedents to set the occasion for committed actions to happen.

## ANTECEDENTS

An antecedent comes before the behavior. There are several ways to categorize antecedent events: 1) setting events, 2) motivational operations, and 3) discriminative stimuli ($S^D$s).

**Setting events.** Setting events are the circumstances that have developed through previous experiences that have an overarching effect on behavior. In other words, setting events have been established in the person's history and have shaped how the environment can influence that particular individual. Bijou and Baer (1961) suggest "a setting event is a stimulus-response interaction, which simply because it has occurred will affect other stimulus-response relationships which follow it" (p. 21). For example, Gregory is a 42-year-old client reporting a history of being reared by an alcoholic mother who exhibited a very passive-aggressive repertoire. Gregory is also a survivor of clergy abuse during his time in junior high school. His childhood was fraught with painful stimuli, and in the past when he tried to assert himself, he was severely punished, while when he simply "took" the abuse, he was left alone or told he was a "good boy." That long series of stimulus-response events can affect other stimulus-response events that come after it. Even now, despite the fact that his mother and the predator are deceased, Gregory still responds to his boss's and boyfriend's abusive attacks by submitting to their demands and failing to assert himself. The early childhood experiences are setting events for his current submissive responses. Extended contextual factors, such as coming from a privileged background, living in a particular subculture, getting divorced, being a military veteran, and so on, are all antecedent influences on a client's potential responses. Setting events are important to a behavioral analysis, and that is why the first therapy session typically includes an assessment of the client's background and relevant history.

**Motivational operations.** A motivational operation (MO) is a more specifically defined setting event. Michael (1993) defined an MO as "an environmental event, operation, or stimulus condition that affects an organism by momentarily altering (a) the reinforcing effectiveness of other events, and (b) the frequency of occurrence of the type of behavior that had been consequated by those other events" (p. 58). The MO can be categorized into two types: establishing operations (EOs) and abolishing operations (AOs). An establishing operation will increase the likelihood that a stimulus will be reinforcing and increases the probability of behavior, and an abolishing operation will reduce the likelihood that the stimulus will be reinforcing and decreases the probability of the behavior. Whether an EO or AO, a motivational operation will temporarily modify how impactful a consequence will be on the response, and how likely the response will be emitted.

For example, Mark is a 49-year-old restaurant owner who struggles with anxiety. He has developed a new pattern recently in which when a stressful event occurs, he goes to his medicine cabinet and takes leftover Vicodin prescribed to his spouse for a wisdom tooth extraction a year prior. The pills have been available to him for over 12 months, but now that stressful events are occurring, those events can be seen by his therapist as a motivational operation: the pharmaceuticals have a greater potential to act as a reinforcer for swallowing them in the presence of high anxiety, and there is an increased likelihood that he will do so under stressful conditions. Including MOs in the behavioral analysis with the client's clinically relevant concerns helps include the physiological, medical, reflexive, and environmental issues that surround and contextualize the person's struggle. ACT therapists who can incorporate this kind of contextual analysis will have a greater likelihood of successfully influencing clients to engage in more committed action.

**Discriminative stimuli.** Discriminative stimuli (S^D) are the antecedent events correlated with reinforcers. They can act as a signal for the opportunity to engage in a behavior that will be reinforced, and this is learned by experience. S^Ds are antecedent stimuli, and after experiencing the contingencies involved with these stimuli, the reinforced response has an increased likelihood to occur in the presence of the S^D. Behaviors that are differentially influenced by these antecedents are under *stimulus control*. In other words, the environment has certain elements that will evoke someone's behavior. The environmental stimuli strongly influence (or "control") the person's actions.

In treatment, the ACT therapist assesses for the antecedents that have stimulus control over clinically relevant responses. Simply put, therapists investigate what cues set the person up to engage in her problematic behavior or, conversely, improved committed actions. When a 12-step sponsor tells a person struggling with addiction to "avoid the faces and the places," he is instructing the person to not come in contact with the S^Ds that might occasion a relapse. The sight of a sink, scrub brushes, and an antimicrobial soap dispenser can act as an S^D for a person dealing with contamination obsessions and compulsive washing. Understand that simply seeing the sink, brushes, and soap does not necessarily evoke the washing. The S^D does not *cause* the operant behavior to occur; however, it "sets the occasion" for washing *if* the setting events and MOs are in place, and there is a history of negative reinforcement related to the washing behavior. Please recall that contextual behavioral science analyzes the act-in-context, so all of the elements related to the antecedent-behavior-consequence are combined to develop a robust analysis.

The antecedent-behavior-consequence model for analyzing behavior is useful for a very simple behavior analysis, but for greater precision, scope, and depth, the additional elements to the consequences and antecedents should be included. When the ACT therapist begins an analysis, she will try to gather as much information as she can about the person and the person's environment and behavior, so that she can be more helpful, and the therapeutic efforts can lead to measurable results. Let's revisit the ABC analysis example about eating unhealthy food earlier in this chapter. An ACT therapist would probably not be satisfied with that ABC model example, but would ask for background information, assess the current environment, and do a functional assessment to discover the purpose or consequential events that come after the behavior. Suppose the person who eats the unhealthy food is used to getting her way, given the manner in which she was reared in her family, and she lives a fairly undisciplined lifestyle. When that person hasn't eaten for some time, she might label herself as "hungry." When she wanders around her kitchen, her favorite unhealthy food is in her environment. Those are the antecedents to the behavior of eating the unhealthy food. Each one of those antecedents acts as either a setting event, MO, or S^D.

| Antecedent | Behavior | Consequence |
|---|---|---|
| *Used to getting her way* (Setting event) | *Eating the unhealthy food* | *Flavor of the favorite food* (Positive reinforcement) |
| *Few skills on self-discipline* (Setting event) | | *Hunger pangs removed* (Negative reinforcement) |
| *Hunger, food deprivation* (Motivational operation) | | *Feeling satiated* (Positive reinforcement) |
| *The presence of a food with highly reinforcing properties* (Discriminative stimulus) | | *Not experiencing the discomfort of self-discipline* (Negative reinforcement) |

In addition, there are different consequences contributing to the increased likelihood that this person will eat the unhealthy food again. The immediate consequences of the flavor of the food and feeling satiated can act as positive reinforcers, while the removal of both the hunger pangs and the aversiveness of trying to control one's behavior is negatively reinforcing. Looking at all the different types of environmental events when investigating the act-in-context gives the ACT therapist much more to work with.

Going deeper than a simple ABC investigation and including more complex perspectives on the surrounding context of the behavior allows a richer intervention to develop. We'll revisit A.J. and Miguel in the next chapter in order to give examples of identifying clinically relevant issues in a functional assessment. For now, recognize how the fundamentals of the ABCs are important for clinical work. Investigating and discussing a client's setting events can even help the person become more accepting of who he is because he understands his unchangeable history. Knowing the motivational operations of problematic behavior could help the client regulate his environment so he doesn't get set up to break his commitments. Discussing the discriminative stimuli helps the client see the cues for action that are important, and could lead to important reinforcers. When teaching mindfulness to clients, the ACT therapist can motivate the client to do his mindfulness exercises because contacting the present moment makes people more aware of their $S^D$s. In other words, the more mindful you are, the better you will be at seeing opportunities to contact important values-based outcomes. Further, analyzing consequences allows the ACT therapist to see what is immediately causing clinically relevant behavior. If the client learns how he is being reinforced for problematic behavior, and therapy focuses on altering the contingencies in the client's life, then there could be solid gains in the therapeutic endeavor. A full discussion of the principles and applications of behavioral science is beyond the scope of this book, but this chapter created a foundation for using those elements to help understand how to build stronger committed actions with the client. In chapter 4, we will discuss functional analysis in the context of therapy, but before proceeding, we need to highlight how the way we use language influences how people react to consequences and antecedents, and how relational framing alters the function of those stimuli.

# Relational Frame Theory and ACT

In addition to understanding how applied behavioral science influences committed action, ACT therapists will also do well to know how client and therapist verbal behavior might support or undermine committed action, too. To explore this topic, we turn to relational frame theory (RFT; Hayes, Barnes-Holmes, & Roche, 2001), a functional contextual theory of language and cognition that informs ACT. Having some familiarity with the processes outlined in RFT can enhance your ability to promote clients' engagement in committed actions.

Our intent in the following brief, relatively nontechnical exploration of RFT is to strengthen your understanding of the role of language in psychological flexibility and inflexibility. If you're interested in a more detailed description of RFT, we recommend reading the seminal RFT book *Relational Frame Theory: A Post-Skinnerian Account of Human Language and Cognition* (Hayes et al., 2001), or *Learning RFT* (Törneke, 2010), a volume dedicated to clinical applications of RFT. Three key features of RFT that are also important to committed action are relating stimuli, transformation of stimulus functions, and rule-governed behavior.

## Relating Stimuli

Human beings, as well as nonverbal animals, can learn to relate stimuli. For instance, in *conditioned discrimination training*, a pigeon or a human child might learn to make a response based on a formal relationship between two stimulus events—one based solely on characteristics that can be perceived with the senses. For example, a pigeon can be put into a chamber with two keys that it can peck and be reinforced with a pellet. Above the keys are slots that can display pictures of different-sized rectangles. When a red light is on in the environment, then pecking the key with the larger rectangle is followed by a food reinforcer, and pecking the other key is on an extinction schedule (no food is given). The experiment can mix up the positions of the rectangles, so that sometimes the larger one is above the left key and sometimes above the right key, but the pigeon only receives the reinforcer for choosing the key with the larger stimulus as long as the red light is on. The experiment continues, but the experimenter changes it a little bit. Instead of a red light, a green light illuminates the chamber, and puts choosing the larger stimulus on extinction (no longer reinforces that choice of behavior), but reinforces choosing the key corresponding to the smaller rectangle. The pigeon soon learns to select "larger than" in the presence of the red light and "smaller than" in the presence of the green light. The pigeon's behavior has been conditioned to discriminate between the physical properties of two stimuli, and the pigeon is then making *a response based on a relationship* between two stimuli. Recognize that the animal is choosing a stimulus not just on the basis of its own properties, but also on the basis of how those properties are related to the other stimuli in that context. If the experiment presents new rectangles of different sizes than the training stimuli, the pigeon will still choose "larger than" in the presence of the red light even when it has never experienced the new rectangles. The pigeon—along with a range of other animals, from bees to fish to monkeys—is capable of relating stimuli based on their *nonarbitrary* features (such as their color, size, or sound). Nonarbitrary refers to the physical, measurable properties of the stimuli. But what if the experiment changed by removing the rectangles and replacing them with a red light over one key and a green light over the other key? Which key would be pecked when presented with a "larger than" stimulus event? The pigeon has no history for choosing the red key, and the likelihood of pecking it would be no better than chance. However, most humans in this experiment would reliably select the red button because of a history of selecting "larger than" in the presence of red. There has been no reinforcement history of selecting *any* colors in this experiment, which is why the pigeon is simply "guessing." The only trained behaviors for the pigeon have been selecting "larger than"/"smaller than" stimuli. In the absence of a previous reinforcement history with selecting red stimuli in the presence of a "larger than" stimulus, a pigeon isn't likely to make such a choice. However, a human being can reliably make this type of choice, and behavioral scientists describe it as "bidirectional relating." Humans typically have a long reinforcement history of learning that if A=B, then B=A; there are two directions to this relationship, thus the term "bidirectional." If red=larger than, then larger than=red. Even if there has been no previous reinforcement for that *exact* relationship in the past, the person does have a history of that kind of relationship from the past. The person may not have been trained to choose red in the presence of "larger than," but *derived* the relationship based on past experiences; thus, the term derived relational responding. The word "derive" means to draw out from, take, deduce, or infer. Derived relational responding is behavior influenced not by direct contingencies, but drawn out from past experience with indirect contingencies such as stimuli that occasion a relationship (Blackledge & Moran, 2009). The ability to engage in derived relational responding helps human beings learn relationships between stimuli in the environment without actually having direct training in those relationships, and that can be very helpful under some conditions, but also problematic under other conditions.

During many daily experiences in childhood, humans learn to bidirectionally relate stimuli in the natural environment. Some of this relating is based on *arbitrary* features— that is, features determined by social convention or whim (Stewart & Roche, 2013). Parents and guardians, while talking to and interacting with the child, can set up antecedents and consequences that reinforce the child's behavior for relating stimuli based on arbitrary concepts of goodness, beauty, scariness, monetary value, and a myriad of other arbitrary ways to relate stimulus events. Through *multiple exemplar training* (in other words, repeated examples of a given stimulus-response relation), verbal humans learn to relate numerous stimuli on the basis of both nonarbitrary and arbitrary features. For instance, a child can be trained to select the smaller of two objects when presented with pairs of objects of varying sizes, shapes, and colors, and this would be a choice based on nonarbitrary stimuli. And the child can also be trained to select the more "beautiful" of the two objects, which would be a choice based on social whim, or arbitrary stimuli. Imagine a 3-year old child with two toys in front of her: a Barbie doll and a 2-foot tall teddy bear. Her uncle says to her, "Which one is the bigger toy?" This question is an antecedent for the behavior of pointing to the teddy bear. The uncle says, "Yes!" and tickles the child as a consequence, and because she likes being tickled, this is a reinforcer for selecting the physically, nonarbitrarily bigger toy when there is a smaller toy in the context, and the language being used in that context calls for a response related to "bigger." Similar instances like this are likely to happen throughout childhood, and a repertoire of successfully interacting with the world using language is being learned.

But imagine the uncle says to the child, "Which toy is more beautiful?" From the point of view of physical properties, neither one is more beautiful than the other one. Broadly speaking, beauty is based on social whim. Selecting one over the other is arbitrary. If the girl picks the teddy bear again, the uncle might grunt in disapproval or say, "No!" This would be a punishing consequence and make it less likely that she would pick the teddy bear in the context of "beautiful." When he asks again, she picks the Barbie doll and receives reinforcement for this arbitrary relational response. There is nothing more or less beautiful about that doll from a nonarbitrary view of the world, but human beings use language to influence behavior with arbitrary relations.

People are reared in the context of relationships through using language during their whole lives. Relating stimuli is a behavior that becomes so well reinforced that we don't even realize we are doing it almost constantly. (This is why mindfulness and defusion can become important for people who are being unhelpfully governed by language.) Arbitrary relational responding is essential for language acquisition, and this complex language skill allows humans to engage in other complex behaviors, such as building airplanes, creating works of art, or devising a numerical system. Relational responding also allows individuals to communicate practical information, such as "I want to get another Barbie doll when we go to the store," and to share private events, such as "I don't think I'm very beautiful" or "I feel angry that you taught me an oppressive viewpoint on beauty!"

Two ways in which relating stimuli is relevant to clinical concerns and psychotherapy are through the processes of cognitive fusion and self-as-content. In cognitive fusion, verbal relations between stimuli govern the person's responses in an inflexible manner. In other words, the language used in the relations is taken to be literally true. For example, "I am going to fail" and "Anxiety is bad" describe relations of correspondence between "I" and "failure," and between "anxiety" and "bad." Likewise, self-as-content is essentially an assortment of stimuli that a person has related in correspondence with the self. As discussed above, this can be useful for descriptions and communicating with others (for example, "My name is Sarah," "I'm a psychologist," and "I'm from New York"); however, such relations can become problematic when evaluative relations dominate (for example, "I'm too fat," "I'm not beautiful enough," and "I am unlovable").

In therapy, helpful stimulus relations can be established between values and committed actions. For example, when a client says, "I'm going to the gym so I can take care of my health," a relationship of correspondence between committed actions and values is established or strengthened. Similarly, when a client is asked, "What's that in the service of?" in regard to a specific committed action, he might notice that this action diverges from behaviors he relates as "values-consistent" and choose not to engage in the activity. Relationships between stimuli are clinically relevant because verbal stimuli carry nonverbal stimulus functions. For example, talking about sad events can lead to the emotion of sadness, and talking about scary events can prompt feelings of fear.

## *Transformation of Stimulus Functions*

*Transformation of stimulus functions* is a second feature of RFT relevant to psychological flexibility, inflexibility, and psychotherapy. This is an aspect of relational responding that occurs when the functions of one stimulus are transformed through its relationship to a second stimulus. If you recognize that Stimulus A is a reinforcer, and you learn that Stimulus A is the same as Stimulus B, you will likely work for Stimulus B even without any prior history of experience with Stimulus B.

Transformation of stimulus functions can even alter the properties of some stimulus events, and change them from aversive to appetitive. For example, a person who has learned that Rembrandt is a great painter or that paintings by Rembrandt are worth millions of dollars might come to appreciate a previously disliked painting upon learning that it was painted by Rembrandt. The stimulus functions of what she learns about Rembrandt transform the stimulus functions of the painting from "ugly," "boring," or "worthless," to "beautiful," "interesting," and "valuable," because the painting has been placed in a relation of correspondence with the name Rembrandt.

Transformation of stimulus functions accounts for much of the psychological relevance of RFT (Stewart & Roche, 2013). For example, a child might develop a fear of going to the dentist, even if she's never been to the dentist, because she already fears the family doctor and learns the relation "A dentist is a type of doctor." Similarly, a child might feel bad about himself if he hears, "Your father was a loser," and then later hears, "You're just like your father." Or consider a student fused with the thought that "anxiety is bad" and the relation that "I feel anxious when I speak in front of others." The combination of those two thoughts would likely make the person avoid speaking in front of people. Now, if that student engaged in goal setting to complete a college degree, and that degree required a course in public speaking, those *arbitrary thoughts* could become an obstacle to reaching the goal. Transformation of stimulus functions is evidenced if the person doesn't attempt an important, valued action because of the relations among the actions and anxiety, and anxiety and bad.

This transformation has implications for ACT interventions. For example, to create an exercise aimed at helping an anxious client engage in more committed action, the clinician can invite the client to simply notice relations that occur when he engages in anxiety-provoking behaviors. As mentioned earlier, committed action means engaging in behavior that aligns with personally authored values even in the presence of difficult private events, including language relations that can impede such actions. The simple defusion exercise restating thoughts with the formula "I'm having the thought that…" (Hayes, Strosahl, et al., 2012) can help clients experience such relations as something to be mindfully noticed, rather than facts that rigidly dictate behavior. These kinds of clinical devices weaken the transformation of stimulus functions that could be impeding committed action.

## Rule-Governed Behavior

When a child touches a hot stove, the consequence of burnt fingers usually leads the child to avoid touching hot stoves again. Fortunately, human beings can use language skills to learn to avoid painful stimuli without actually experiencing the pain, so most children can learn not to touch hot stoves without getting burned. This is made possible by *rule-governed behavior*. In this context, a rule is a verbal antecedent that affects behavior without the necessity of contacting contingencies in the natural environment (Törneke, Luciano, & Valdivia Salas, 2008). For example, a person can listen to and follow the rule "Don't touch the hot stove, or you'll burn your hand." The relations between the stimulus events of "you," "don't," and "touch," can have an effect on the person's actions. This would be especially effective if the person has a history with experiencing pain related to the verbal event "burn." The rule creates temporal relations and relations of coordination between "you," "touch," "stove," "will," and "burn." The ability to engage rule-governed behavior via language allows for a variety of behaviors to serve as reinforcers or lead to valued outcomes simply through the influence of language. People can follow rules to bake a cake, program a computer, build a birdhouse, start a family, or create meaningful spiritual experiences. The power of language and rules over human actions is vast.

Rules are especially useful when they allow us to avoid aversive consequences or to contact desired consequences without taking the time needed to learn the target behaviors through natural shaping processes. For example, would you rather learn to wear your seatbelt by the natural shaping process of getting injured in car crashes a few times and then discovering that if you are wearing a seatbelt during a collision, you are less likely to get injured, or would you rather just be given the rule: "Wear your seatbelt." As mentioned throughout this section, human beings can learn things without actually coming into contact with direct contingencies, thanks to relational responding, and that shows how very helpful language can be.

However, rules can potentially be problematic in two ways that are relevant to mental health problems and their treatment. First, control by rules can make individuals insensitive to the actual contingencies operating in the environment (Hayes, Kohlenberg, & Melancon, 1989). For example, a recipe for soup with an error in it might call for adding a tablespoon of salt once the liquid starts to boil, instead of a teaspoon. The rule is faulty, whereas if the cook had instead gradually added salt and tasted, the natural consequence of a desired level of saltiness might have prevented an excess of sodium. For a more clinically relevant example, a person might learn "People cannot be trusted" and therefore not attempt to have deeper, more intimate relationships, thereby missing out on the opportunity to learn how to discriminate between those who can and cannot be trusted.

A second way in which rules can be problematic is when they generate or maintain dysfunctional behavior (Hayes et al., 1989). For example, the rule "If you never get intimate with someone, you can avoid the pain of a breakup" is accurate. At the same time, a breakup is not the only possible outcome of a relationship, and avoiding relationships means avoiding the possibility of an enduring relationship as well as avoiding the pain of a breakup. Additionally, avoiding potential romantic relationships might be counter to the person's values. So, although following the rule of staying out of potential intimate relationships in order to avoid pain may be "successful," it wouldn't be functional when measured against the person's values.

# What Does RFT Have to Do with Committed Action?

We believe that learning about RFT at a basic level can contribute to your effectiveness as an ACT therapist, both in delivering ACT and in understanding the theory behind it. Westrup suggests that "familiarity with RFT is clinically helpful, because in clarifying how our relationship with language can cause so much difficulty, we see that these difficulties are a fundamental aspect of being human" (2014, p. 17). The power of arbitrary relational responding on overt behavior can be very helpful to shape up values-based committed actions, but relational responding also creates obstacles for committed actions at times. Accordingly, and where applicable, we'll briefly discuss ways in which language can affect behaviors in case examples throughout this book. Now that we have reviewed the fundamentals of behavioral science and relational frame theory, we can move forward with identifying and planning committed actions.

## Summary

This chapter took a look at the philosophical assumptions of contextual behavioral science, as well as the general basic principles of behavior change. We investigated how to perform a behavioral analysis with the ABC approach, discussed the details involved with antecedents and consequences, and suggested how this approach is important for clinical work. In addition, we looked at language from a relational frame theory point of view, and reviewed how language is involved in behavior change. In chapter 4, we'll discuss strategies for assessing, identifying, and evaluating execution of committed actions.

# Assessing and Planning Committed Actions with Contextual Behavioral Science

As a therapist, before you can help clients select relevant or immediate committed actions, you first need to complete a thorough assessment of their current needs and context so you can fully understand the presenting complaint and identify appropriate treatment goals. ACT utilizes functional assessment to accomplish this.

## Functional Analysis of Behavior

A functional analysis is a form of behavioral assessment useful for understanding behavior and developing and evaluating behavioral interventions. All of the contextual variables that we discussed in chapter 3 are considered when using contextual behavioral science for analyzing a client's clinical issues. According to Follette, Naugle, and Linnerooth (2000), a functional assessment has six steps:

1. Identifying clinically relevant behaviors and the contextual variables that maintain them.

2. Identifying which functional variables have the greatest impact on the behavior—that is, which consequences, environmental cues, states of motivation, and other functional variables maintain the behavior of interest.

3. Developing an intervention plan based on the resulting understanding of the behavior.

4. Implementing the intervention developed in step 3.

5. Assessing the outcome of the previous four steps—determining whether there was a change in the target behavior.

6. Evaluating the outcome of the functional assessment—determining whether the functional variables that maintain the behavior are correctly understood, whether behavior change follows application of the intervention, and whether the change in behavior is maintained.

Note that the terms "functional assessment" and "functional analysis" are used somewhat interchangeably, though technically a functional analysis is more thorough, with a functional assessment not becoming a functional analysis until steps 5 and 6 are completed.

# Functional Assessment in Clinical Work

Once the therapist understands these six steps and the ABCs that go into this process, she can begin to do a clinically helpful functional analysis. The clinician will certainly begin to have greater impact with the functional assessment when also incorporating how relational framing has an influence on how people respond to their environment. (We will explore that perspective in the "Using Values Clarification to Identify Target Behaviors" section of this chapter.) Let's take a closer look at how functional analysis is important for A.J.—the client who has significant struggles with crack cocaine—by discussing the first two steps in the Follette et al. model: identifying clinically relevant behaviors, and identifying which functional variables have the greatest impact on behavior. The clinically relevant problem is very obvious to the client and the clinician. This could be described as "getting high," and that term could be used throughout therapy, but the therapist might want to be more precise. The problem could be operationally defined as "inhaling the smoke from heated, crystalized cocaine," but from a practical perspective, the therapist does not have to be so precise, because the client might find ways around the definition. The clinically relevant behavior could simply be defined as "purposefully creating conditions that lead to intoxication with drugs or alcohol." Once defined, using the colloquialisms will likely be fine during therapy sessions.

After defining the behavior, A.J. could be asked about the characteristics of this behavior. The therapist could look at the intensity of his high on a scale of one to ten, or how this problematic behavior happens with short latency after he wakes up in the morning, but perhaps the most useful characteristic to measure for A.J. is rate. The therapist queries how many times a week A.J. purposefully creates conditions where he is intoxicated by crack cocaine. (Of course, self-report is often unreliable from clients, especially someone who engages in frequent drug abuse. We're simply describing how a functional analysis is completed in this section. For further information on improving the veracity of drug addiction data, see the National Institute on Drug Abuse archives; NIDA, 2017). The clinician, with informed consent from A.J., will endeavor to work with him to reduce the rate of this clinically relevant behavior.

At this point of the description, you might be thinking that this aim is missing out on the richness of acceptance and commitment therapy. You could be concerned that the therapist is not trying to help A.J. accept his cravings or defuse from his negative self-talk. The goal of reducing the rate of the response might seem like it is missing a nuanced discussion of values and the core self, and it is not including the power of mindfulness interventions. This book is focusing on the committed action component of the ACT hexagon model. All those other components of the intervention are inextricably intertwined with committed action, and we're simply highlighting that one domain in this book. In the case of A.J., reducing the rate of his substance use, no matter how sterile that may seem in the context of ACT, is the aim.

With this objective in mind, the ACT therapist analyzes A.J.'s drug abuse using the ABC approach discussed in the last chapter. Such a therapeutic assessment process helps define the act-in-context with precision, scope, and depth, and assists the therapist in assessing how the client's behavior is influenced by environmental variables. The initial evaluation assesses the context of the presenting problem, and includes an investigation of the client's history and current stressors. In the initial interview, A.J. reports that his parents were also drug users, as are many other people in his family. This information could lead the therapist to surmise that there might be a genetic proclivity toward addiction and realize that this genetic influence and the way A.J.'s parents reared him are setting events for his addictive behaviors. There are rarely interventions available to the psychotherapist that would directly alter the setting events, and it is still good to know these contextual variables during the therapeutic endeavor. For example, when A.J. becomes harshly critical of himself, discussing how there are events that were not under his control that led to his problematic behavior, awareness of these historical facts could help engender more effective self-compassion and self-acceptance. In addition, knowing the setting events might support defusion when A.J. says, "This is all my fault!" The therapist wouldn't necessarily dispute that denigrating thought but would ask, "How is thinking that working for you?" to see if the influence of that verbalization could be depotentiated or weakened, so as not to exacerbate the stress that he is experiencing, which could occasion further drug use.

During assessment, the ACT therapist also explores other antecedents that set up A.J.'s drug use. Because A.J. reports that he hates his job and feels overwhelmed, those emotional stressors can act as motivational operations that set up the crack cocaine to be a reinforcer. For example, if A.J. actually enjoyed his job and found it meaningful, getting high on crack cocaine during his free time might not be as attractive. A therapist might consider using several approaches to reducing the workplace stress that occasions drug use. Relaxation therapy could reduce the stress reactions, or finding a new job could assist with addressing the difficulties in his life that make him want to seek the reinforcing consequences of getting high. Keep in mind that some antecedent interventions are not very practical—for example, A.J. might not have opportunities to get another job. However, this chapter is highlighting clinical functional analysis, and aims to discuss a full array of different influences on behavior and how they might be altered.

Another influence on the drug use is the discriminative stimulus of the availability of the crack cocaine. Clearly the drug use wouldn't be possible if A.J. could fully avoid situations that present the substance to him. Some therapeutic approaches would suggest, as a method of reducing temptation, that A.J. take a different way home from work rather than pass by his crack house. The phrase often used in recovery, "Avoid the faces and the places," instructs him to diminish his contact with the discriminative stimuli correlated with all the immediate positively reinforcing consequences of smoking crack.

Assessing the antecedents for problematic behavior is important because ACT therapists choose to look at the act-in-context, and this is a practical focus for treatment plans. A person who uses drugs only to magnify his euphoria in order to have fun at a party has a different motivational operation than a person doing drugs to escape the experience of work and life stress. At the same time, antecedent interventions are unlikely to be sufficient, so the therapist must also look at consequences and how language influences the client's behavior.

| Antecedent | Behavior | Consequence |
|---|---|---|
| *Genetic proclivity to addiction* (Setting event)<br><br>*Parents were drug users* (Setting event)<br><br>*Workplace stress* (Motivational operation)<br><br>*Availability of crack cocaine* (Discriminative stimulus) | Smokes crack | *Feeling of euphoria* (Positive reinforcement)<br><br>*Removal of tension from stress* (Negative reinforcement)<br><br>*Removal of negative self-talk* (Negative reinforcement)<br><br>*Withdrawal symptoms* (Positive punishment, but not immediately, so it is unlikely to affect his behavior) |

Immediately following the first inhalation of the crack cocaine, A.J. experiences euphoric feelings, and given his repertoire, this euphoria functions as a positive reinforcer. The feelings of stress wash away temporarily, as does his self-denigrating verbal behavior, and these consequences likely function as negative reinforcers. Both of these immediate consequences function to increase further likelihood of crack smoking. A person might argue that the uncomfortable physiological withdrawal symptoms that occur after using crack would act as something added to his world, and that it should diminish the use of drugs, and therefore introducing a positive punisher to the analysis. Although it might be a positive stimulus and be uncomfortable, that consequence happens too long after the behavior to actually have a direct influence on the probability of the behavior.

This kind of functional analysis helps in conceptualizing how to plan treatment for A.J. Knowing that there are contextual variables that function to increase the likelihood of A.J.'s addictive behavior helps to broaden the treatment perspective. His drug misuse is no longer blamed on "lacking willpower" or his culture or upbringing. We would not say that his use is exclusively caused by a mental illness or his substance use disorder. (Concerns regarding formal diagnosis will be further addressed later in the chapter.) Now the functional contextual therapist can analyze how his behavior functions in that context.

But just knowing that environmental consequences encourage further misuse is not enough; that knowledge just contributes to the clinical picture. It is not always possible to take away the reinforcing properties of some stimuli. (If A.J. were addicted to alcohol, perhaps administering the drug Antabuse could have such an effect because it reacts with the alcohol and nauseates the client. This would function as a punisher for imbibing. But this kind of intervention is not currently possible for A.J.'s cocaine problem.) It will be impossible for a therapist to directly make cocaine less positively and negatively reinforcing from a physiological perspective. But the power of language can alter the reinforcing properties of the substance use. Asking A.J. to discuss the purpose of the drug use, clarify his values, and learn from verbal discussions about how the drug use is actually exacerbating the problems that he is trying to escape from could be helpful. Before we explore values and how the language-based interventions of ACT might help A.J. start living a healthier, psychologically flexible life, we need to cover a few other ideas related to assessment and planning committed actions in therapy.

# Distinguishing Between Formal and Functional Assessment

Developing an effective ACT treatment plan, including identifying and planning committed actions, typically relies less on a formal diagnosis and more on an assessment of the client's behavioral repertoire and values. As previously mentioned, A.J.'s problems are not caused by having "an addiction" or because he "has a substance use disorder."

Those are just verbal descriptions of his repertoire, not an analysis of the function of his clinically relevant behavior. Functional analysis gives us some observable, measurable, and even manipulable environmental events that can be influenced. If the therapist values the contextual behavioral approach and keeps the assumptions of functional contextualism, then she has to go beyond just talking about a formal diagnosis or a mental illness as the cause of the problem.

To clarify the distinction between formal and functional assessments, let's consider a different client: Kyla, a 28-year-old single woman. In her first session, she reported that she had previously been diagnosed with obsessive-compulsive disorder and had been to several therapists in the past seven years. She felt that she hadn't made much progress on improving her symptoms. She continued to be plagued by obsessions about hurting people and checking compulsions that revolved around making sure that she hadn't hit someone with her car or bicycle, or that she hadn't inadvertently left an appliance or other device turned on that might explode and kill someone. She noted that she had dropped out of college twice in order to control the frequency of her symptoms. She was taking a benzodiazepine when she felt she needed one, yet continued to experience frequent symptoms. Kyla said that a friend of hers had read a magazine article about ACT and suggested that she try an ACT therapist. She also said that she felt motivated to get better and deal with life.

A diagnosis such as obsessive-compulsive disorder can be useful for completing an insurance form or assessment report, communicating with other behavioral health professionals, or discussing the presenting complaint with a client. However, a diagnosis alone won't take an ACT therapist very far in developing a comprehensive treatment plan.

A conflict arises because ACT is a functional contextual approach to treating mental health problems, and the *Diagnostic and Statistical Manual of Mental Disorders* (*DSM*) isn't based on functional diagnoses. Debates about the clinical utility of the *DSM* have raged for decades. On the one hand, some writers, such as Kendell and Jablensky (2014), conclude that *DSM* diagnoses are useful to clinicians because they provide important information about the probable etiology and course of the difficulty, as well as insight into how the client might respond to treatment. On the other hand, some argue that such diagnoses are too generic: "The main problem with psychiatric diagnosis is that groups identified by a common label, for example schizophrenia, in fact have little in common. The level of heterogeneity in terms of psychopathology, need for care, treatment response, illness course, cognitive vulnerabilities, environmental exposures and biological correlates is so great that it becomes implausible that these labels can provide much clinical utility" (van Os, Delespaul, Wigman, Myin-Germeys, & Wichers, 2013, p. 113). Although the purpose of this book is not to debate the clinical utility of the *DSM*, we do take the position that, in contrast to a diagnostic assessment, a functional assessment can provide information essential to creating a treatment plan that addresses the individual's presenting complaint while also being sensitive to the present and historical contexts of the client, including personal goals and values, regardless of whether the client has a *DSM* diagnosis (or a diagnosis within any other classification system).

Returning to Kyla, observation and functional assessment suggested that she thought about harming other people much of the time and especially after spending time around other people. Her checking compulsions functioned to momentarily decrease her obsessions about harming someone and briefly decrease her anxiety. Further, her checking behavior increased when she was alone, when her anxiety was high for any reason, and just after she had recently been around other people.

| Antecedent | Behavior | Consequence |
|---|---|---|
| *Ongoing obsessive-compulsive repertoire experiences* (Setting event) | Goes back into her house and checks the stove | *Seeing the stove is not on* (Positive reinforcement) |
| *Being around other people* (Motivational operation) | | *Removal of tension from stress* (Negative reinforcement) |
| *Heightened arousal; feelings of "anxiety"* (Motivational operation) | | |
| *Thinking "I might have left the stove on."* (Verbal discriminative stimulus) | | |

Because her obsessions and compulsions increased after being around other people, it might seem—at first glance and to the uninitiated in functional analysis—that an appropriate intervention for decreasing both her obsessions and her compulsions would be to decrease the time she spends with other people in order to reduce the motivational operation. To test this hypothesis, Kyla's therapist could ask her to monitor her obsessions and compulsions while carrying out her usual activities for several days, and then have her monitor her obsessions and compulsions after reducing her contact with others by 50 percent. Alternatively, since her obsessions increased when she was more anxious, the therapist might try to decrease her heightened arousal and feelings of anxiety by increasing the dosage of her medication or prescribing a different anxiolytic. This intervention may be helpful, given that the functional assessment suggests that Kyla's compulsive checking increases when her anxiety is high, so anything that decreases her anxiety might be followed by a decrease in compulsive checking.

On the one hand, these interventions might be helpful for Kyla, and she may end treatment feeling grateful that her compulsive checking has decreased. On the other hand, we don't yet know whether these interventions would be acceptable to her. Perhaps she would actually value increasing her social engagement, in which case decreasing her interactions with others would be undesirable. Perhaps she would personally value reducing or ending her reliance on anxiolytic medication. Although the proposed interventions might be useful for decreasing compulsive checking, the therapist needs to determine whether Kyla sees decreased checking as an important treatment goal. As mentioned, she read about ACT in a magazine article, and she may have read that ACT does not primarily focus on symptom reduction.

# Using Values Clarification to Identify Target Behaviors

The preceding example illustrates a noteworthy limitation of considering client problems largely in terms of clinical disorders and levels of symptoms. When we see them through a lens of syndromal classification, it's easy to focus only on symptoms that should be targeted for reduction. And while functional assessment is useful for understanding the functions of behaviors and essential for selecting behavior change strategies that are likely to be effective, it too has limitations, one being that many functional assessment procedures were developed for the treatment of simple behavior problems, rather than complex presentations (Dahl, Plumb, Stewart, & Lundgren, 2009). Therefore, although these techniques can help therapists identify and evaluate interventions that could be effective for behavior change, functional assessment alone only goes so far in deciding which interventions will be most useful for a specific client with a specific presenting complaint. One more step is needed in order to identify behaviors that can be called committed actions. In ACT, that step is values clarification. This is where the clinician will begin to have greater influence with the functional assessment by incorporating how language has an influence on people's response to the environment.

Values clarification can be used as a standpoint from which to identify committed actions that are consistent with an individual's values. In ACT, "values are used to help clients select directions for their lives that are congruent with what is deeply important to them and establish goals supporting movement in those directions" (Dahl et al., 2009, p. 1). Thus, while functional analysis can aid in identifying the variables influencing problem behaviors and point to interventions that might be effective for behavior change, the addition of values clarification ensures that proposed interventions are consistent not only with the functional analysis, but also with what matters to the client.

Although values clarification is an ongoing part of treatment, a thorough values assessment can be useful relatively early in treatment because it can aid in identifying appropriate committed actions for the client and help build motivation for change. As noted in chapter 2, values are defined in ACT as "verbally construed global desired life consequences" (Hayes et al., 1999, p. 206). Importantly, values are not just attitudes or judgments about what's important. Values are linked to actions in that it's generally possible to identify people's values by observing their actions, more so than by what they say they value. For example, someone might say, "I value being active in my community." However, this statement alone may not provide much evidence of the person's values in this domain; it's also necessary to know how important this value is to her and what actions she takes in the service of being active in her community, such as being informed about community events and issues, voting, volunteering, and so on. More colloquially, in ACT it's often said that "you value with your feet." In other words, we can talk about our values, but ultimately they're expressed and lived in actions, not words. So, an important goal in ACT is to use values clarification exercises to help clients identify their values and also identify how their behavior is values-consistent or how it can become more values-consistent.

Values clarification work most often begins in the form of a semi-structured interview with clients in which the clinician first explains what values are in the context of ACT and then helps clients identify their values, the relative importance of those values, and how they are currently acting in the service of their values. There are also worksheets that clinicians or clients can use to facilitate this process, such as the Valued Living Questionnaire-2 (VLQ-2; Wilson, 2008). The VLQ-2 lists 12 life domains, including areas such as family, marriage, work, friends and social life, recreation, and physical self-care. Clients are then tasked with identifying how possible it is that something meaningful could happen for them in each domain, assessing how important each domain is, and identifying actions they're currently taking in each domain. Finally, they're asked to evaluate how satisfied they are with their level of action in each domain and to note any concerns regarding each.

Returning to Kyla, when she considered the domains of family and friends in values clarification, she identified "being there for those I care about" as an important value. When her therapist asked her to elaborate by describing her actions in the service of this value, she said, "I let my brother borrow my car when his car broke down, and I went to the pharmacy for my friend when she was sick." When asked about how satisfied she was with her actions in the service of being there for others, she said, "I did those things more than a year ago. After I let my brother use my car, I worried that maybe there was a problem with the engine and he could be killed and it would be my fault. I kept texting him and calling to make sure he was okay, and then he got mad and said he never wanted to borrow my car again. And with my friend, well, after I got her medication, I worried that maybe I got the wrong medication and she would get even sicker. I probably checked the label 50 times. Then, after I gave it to her, I called to check on her several times, and I even used my spare key to get into her house and check the medication while she was sleeping. I want to help people, but it gets messed up. So no, I'm not satisfied with my actions."

Returning briefly to the limitations of functional analysis in the absence of values clarification, for Kyla, an intervention aimed at decreasing her social interactions as a strategy for reducing her checking behavior might indeed reduce that behavior. However, it wouldn't help Kyla increase her values-based behavior in the service of being there for others. If her therapist hadn't engaged in values clarification work, he wouldn't know this. Functional analysis should not stand on its own without an investigation of values.

A growing number of clinical resources are available to assist clinicians in conducting values assessments and evaluating values-consistent behavior. For example, in the series of which this book is a part (the Acceptance and Commitment Therapy Series), there is an entire volume dedicated to values clarification: *The Art and Science of Valuing in Psychotherapy* (Dahl et al., 2009), and values clarification is addressed in most book-length ACT clinical manuals. There are also book chapters and a growing body of research articles and assessment instruments available on this topic. In addition to aids for conducting an initial values assessment, there are values clarification tools aimed at specific populations, such as the Chronic Pain Values Inventory (McCracken & Yang, 2006). There are also instruments for helping clients monitor how consistent their actions are with their values, such as the Bull's-Eye Values Survey (Lundgren et al., 2012).

Values can move clients toward committed action in a few different ways, even if the context for that behavior is not immediately reinforcing. With regard to specific behaviors, values can provide an answer to the question "What's that in the service of?" Kyla's therapist could ask, "How come you show up to therapy on a regular basis? What is that in the service of?" When Kyla says, "I really wish I could get more integrated with my friends and family," she would be verbalizing her values. Values clarification can also be a powerful tool for helping clients identify behaviors that aren't working (in other words, behaviors that aren't congruent with their values) as well as behaviors they may want to increase or skills they may wish to learn in order to enable them to engage in more values-consistent behavior. Kyla might articulate that when she obsesses about potential problems in her home after she leaves her apartment, her compulsive behavior of going back to check sometimes makes her late or totally miss events with her social group. Her therapist would do well to capitalize on relational framing in order to alter the contingencies that show up during an exposure exercise. When Kyla is asked to leave her house without going back in and checking the stove, she could be doing that not to reduce the OCD "symptomology," but as a broadening of her repertoire so she has more time with friends and family, since she's no longer wasting time checking.

To facilitate identification of client target behaviors, therapists can ask clients which behaviors they most want to change. The therapist may ask questions to determine which changes will lead to the greatest change in other behaviors of interest, which behaviors are easiest or fastest to change, or which changes will have the most significant impact on the client's quality of life (Bach & McCracken, 2002). There's no single "right" way to begin taking committed action. Beginning with the committed action the client most wants to engage in can obviously provide a great deal of motivation for change. (In fact, such a values articulation can be viewed as a verbal motivational operation.) Selecting the easiest behavior to change might improve motivation by allowing for early success. Alternatively, selecting a committed action that will have beneficial effects on other behaviors might widen the scope of an intervention. For example, making a commitment to improve social skills might have wider effects on a client's social behaviors and outcomes, or making a commitment to practice an anger management technique might have broad benefits in terms of a client's occupational behaviors and outcomes. These are just a few suggestions for ways to identify effective, individualized committed actions. Whatever strategy you use, be sure to include input from clients about what outcomes they'd like to aim for with their committed actions. In other words, what is any given choice in the service of?

# The Challenge of Using Committed Action to Decrease Behavior

Clients are frequently as interested in decreasing problematic behaviors as they are in increasing workable behaviors. Although decreasing behavior is often an important part of effective treatment, we recommend that ACT therapists be wary of commitments "to not do X." Ogden Lindsley famously noted, "If a dead man can do it, it isn't behavior and shouldn't be taught" (1991, p. 455). Put another way, if a behavior change plan can be successfully executed by a dead person, then it probably isn't an effective plan. The point is that behavior change plans that emphasize what *not to do* rather than what *to do* are problematic. For example, a dead person won't smoke or drink to excess, swear at people, hit others, gossip instead of working, spend too much money, have panic attacks, spend too much time on social media, or check the stove excessively. Simply avoiding unwanted behaviors doesn't meet the aspiration of creating a life worth living.

Consider Jason, a client who exemplifies the problem with "not doing" as a goal. Jason's problem developed soon after he started dating Serena. He was crazy about her and couldn't believe his luck that Serena, an attractive 25-year-old student working on her master's degree, wanted to date him. Jason thought it was unbelievable that she could find him attractive given that he is an overweight, twice-divorced, 38-year-old accountant. He was in love and also feeling insecure. He tried to reduce his insecurity the only way he knew how. He called Serena or sent a text message each time he felt insecure. His messages were usually brief but frequent: "I love you babe." "Thinking about you ❤ ❤ ❤ ☺." "I miss you ❤ ❤ ❤." "Are we getting together tonite?" However, as his insecurity grew, Jason found it more difficult to keep his tone light: "Are we okay??!!" "Do you still love me?" "Why don't you reply? ☹" The more Jason texted, the less reliably Serena replied, and Jason's angst grew in tandem with the time between Serena's replies. And increasingly, Serena sounded annoyed when he called or turned down his invitations to go out. He wanted to make weekend plans by Monday or Tuesday, while she preferred to wait until Friday to commit, "in case something more fun comes up."

Jason sought therapy when he noticed that his anxiety had increased to an extreme level and realized that he was coping with his anxiety by drinking to excess. Meanwhile, he was calling and texting Serena even more frequently, or thinking about calling or texting her. He acknowledged that this wasn't a new pattern of behavior, but rather an old pattern that had reached new levels. He wanted to call and text Serena less frequently, and felt sure that if he did so, their relationship would improve and his anxiety would abate. He was ambivalent about drinking less and believed that excessive drinking was only a problem to the extent that it was associated with excessive calling and texting.

Against the recommendations of his therapist, Jason initially came up with a behavior change plan founded on "not doing" and "doing less." He committed to not drinking before 8:00 p.m., limiting his calling and texting to no more often than once every two hours, and waiting longer before inviting Serena on dates. On the face of it, his plan might make sense: if he was successful, his problem behaviors would decrease, and perhaps this would reduce the strain on his romantic relationship.

After one week, Jason reported that he'd been able to decrease his calling and texting and that he hadn't had a drink before 8:00 p.m. But he was dismayed because he continued to feel anxious and insecure about his relationship with Serena. When his therapist asked him to elaborate on how things had gone more specifically over the previous week, the following dialogue ensued.

*Jason:*     I called Serena last Sunday and said, "Your favorite band is going to be in town. Do you want to go to their concert on Friday?" She said she didn't know and told me she'd get back to me later. I waited two hours—in fact, I waited almost three hours, and then I texted her to ask how she was doing. She didn't reply, so I waited another two hours and then sent another text. She didn't reply, so I sent another text. By then it was after 8:00, so I had a couple of beers, and then I started texting more. Now it's Wednesday, and she still hasn't told me whether she wants to go to the concert.

*Therapist:* Tell me, what were you doing during the time between those calls and text messages?

*Jason:* Nothing much. I was kind of watching the clock to make sure I didn't call or text too early, and the time went really slow. The Sunday football games were on, so I watched for a few minutes to pass the time.

*Therapist:* Do you enjoy spending your Sunday watching football?

*Jason:* Not especially. It was more like a way to make the time go by and not think about Serena. I thought it could help me calm down while I was watching the clock.

Unfortunately for Jason, not doing something is not a behavior. So, while not texting, not calling, and not drinking, he was thinking about calling and texting and drinking. To the extent that he engaged in actual behaviors that he did not enjoy, this was aimed at decreasing his thoughts about texting and calling and drinking, and at reducing his anxiety. Basically, his efforts at "not doing" weren't improving his mood or his relationship, nor were they moving him toward his values.

In terms of committed action, it's generally more helpful to make commitments based on what to do, rather than what not to do. Instead of merely not calling (not a behavior), Jason might be more effective if he increases valued behaviors that are incompatible with texting and calling, such as socializing with others, exercising, or engaging in almost any other activity he values. This is not to say that that people can't successfully stop performing an undesirable behavior by gritting their teeth. And, of course, a reduction in some forms of behavior can certainly be values-consistent. However, it's generally more effective to conduct a functional assessment and engage in values clarification to help clients contact what they value so they can identify alternative behaviors that are more aligned with what's important to them. This brings us to a salient ACT slogan: "Outcome is the process through which process becomes the outcome" (Hayes et al., 1999, p. 219).

Decreasing behavior is often regarded as the end goal. For instance, smokers and problem drinkers are considered to be successfully treated when they stop smoking or drinking. However, more often than not, this type of behavior change isn't really the person's ultimate aim. Smokers and drinkers often have other goals and values, such as improving their health, being more effective at work, or being a good role model for their children. When these types of more global outcomes are regarded as the ultimate goal, quitting smoking, abstaining from drinking, and similar aims can become process goals on the way to more global outcomes. In this scenario, committed actions can include an entire menu of behaviors that move clients in the direction of their values.

For a more specific example, let's return to Jason. His attempts to stop texting and drinking were largely unsuccessful, yet he acknowledged that these weren't effective behaviors if he wanted to stay with Serena. Values clarification helped him identify drinking to excess as a behavior that interfered with most of his relationships and with his productivity at work. He also noted a long-term pattern of decreasing his contact with friends and family and reducing many activities he enjoys in the service of pleasing a woman he's dating. He could see that this behavior harmed his relationships and left him feeling like a bad friend, as well as an overly dependent boyfriend.

Based on these realizations, Jason decided to work toward engaging in more behaviors in the service of his values, and identified committed actions that were more about doing than "not doing." For example, if Serena didn't choose to go to a concert or sports event in a timely way, he invited a friend or relative instead. That allowed him to attend events he enjoyed while also spending time with people he cares about. He also committed to exercising more, and when he noticed that drinking in the evening was usually linked to a reduced likelihood that he'd go for his morning jog, he found it easier to choose to drink tea instead of alcohol in the evening.

To Jason's surprise, after he began scheduling activities with others when Serena was reluctant to say that she would go with him, her behavior changed, and she began to accept his invitations earlier and more often. However, the biggest surprise came a few months later when he broke up with Serena. In reflecting on his own journey, he said, "I was so caught up in fear of rejection that I never stopped to ask myself what I want in a relationship." He realized that although he was attracted to Serena, he also valued reliability in a partner. He found himself curious about whether, as he became more independent and less needy, he would attract more reliable women, and looked forward to learning the answer the next time he met someone he wanted to date.

The lesson here is that attempts to decrease behavior will often be more successful when they're replaced by alternative behaviors linked to the individual's values. Another key point is that Jason's actual aim wasn't to change his own behavior; rather, it was to change Serena's behavior. A good rule of thumb is that committed actions aimed at changing the behavior of another are usually doomed to fail.

Returning to Kyla, her case also illustrates the importance of linking behavior change to values. When Kyla was motivated primarily by the desire to decrease her symptoms of OCD, her behavior was avoidant, and she frequently used medication to deal with her anxiety. After values clarification, she articulated values of being a reliable friend and being self-supporting. Once she identified committed actions linked to these values, she became more willing to consider exposure and response prevention to help break her pattern of avoidance. Interestingly, although exposure and response prevention is a highly effective treatment for OCD, one of its significant drawbacks is that many clients refuse to engage in such a therapy, or drop out after beginning the treatment (McLean et al., 2001). ACT therefore serves as a powerful complement to exposure and response prevention—and to other challenging treatments—as values clarification aids in both identifying appropriate committed actions and building willingness to take the difficult steps necessary to move forward.

# Using Committed Action to Work with Verbal Behavior

Back in chapter 3, we suggested that learning a little something about RFT might be helpful for understanding and conducting ACT. RFT is a theory of verbal behavior, and verbal behavior is an important part of ACT. We can assess how client verbal behaviors contribute to problem behaviors, and interventions such as cognitive defusion techniques necessarily entail verbal behavior. Most people, at least occasionally, have thoughts they might evaluate as strange, excessive, or inappropriate. For example, an angry driver might have thoughts of smashing into the car that cut him off, or a frustrated mother might have thoughts of leaving her family. For many people, such thoughts are generally easy to dismiss ( "Wow, I must be stressed-out today!"). People with OCD, on the other hand, might take these thoughts to be literally true or dangerous.

For Kyla, thoughts about harming someone have the same functions as actually harming someone. She feels just as guilty and horrified as she would if she actually had harmed someone. For Kyla, an effective cognitive defusion technique might be to have her begin to use a verbal convention of saying to herself, "I am having the thought that I'm going to harm someone." If Kyla can see thoughts as thoughts, then their stimulus functions will be transformed, which might allow her to respond in a less reactive way. Practicing this defusion technique could therefore be a committed action that Kyla engages in to cope with her obsessions.

Jason also uses language in ways that contribute to his difficulties. For him, having a girlfriend is in a frame of correspondence with being successful or worthwhile. Engaging in values clarification could help highlight other worthwhile outcomes so that his sense of self and well-being won't rely on having a girlfriend, or he might use values clarification to focus on how he treats people and explore the qualities of relationships that are desirable to him. Alternatively, he might transform the stimulus functions of not having a girlfriend by considering the advantages of being single, or he could reduce the significance of being in a relationship by viewing it as one of several values he might pursue.

Jason was also plagued by recurring thoughts about whether Serena would return his calls and texts. To transform the functions of those thoughts, he too might use cognitive defusion skills, telling himself, "I notice that I'm having the thought that Serena is leaving me." Notice that any of these actions constitute new behaviors and would therefore require committed action on Jason's part (such as engaging in values clarification, modifying his verbal behavior, and changing his behavior in relation to women). These examples of both Jason and Kyla illustrate the importance of considering both verbal and overt behaviors when assessing client problems and planning ACT interventions.

# Size Doesn't Matter

In ACT, the aim of committed action is increased psychological flexibility. Most effective committed actions are values-consistent behaviors that reduce problematic consequences and increase opportunities for positive reinforcement. When evaluating committed actions, commitment can be measured by the dimensions of behavior change discussed in chapter 2 (rate, duration, and so on), but not necessarily by magnitude.

The size of the commitment doesn't determine its importance; rather, the execution of a committed action of any magnitude is a marker of success. For example, Kyla doesn't have to commit to socialize with others several times a day; she's successful if she commits to inviting a friend out once a week—and she's successful whether or not her friends accept her invitations. Jason doesn't have to commit to stopping drinking or texting in order to be successful in his goals. He's successful if he commits to reducing his drinking and texting and meets a target goal, by monitoring the number of drinks consumed or his phone usage, and so on.

Likewise, a smoker doesn't have to quit smoking to be successful at committed action. She succeeds if she commits to and carries out actions such as reading a book about smoking cessation, scheduling an appointment with her physician, purchasing a nicotine replacement product, or smoking less in accordance with a harm reduction plan or other plan for cutting down. Similarly, a father doesn't have to commit to spending 20 hours a week playing with his children in order to live in alignment with his value of being an engaged parent. Instead, he's successful to the degree that he engages in behaviors he commits to, such as taking his son to the park on Saturdays or helping his daughter with homework after school on weekdays. The ACT exercise "Jump" (Hayes, Strosahl, et al., 2012, p. 280) helps clients experience this quality of willingness by illustrating that whether the client is jumping off a chair or a piece of paper, the behavior of jumping is the same. Committed action is like that. Consistent movement in a valued direction is the key.

# Summary

In this chapter, we introduced the importance of functional analysis of behavior, and showed that although formal diagnosis might be important in some contexts, functional analysis contributes a great deal to treatment from a contextual behavioral perspective. We also discussed how values clarity can assist with identifying relevant target behaviors for committed action. As you may recall from chapter 2, our concise definition of committed action includes the phrase "even in the presence of obstacles." We'll turn to that topic next, in chapter 5, as we discuss how to identify common obstacles to committed action, such as mindlessness, cognitive fusion, and avoidance.

# Identifying Obstacles to Committed Action

In chapters 1 through 4, we discussed what committed action is and what it means to make a commitment, and also explored how to identify appropriate committed actions and make plans for engaging in them. Because this book focuses on how to strengthen the process of committed action, we also need to look at what can weaken or obstruct committed action. If we look at the flip side of the concise definition of commitment offered in chapter 2—acting in the direction of what you care about even in the presence of obstacles—we can say that the experience of lacking commitment is related to inaction influenced by insufficient personally relevant motivation and being impeded by private events, such as emotions, thoughts, unhelpful self-descriptions, and distraction. In fact, the three parts of that definition—inaction, lacking values-based motivation, and being hindered by private events—encapsulate psychological inflexibility. Any single one of these issues contributes to psychological inflexibility and hinders commitment.

## The ACT Model of Inflexibility: Six Obstacles to Committed Action

As a reminder, ACT aims to promote psychological flexibility using the six core processes of the hexaflex model: acceptance, defusion, contact with the present moment, self-as-context, values, and committed action. For each, there is an opposing process that contributes to psychological inflexibility: experiential avoidance, cognitive fusion, mindlessness, attachment to the conceptualized self, unclear values, and inactivity, avoidance, or impulsivity. Together, these six processes give rise to an obverse model: the ACT inflexahex, depicted in figure 2.

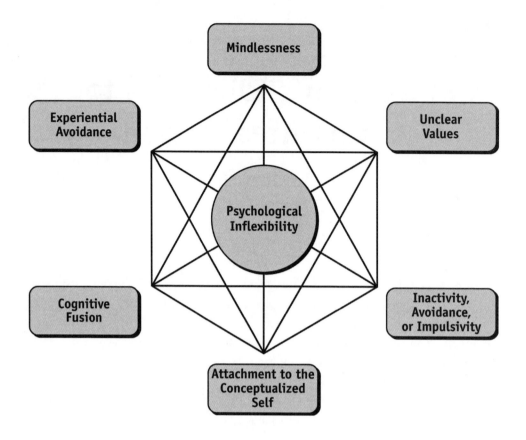

**Figure 2.** The ACT inhexaflex.

When assessing clients' presenting problems during intake, and during every session, it's prudent to conceptualize clients' behavior in terms of these processes. In the sections that follow, we'll briefly describe each process and provide case examples.

## Inactivity, Avoidance, and Impulsivity

Because this book specifically targets committed action, we'll begin with the opposing processes that lead to and maintain ineffective behavior: inactivity, avoidance, and impulsivity. Indeed, this entire book is dedicated to addressing these processes. Therefore, in this section we'll review this inflexibility model in a streamlined manner in order to provide a context for how to best facilitate committed action in the next chapter.

Well-established repertoires of inactivity, avoidance, or impulsivity often pose barriers to committed actions. When people are suffering and come to therapy, therapists typically explore what they're doing too much of or too little of, or what they're doing in inappropriate contexts. Sometimes the obvious presenting problem is related to these three aspects of behavior, so the therapist creates an evidence-based plan to address these issues. Sometimes clients are already well aware of how these aspects of behavior are involved in their problem. For example, a client who comes to therapy for smoking cessation implicitly acknowledges that the problem is consuming cigarettes excessively, or an overweight client may admit to engaging in too little exercise. And a self-referred anger management client probably already understands that he needs to stop impulsively displaying aggressiveness in inappropriate contexts.

However, sometimes clients aren't aware that behavior change is necessary, making it incumbent on the therapist to bring this to the client's attention and work together collaboratively to develop a plan for meaningful behavioral change. For instance, a client may come in because she's feeling sad and is consumed with hopeless thoughts. The therapist might address her depressive symptoms with acceptance, defusion, and mindfulness, but the therapy would generally be incomplete without behavioral activation (Martell, Dimidjian, & Herman-Dunn, 2013). Therefore, an ACT therapist would leverage the empirically supported treatment of behavioral activation in an effort to help the client stop engaging in operationally defined unhealthy behaviors (such as staying in bed too long and impulsively eating too much junk food) and start engaging in healthful, personally appetitive behaviors (such as doing an enjoyable form of exercise, socializing, or working). Creating a therapeutic context that effectively addresses inactivity, avoidance, and impulsivity is very important in ACT.

## Unclear Values

A core principle of applied behavioral science is that behavior is a function of environmental consequences. As discussed in chapter 3, when human behavior is positively reinforced, that behavior is likely to occur again in situations where there are similar stimulus properties. For example, if someone is at home and is hungry because he hasn't eaten for several hours, and then he opens the refrigerator and is able to contact and enjoy the delicious, high-calorie foods inside, the next time he's hungry while at home there's an increased likelihood that he'll open the refrigerator to obtain those edible reinforcers. Consequences that provide positive reinforcement, such as discovering delicious food, increase the probability of the actions that preceded the consequence. But that same man can say to himself, even while hungry, "I'm aiming to manage my weight better because I care about being healthy, so I'm just going to drink some water and wait until dinnertime to eat." This verbal behavior—relating that set of stimuli with specific language—can have an influence on whether or not he engages in the previously reinforced behavior of finding food. This verbal behavior of articulating his value of being healthy can reduce the reinforcing qualities of the food he might find. Such is the influence of transformation of stimulus functions through relational frames. By verbalizing his higher-order values, this individual may influence himself to drink water instead of eating the high-calorie food he finds in the refrigerator, even though that might be immediately more physically satisfying.

Now think about what would probably occur if he doesn't leverage the power of verbal behavior in the direction of the value of being healthy. What if he can't articulate why he might want to drink water instead of eating high-calorie food? What happens when a person cannot or does not state a reason for engaging in healthy abstinence in the presence of positive reinforcers—like delicious food, for instance? Again, behavior is a function of consequences. If there is a history of positive reinforcement for eating high-calorie food and no verbal behavior to redirect overt behavior toward more valued, personally relevant, longer-term outcomes, the person will be more likely to engage in behavior that will be immediately gratifying, even if, over the long haul, it's less healthful. In the absence of clarity about values, the client won't have established verbal relations between his behavior and stimuli that are unhealthy in the long run but also immediately gratifying. And in the absence of transformation of stimulus functions related to the unhealthiness of those stimuli, a commitment to healthier eating patterns isn't likely to be supported.

When clients are unclear regarding what they care about, they're prone to engaging in behaviors that are gratifying in the short term, even though immediately reinforcing outcomes aren't always the most healthy or meaningful. If clients have unclear values, meaning that they can't verbalize purposeful, broad, desired outcomes that reflect living life in a certain way, they're more likely to simply engage in actions that get them the next "feel-good" experience. Here are some examples:

- A woman stays home and listens to podcasts rather than meeting new people at the happy hour hosted by her workplace, because that feels more comfortable now—without realizing that this has a negative impact on her social skills, interpersonal network, and career opportunities.

- A man smokes a cigarette because of the immediate gratification of the buzz it gives him—without truly connecting that behavior with the detrimental impact it's having on his cardiovascular health and longevity.

- A fraternity member stays in his house with his friends on a Wednesday afternoon playing video games instead of going to class—without attending to the fact that the immediate gratification of having fun is reducing his exposure to the educational experiences he paid for when he signed his student loan promissory note, and making it less likely that he will keep his partial scholarship.

These are just a few examples of the many ways in which people engage in immediately gratifying actions when doing so has a negative impact on healthful, meaningful, long-term consequences. When ACT therapists help clients clarify what's important to them (for example, career success, physical health, or obtaining an education), those values can assist clients in making choices that help them forgo the currently accessible short-term reinforcer and put them in contact with the long-term consequences. To achieve transformation of functions and alter behavior through longer-term contingencies, it's necessary to establish relational responding in a valued direction. Therefore, values clarification is essential to acceptance and commitment therapy.

As Nietzsche said, "If we have our own why in life, we can bear any how" (1895, p. 3). This speaks to the ACT approach of developing a treatment plan with a target of reducing clinically relevant inactivity, avoidance, and impulsivity, wherein the clinical process will benefit from discussing the purpose and meaning of choosing behaviors that are more personally worthwhile. This will help clients engage in these behaviors even when they're tempted to avoid them, as this verbal behavior can motivate actions even in the absence of immediate reinforcement. Because commitment means acting in the direction of what one cares about, ACT therapists aid clients in figuring out what they care about and verbally expressing these values to increase the reinforcing qualities of certain choices.

## Experiential Avoidance

In the previous section, we discussed clinically relevant processes stemming from positive reinforcement. You may have wondered about the opposing process in regard to consequences: negative reinforcement. If you look at the preceding examples, you could conceptualize each person's behavior as not just positively reinforced by the characteristics of the choices they made, but also influenced by negatively reinforcing contingencies. For instance, the hungry man is escaping hunger pangs in addition to getting food, so opening the refrigerator is both negatively and positively reinforced. Likewise, the woman who doesn't attend the company happy hour is avoiding feeling anxiety symptoms that might arise upon meeting new people, such as heart palpitations and muscle tension. The smoker is escaping uncomfortable nicotine cravings, and the college student may be staying away from feelings of boredom or intellectual inadequacy that arise during his Wednesday afternoon class.

From this perspective, we can say that the people in those examples are engaging in experiential avoidance: attempts to mitigate or evade contact with unwanted psychological events. Experiential avoidance becomes clinically relevant if it promotes acting in an unhealthy manner or prevents moving in valued directions and toward meaningful outcomes. Notice that we used the tenuous word "attempt" in defining experiential avoidance. It's important to understand that actions aimed at reducing contact with private events—such as emotions, sensations, and feelings—don't ensure that these events will go away or won't arise again. In fact, avoidance moves might eventually exacerbate the problematic repertoire.

Returning to our examples: After avoiding social events with coworkers, is the anxious woman going to feel any more comfortable at the next event, or might she feel less comfortable because she will still have underdeveloped, underpracticed social skills, and meanwhile, social ties between her coworkers have become stronger? And each time the man smokes another cigarette to reduce his uncomfortable cravings, isn't he simply causing his body to become more addicted to the nicotine? As for the college student who's avoiding class because it fires up feelings of self-doubt and intellectual inadequacy—after missing a few lectures, he may be so far behind that he won't be able to catch up, thereby increasing his feelings of insecurity. These are just a few examples of how avoidance can actually increase the influence of the unwanted private events on behavior in the long run.

Attempts to avoid psychological experience are a major obstacle to committed action. The crux of ACT work builds upon clinical tools for addressing culturally influenced repertoires for avoiding private events. Social norms often suggest that certain feelings are to be avoided. Children are given many instructions that suggest they should quash certain emotions: "Stop crying or I'll give you something to cry about;" "Cheer up, kid. Everyone loses a game from time to time;" "I don't see why you just can't be happy about this;" and so on. These oft-used language events set up relations that can be counterproductive. Consider the relations set up when the stimulus event "stop crying" is placed in a conditional relational frame with "or I'll give you something to cry about." Such a threatening message might make the child even more anxious and tearful. The way authority figures talk to children can perpetuate the cultural idea that certain emotional experiences are problematic and should be avoided—a rule-governed approach to private events that often persists into adulthood and manifests as psychological inflexibility. Adults often say the same types of things to other adults in an attempt to make them feel differently: "Don't worry about it; everything will work out in the end;" "You have nothing to be depressed about—your life is great;" or "Don't get angry at me—this situation is not my fault."

Even mental health practitioners and researchers refer to certain feeling states as "negative emotions," and many therapeutic endeavors attempt to get rid of or diminish certain feelings. From the ACT perspective, practitioners can simply replace the word "negative" with "natural." When so-called *negative* emotions are perceived as *natural* feelings, both therapist and client may relate to them differently, which supports the broader ACT approach. When leveraging the ACT model to help people maintain stronger, measurable commitments, therapists need to recognize the difficulty that can arise if clients have a control agenda regarding their own private events. In chapter 6, we'll discuss acceptance, a process and skill that therapists can leverage to help clients stick to their commitments and not get sidetracked by private events that they deem unpleasant.

## Cognitive Fusion

As discussed earlier in the book, human beings are both blessed and cursed by our ability to use language. One of the blessings of our language abilities is that they allow us to describe, evaluate, and problem solve, influencing our behavior and the way we work with the world around us. They also allow us to verbally influence individuals' overt behavior without them having to contact the natural contingencies. As mentioned in chapter 1, someone can tell a child, "Don't touch the hot stove or you'll burn your hand," and the child will probably keep her hand away from the stove during that particular time frame. The child doesn't have to directly contact the aversive stimuli (getting burned) in order to ensure that she'll keep her hand away from the stove. Language can be very helpful in these sorts of situations.

Now, to get a sense of why language can be a double-edged sword, let's take a look at a similar verbal rule that can sometimes be helpful: "If you think your hands are contaminated, you should wash them." A mother may teach this conditional relational response to her teenage daughter when she's cutting up raw chicken, and it's helpful because it reduces risk of salmonella cross-contamination. Then, after the girl shakes a lot of hands at a high school mixer, she may feel compelled to wash her hands because she's been reinforced to think, *If you think your hands are contaminated, you should wash them*. As a natural extension of the rule, this isn't a problem and can actually be helpful. But here's where the potential curse of language comes in: What happens when this same girl starts to develop a budding OCD repertoire? Even though she may have no contact with items that would measurably increase her risk of contamination, she may still have the thought, *I think my hands are dirty; I should wash them*. She can't stop herself from having this thought, and the rule becomes highly influential.

This is an example of the automaticity and power of language. People automatically have language-based relational responses, and they can't control the fact that certain thoughts come up in their private experience. When certain relational stimuli occur, they evoke the private verbal repertoire that dictates a particular response. For example, what private experience do you have as you read the next sentence? "On the night before Christmas, Santa Claus comes down the chimney and brings _____ for all the good little boys and girls." It is highly likely that you said "toys," "presents," or "gifts" to yourself because of the context that was set up. It doesn't matter if you believe it. It doesn't matter that such a thing has never happened in your direct, observed experience. Verbal relations are established through various experiences and then those verbal responses simply show up, even if we try to resist them. In fact, trying to resist thinking certain thoughts can actually accelerate the rate of those private verbalizations (Abramowitz, Tolin, & Street, 2001).

In addition to being automatic, thoughts are also powerful. Relational responding can have a significant impact on people's feelings and actions. When hearing a sad story, people may cry. When hearing about injustice, people often get mad. The sad story or injustice doesn't have to happen directly to the listener to have an impact. Because of the power of relational responding, the listener can feel the emotional event and might even do something about it, even without contacting the events as direct contingencies. Again, this power of language is a double-edged sword: it can motivate action toward rectifying a situation, but it can also cause unnecessary suffering.

Cognitive fusion is the domination of behavior regulatory functions by verbal networks, especially when there's a failure to distinguish the experience that the person is having as a thought, rather than being beholden to the content of the thought (Hayes, 2006). Going back to the girl with a burgeoning OCD repertoire, she can't help but say to herself, *I think my hands are dirty; I should wash them*, because of the automaticity of thinking. Unfortunately, in this scenario, the power of that relational responding might lead her to wash her hands again and again, perhaps even 60 times a day. Unwanted, unintended verbal events are regulating her actions, and she doesn't recognize that this is simply a thought or private event and there's no risky contaminant on her hands that she needs to sanitize. Her fusion with these cognitions is influencing her to engage in behavior that's avoidant, repetitive, and potentially competing with doing other things that could be more meaningful and rewarding. If, as an adult, she makes a values-based commitment to get a job and make more friends, this will require shaking hands with people and coming into contact with potentially contaminated public stimuli, such as doorknobs and elevator buttons, on a more frequent basis. She might not be able to follow through on these committed actions if her verbalizations generalize more broadly to *I have to stay away from contaminated stuff*. This kind of cognitive fusion, leading to responses that aren't based on direct contingencies, is an obstacle to following through on commitments.

## Attachment to the Conceptualized Self

Clearly, language can have a significant impact on behavior. Beyond the types of rules and judgments about the external world discussed in the preceding section, people often use relational responding to engage in self-descriptions: "I am 6-foot-3," "I'm fun to be around," "I'm an electrician," "I'm from Mexico," "I'm tired," "I'm angry," and on and on. This use of language is also a double-edged sword. Being able to describe your body, your personality, where you're from, how you feel, and what you do is helpful in our social world. Yet sometimes people get attached to their self-descriptions, or conceptualized self, which can impede them from following through on more flexible behavioral repertoires in the service of values-based committed actions.

Consider Loren, a former alcoholic who is married and has one son, Anthony. Early in Anthony's life, Loren made a commitment to be an involved father. He's chosen to spend as much time with Anthony as possible and to earn good wages to provide him with opportunities. He also gave up drinking alcohol on Anthony's third birthday. When Loren struggles with his abstinence, he follows through on his commitment to go to Alcoholics Anonymous meetings to help him stay sober. During the meetings, he is taught to refer to himself as an alcoholic, and is reinforced when introducing himself to the crowd at the AA meeting by saying, "Hi, I'm Loren, and I'm an alcoholic." This type of relating can be helpful to his commitment to abstain. He is coordinating his sense of his own self as someone with a significant problem with alcohol, and this verbalization could facilitate a commitment to a sober lifestyle.

Suppose Loren gets his life together and shows up at all of Anthony's drama club events and dance recitals throughout the boy's childhood and high school years, and that he works extra hard to pay for Anthony's tuition at an exclusive art school. Let's also say that near the end of Anthony's final year at college, Anthony lands a movie contract paying him millions of dollars. Unaware of his father's history of alcoholism, Anthony chooses to throw himself a graduation party at a fancy restaurant with a bar. Loren hasn't had a drop of alcohol for 19 years, but he agonizes over attending Anthony's graduation party because of his attachment to his "alcoholic" self-identity. He has rigorously trained himself to say, "I am an alcoholic," "As an alcoholic, I can't be anywhere near alcohol," and "Alcoholics must avoid the faces and the places." Because of fusion with this conceptualized self, and the rules that coordinate with such a verbally evaluated "self," he decides not to attend the graduation party. Because of the way he's learned to relate to this aspect of his self-identity, he breaks his commitment to be an involved father on one of his son's most important days—a day Loren helped Anthony achieve. Fusion with the rule "I can't be anywhere near alcohol," in combination with fusion with the self-identity "I am an alcoholic," severely limits Loren's behavioral flexibility. This example highlights the blessing and curse of language. In one context, "I am an alcoholic" is helpful, and in another, it becomes a problem. Contacting the self-as-context—realizing that you are not your content, but rather, the context for your life—and also using defusion skills can be helpful with this concern.

## Mindlessness

People tend to experience an ongoing stream of consciousness. Verbal behavior is so helpful to human beings, and it is so frequently reinforced that we have a very hard time ceasing relational responding. And within this neverending stream of thoughts, on average, people tend to not think about what they're doing for about 47 percent of their waking day—almost half of the day (Killingsworth & Gilbert, 2010). When people are thinking about something other than what they're doing in the present moment, they're often lost in thoughts about the past or future. Relational responding also enables this, and sometimes it is a problem. Using language to consider the past and to plan for the future can be a fruitful behavior. However, it can also cause people to lose contact with the present moment and miss important cues for action. Because committed actions can only happen in the present moment, ACT therapists help clients see that thinking about the "there and then" instead of "here and now" can sometimes diminish optimal behavior in the present moment.

Further, this language ability allows people to compare their current experience to past events, in which case they may get caught up in attempts to change their environment to be similar to a past ideal situation. Or sometimes people suffer by becoming overly anxious about an event that may never occur. Similarly, relational responding allows people to casually reminisce about the past and plan future events in an attempt to create a more reinforcing environment. Once again, this aspect of language is a double-edged sword, and whether the process is helpful depends on the context and the person's values.

To give a broader clinical picture of the problem on mindlessness, let's take a look at Ephraim, a 35-year-old sales professional who was told by his wife that he needed therapy. During the initial meeting, Ephraim said, "My wife thinks I'm a workaholic. I don't think I am, but I do work a lot for my company."

"Why do you work so much?" queried the therapist, starting to probe for values in this question, which sounds quite like *What is that in the service of?*

"I love my children so much, and I really want to provide a nice life for them. I grew up poor, and I don't want them to want for anything. I want them to have a full life."

The therapist and Ephraim discussed how important quality time is for youngsters, and that they would probably appreciate personal attention more than material items coming from their father. Ephraim seemed to agree, but mindlessness took over on the way home from that therapy session. While sitting in the back of a taxicab, he started to ruminate about a sales pitch that he had to put together for the next day. He was still thinking about the slide deck he was going to prepare when he got to his home office. Under these situations, thinking about there and then is not a major concern. As long as he "keeps his wits about him," planning behavior in a safe environment is not unhealthy. The problem began when he walked in the front door and his young son shouted, "Daddy!" Ephraim barely glanced up at the boy because he didn't want to forget what he was going to write in his PowerPoint presentation. "Daddy, look!" the boy exclaimed. "I painted a picture of me and you playing soccer last weekend. Remember that? My kindergarten teacher gave me an A-plus. What do you think?"

Ephraim looked at the painting for a second and said, "Hey. Good job." He turned on his heels and started walking down the hall, and then called out to his son as he ascended the stairs to the home office, "Hey, pal, I can't have dinner with you all tonight. I have a big presentation tomorrow and I have to work in my office. But I'll try to tuck you guys into bed tonight."

Ephraim never did tuck the kids into bed that night. His mind was thinking about there and then instead of the here and now. He had a perfect opportunity to spend time with his son, compliment him on his artistic abilities, and maybe even spend 10 minutes playing soccer with him in the backyard. Of course, Ephraim has a job to do and he needs to earn money, but engaging in a brief values-based parenting interaction would have been just a minor interruption to the work flow, and on balance, not likely to make a negative impact on the next day's sales pitch. It also could have had a major impact on the little boy to get such positive and fun attention from dad. Ephraim was mindless and, for that moment, psychologically inflexible, by not engaging in a simple committed action based on his values. Mindlessness can have a major influence on psychological flexibility, which is why ACT therapists strongly suggest building a mindfulness repertoire through exercises and practice.

# Additional Obstacles to Committed Action

We spent much of this chapter identifying the obstacles to committed action using the Inflexahex model, but there are two other areas of consideration that every ACT therapist should keep in mind during case conceptualization. Sometimes clients are doing well with their psychological flexibility, but when they try to engage in a committed action, they lack support from their personal environment to complete their goal. Other times, clients are impeded by skills deficits, and need to be taught how to successfully engage in a particular action. A dedicated ACT therapist can use her networking skills to help the client obtain more support from the environment, or engage in psychoeducation and training to assist the client with skills acquisition. In addition, the ACT clinician could collaborate in an interdisciplinary fashion by asking a professional social worker to help the client access needed support, or ask a counselor or educator to help with whatever skills deficits are observed. Let's briefly review those two additional obstacles to committed action.

## *Lack of Environmental Supports*

The six inflexibility processes described in this chapter generally present internal obstacles to committed action. Of course, *external* obstacles also exist, so in order to be effective, ACT therapists must also work with clients to identify external obstacles and come up with plans for overcoming them. Often, clients simply lack resources needed for committed action; however, they may also face significant aversive events. For instance, Karl is a 22-year-old architect who recently graduated from college. He chose to enter therapy to deal with newfound sadness and loneliness because he recently moved and has no friends in his new neighborhood. His ACT therapist would prudently aim to give him a more psychologically flexible perspective on his lot in life with the concepts of defusion and acceptance, but an effective therapist also knows there is much more to be done. The clinician should allow open and honest discussion of aversive environmental variables present in Karl's life (not just how he is coping with those circumstances), and respect that the client's lack of resources has a deleterious impact on his ability to engage in valued actions. Part of the therapeutic endeavor is to help clients deal with obstacles from a standard psychoeducational perspective. When working with this client, the ACT therapist might also discuss community events and social opportunities where Karl can meet new friends. Reviewing the opportunities to attend social events or hobby-related clubs for young adults would help create support for more real-world social networking. Collaborating with the client to learn about occasions for values-based action is often a crucial part of treatment. And while giving this particular client the prospects for social situations, his therapist should also teach social skills so he is successful when entering new environments.

## Skills Deficits

After working with his ACT therapist on choosing how he can create a robust support network, Karl makes a commitment to attend a running club at the local park. This commitment would be bolstered if Karl had the appropriate repertoire for introducing himself to new people, and to carry on conversations with them. Karl may need to change his skill set to be more effective with people if he wants to successfully engage in committed actions aimed at dealing with his loneliness, and increase values-based social interactions. The therapist can utilize a social skills training approach that teaches Karl about making proper eye contact, using a firm handshake, using appropriate communication during introductions, reflective listening, and sharing personal anecdotes. Not only is it worthwhile to commit to engaging in socially appropriate communication at the running club, but doing the social skills training in therapy is also a committed action for Karl. As discussed in chapter 2, effective committed actions involve measurable behavioral changes, and the actual content of those changes depends on individuals' contexts—their resources, strengths, and weaknesses—along with a good functional analysis to inform the process of altering clinically relevant responses. Therefore, the varieties of potential skills-building approaches are innumerable.

# Summary

This chapter reviewed a variety of obstacles to committed action: impulsive and avoidant behavior, unclear values, experiential avoidance, cognitive fusion, attachment to the conceptualized self, and mindlessness. Using ACT to build stronger commitments hinges upon developing an evidence-based treatment plan with significant measurable actions. While collaborating with clients to create such plans, clarifying their values will support them in following through on treatment goals. In addition, an effective treatment plan will promote experiential events that strengthen acceptance, defusion, perspective taking, and mindfulness. In chapter 6, we turn to developing such a plan and ensuring that it addresses the obstacles we've described in this chapter.

# Addressing Obstacles to Committed Action on the Part of the Client

The previous chapter examined obstacles that weaken committed action. The aim of this chapter is to explore the use of ACT's core processes to overcome those obstacles. Committed action rarely stands alone without the support of other ACT processes. For example, a client may be afraid to make behavior changes because she doesn't like the feelings that show up when she engages in committed action, in which case acceptance may be helpful. Alternatively, a client may resist committed action because he buys into stories he tells himself about why he cannot or should not change, in which case defusion will be helpful. A client may be unsure of which specific committed actions would make her life more workable, in which case values clarification may be in order. A client may struggle following life changes such as job loss, divorce, or retirement, in which case self-as-context work may help him distinguish the self from his roles. And even willing and motivated clients may focus excessively on the future or past and therefore miss opportunities for committed action, in which case it could be helpful to promote present-moment awareness. The core ACT processes overlap and work in concert. Thus, committed action is more likely when supported by other core ACT processes. And in many instances, committed actions may themselves reflect engagement with other core ACT processes.

## Acceptance and Committed Action

Although clients occasionally show up at a first session ready to engage in committed action, more often they understandably arrive wanting to change private events without necessarily wanting to change their behaviors, stating goals such as reduced pain or improved mood. Other clients understand that behavior change could be helpful, but want to make changes without experiencing discomfort, as when a client wants to lose weight or stop misusing substances without having cravings. Yet other clients may be unwilling to change their behavior because they don't accept the events that brought them to their present circumstances—as in the case of a client who doesn't accept that a loved one is addicted to drugs. In all of these circumstances, along with others, interventions that promote acceptance can be a powerful way to build willingness to take action.

Consider Michelle, a 54-year-old married woman who sought therapy to help her lose weight. Earlier in life, she'd had a very active lifestyle, but after a back injury 15 years ago, her weight had steadily increased, especially after she developed a habit of binge eating most evenings. Several years ago, she was diagnosed with diabetes and high blood pressure, and during her most recent physical, her physician informed her that her weight now qualified as morbidly obese. In her first therapy session, Michelle noted that she'd dieted many times. "I've tried every diet there is. I've lost anywhere from five to 25 pounds, and I always gain it back and then keep on gaining more." Describing her previous weight loss efforts in more detail, she said, "I want a psychologist who can help me lose weight as quickly as possible without feeling hungry all the time or feeling like I'm on a diet."

When asked about her eating habits, she became defensive, saying, "I can't stop eating out. That's a big part of our social life. I know that I binge on snacks when I watch TV, but keeping snacks out of the house would be rude to my husband, and he shouldn't suffer just because I want to lose weight." Essentially, she was saying that she wanted to lose weight quickly, didn't want to change most of the behaviors or contexts that were contributing to her weight problem, and didn't want to feel uncomfortable while losing weight. In essence, she preemptively stated what she was unwilling to do.

Michelle clearly has a control agenda. She doesn't want to feel "negative" emotions and doesn't want to change certain behaviors. Acceptance work might help her build willingness to engage in committed actions even while feeling unpleasant emotions or having thoughts that she doesn't want to give up her favorite foods. To that end, the therapist might work to engender *creative hopelessness*. In this approach, the ineffective strategies that a client has been using are identified as part of the problem, rather than the solution (Hayes & Wilson, 1994). Moving from creative hopelessness to acceptance means undermining the control of faulty rules—those that aren't accurate or aren't helpful in the context of weight loss—and instead promoting openness and willingness to try something new.

As you can see, Michelle currently follows many rules that aren't effective in the context of her stated agenda of losing weight (for example, "I can't stop eating out," "I have to keep unhealthy snacks in the house," and "It's bad to feel hungry.") To help her explore creative hopelessness, Michelle's therapist might review the effectiveness of her previous weight loss efforts and might also point out the control agenda she's bringing to the table. (Of course, cognitive defusion, mindfulness, values clarification, and other strategies could also be helpful, but here we're focused on acceptance.) Before she will change behavior, it will be helpful to explore her avoidance and control agendas. This work can be challenging, especially if patterns of avoidance are highly entrenched, as they were for Michelle. She eventually left treatment after a few weeks, complaining that, after modifying her behavior, she missed eating whatever she wanted to. Six months and five pounds later, she returned to treatment ready to try again. The second time around, she was ready to accept that committed action would sometimes be accompanied by uncomfortable feelings.

Avoidance can take many forms, some more obvious and some more subtle, but whatever the form, avoidance is usually a barrier to committed action. Consider Rita, a depressed client who came to therapy saying that she had difficulty completing homework assigned by her therapists in the past, and that she wanted to make completing homework a priority this time. In an early session, her therapist gave her a homework assignment to read some information about depression and complete a worksheet. In the following session, she brought in a self-help book by a different author using a different approach to treating depression, and noted that she thought this workbook might be more helpful than the assignment her therapist had given her. Further exploration with her clinician suggested she was afraid of failure and perhaps intimacy or loss of autonomy, as she noted that she did not want to "give myself over to a therapist as if I can't do it myself." That is experiential avoidance.

Or consider Jason, from chapter 4, who was agonizing over his relationship with Serena. He committed to engaging in social activities with his friends, but initially didn't follow through for fear of missing out on an opportunity to go out with Serena. By maintaining his dysfunctional behavior, he avoided worry. Only after he was willing to accept the distress he felt when he didn't text her, talk to her, or generally make himself available at all times was he willing to make behavioral changes.

Finally, consider Mark, a 32-year-old veteran who lost a leg and part of an arm in an explosion during combat. He feels depressed and angry and has several symptoms associated with post-traumatic stress disorder. He's told his therapist that he feels lonely and is certain that he'd be happier if he were in a romantic relationship. However, he hasn't attempted to date because he believes that no one would date a double amputee. He rarely goes out because he feels embarrassed and self-conscious when others look at him, and he's convinced that others find him gross or pity him. Mark's unwillingness to venture out and socialize suggests that avoidance may be a key part of his current problem. Specifically, he may be avoiding unwanted private events such as feeling embarrassed or thinking he's being rejected by others.

Hayes and colleagues have noted that one of the circumstances in which acceptance is particularly useful is when the client hasn't accepted something that isn't changeable (Hayes, Strosahl, et al., 2012). In Mark's case, his injuries cannot be undone. Mark's unwillingness to go out of the house or try to date because he's a double amputee suggests that he may not have fully accepted his loss. Acceptance of himself as he is in the present moment might increase his willingness to engage in behavior change. More specifically, acceptance of his feelings, along with acceptance of the reactions of others, could increase his willingness to engage in committed actions that would provide opportunities for positive experiences, even though they may also increase his chances of having negative private experiences. In such situations, building willingness to have negatively evaluated thoughts and feelings can increase clients' willingness to engage in committed actions.

Mark initially resisted this approach and seemed to equate acceptance with giving up and liking or wanting his present circumstances, saying things like, "I'm a warrior; I don't give in" and "Why would I like being an amputee?" Mark's therapist used the classic ACT exercise, the Chinese Finger Trap (Hayes, 2005, p. 37) to help him contact the futility of a control agenda and willingness to have difficult experiences at a more experiential level.

Acceptance can also help clients maintain willingness when they engage in committed action and don't attain a desired outcome. For Mark, this could be useful if he goes out in public and feels pitied by someone he speaks to, or if he asks someone on a date and is rejected. In Michelle's case, she might binge on junk food one evening or reach a plateau and fail to lose weight for some period of time. If so, acceptance can help her maintain willingness to stick with new eating habits instead of giving up.

Avoidance behaviors are often related to cognitive fusion. For example, Michelle is fused with the belief that changing her eating behaviors will inconvenience her husband, and Mark is fused with the belief that no one could love him. In such cases, cognitive defusion will be helpful for loosening the hold that thoughts and beliefs have on clients' choices—which brings us to our next topic.

# Cognitive Defusion and Committed Action

Fusion with thoughts can interfere with committed action in several ways. Under the sway of fused beliefs, clients may convince themselves that they can't act just yet, that they're doomed to fail, or that change wouldn't be helpful and could even be harmful. Fusion can also contribute to missing opportunities for committed action if the opportunities don't fit with the stories people have told themselves. Another issue is that clients sometimes focus on behavior changes they want others to make and fuse with the belief that they must change others or can't experience happiness if a loved one is unhappy.

Returning to Mark's case, he was fused with stories that fed his avoidance and kept him stuck. Mark was convinced that no one could fall in love with an amputee, that his depression made him defective, and that other people pitied him or were disgusted by him. To address this, Mark's therapist used a metaphor of wearing colored glasses (Luoma et al., 2007, p. 13). When wearing funky colored sunglasses, everything you look at is biased or tinted. Things do not look as they naturally are, and after a while you don't even realize how your view is colored. Biased, darkened thinking makes people see the world in problematic ways, especially when fused to such content. This explanation helped Mark notice that when he looked at the world *through* his beliefs, rather than looking *at* his beliefs, he often missed opportunities to have a different experience of the world. For instance, when he was fused with memories of women rejecting him, stigmatizing comments about depression, or people expressing pity toward him, he minimized positive encounters with women, refused to join a veteran support group, and ignored people who respectfully acknowledged his service to his country. When fused, Mark experiences a dark, unwelcoming world. When defused, he was more likely to see opportunities to have positive experiences. Notice that he doesn't have to believe that the outcomes of committed actions will be positive. All he has to do is notice that he has an opportunity for committed action and then engage in action no matter what his mind is telling him. In this way, cognitive defusion alters verbal relational networks so that they no longer serve as barriers to committed action.

For another example of defusion, we turn to Loretta, whose first words upon being asked, "What brings you here today?" were "I hope you can help me figure out how to get my 31-year-old daughter to stop depending on me and become more motivated to get a job." It is not uncommon for clients to come to therapy with an agenda that emphasizes change in others—especially significant others, parents, or children. What's far less common is for these clients to have a clear intention to change their own behavior. Loretta was contemplating retirement and feared it would be financially unfeasible because she was supporting her adult daughter, Megan, and there appeared to be no end in sight. According to Loretta, Megan had a substance use problem and wasn't motivated to take action to become self-supporting.

Creative hopelessness was easy and straightforward. Loretta was able to describe a long list of things she'd already done in attempts to change the situation. For example, she'd promised Megan a new car if she got a job and followed through—and then Megan quit her new job three weeks after getting the car. She'd thrown away Megan's stash of marijuana several times, only to have Megan purchase more. And she'd repeatedly refused to pay Megan's debts, but eventually gave in each time so Megan wouldn't feel deprived or get into more financial trouble. Loretta was aware that what she was doing wasn't working. She also noticed that she told herself many sad and scary stories about what could happen to Megan, which bolstered her willingness to try something new. However, rather than focusing on committed actions she might engage in, Loretta focused exclusively on things Megan might do to improve her life, and how she could persuade Megan to engage in those actions. At the same time, Loretta was certain that Megan would end up in prison or never speak to her again if they didn't continue in their entrenched pattern. She believed that it was her duty to take care of Megan and said she owed it to her because things had been rough for Megan after her dad left. In short, Loretta didn't want to change her own behavior and was fused with the belief that changing her behavior would lead to a destructive outcome for Megan. Defusion would be necessary before she could engage in committed action.

A classic defusion technique is the "and/but" convention (Hayes, Strosahl, et al., 2012). When we use the word "but," we tend to negate the content that precedes it. For example, when someone says, "I wanted to go to the party, but I was anxious," it is regarded as synonymous with saying "I did not want to go to the party." The and/but convention is simply replacing *but* with *and* to reduce fusion with thoughts and feelings as causes of behavior. For example: "I wanted to go the party, and I was anxious." The and/but convention is "simple, and not easy," in the sense that it takes practice to get used to. And it allows people to have the experience that words don't cause behavior and that they can have conflicting thoughts, feelings, and desires at the same time. To experience the power of the and/but convention, try it yourself!

The therapist used the and/but convention to facilitate Loretta's fusion with the story that she had to do what she did in order to protect Megan.

*Loretta:* I want to save more money, but my daughter won't get a job.

*Clinician:* I want to save more money, *and* my daughter won't get a job.

*Loretta:* I want Megan to move out, but I'm worried she would be homeless.

*Clinician:* I want Megan to move out, *and* I'm worried she would be homeless.

In those examples, the clinician is aiming to cut through Loretta's fusion with stories she tells herself about how various action (or inaction) would affect her situation, and to gently shift the focus from Megan's behavior to something Loretta can more directly influence: her own behavior.

Loretta's therapist also used several other cognitive defusion techniques for changing language parameters and undermining verbal rules and narratives that were serving as obstacles to commitment—techniques such as *contrasting thoughts with the present moment* and *reasons aren't causes* (described in *Cognitive Defusion in Practice*; Blackledge, 2015, pp. 105 & 131). This helped Loretta approach the topic of committed action without immediately defending her inaction or focusing on reasons why various solutions wouldn't succeed. The therapist also targeted acceptance to help Loretta gain more willingness to have anxious thoughts and feelings about Megan. For instance, in noticing that "if you're not willing to have it, then you've got it" (Hayes, Strosahl, et al., 2012, p. 185), Loretta accepted that she had always worried about Megan and would continue to do so, whether or not Megan changed her behavior.

Loretta was eventually ready to engage in committed actions in relation to Megan. For one, she stopped asking Megan to look for a job, and instead of insisting that Megan never smoke marijuana or drink, she enforced a rule that Megan wasn't permitted to smoke marijuana or drink in Loretta's home. And while she continued to pay some of Megan's bills, she didn't purchase luxuries for her. With time, and thanks to these new contingencies, Megan gradually took steps toward taking more responsibility for herself.

Even at this stage, Loretta's therapist continued to work with cognitive defusion, as Loretta's committed actions were frequently followed by dramatic reactions from Megan. (Contextual behavioral science would predict that from Megan, because behaviors that were previously reinforced are no longer being reinforced, and that would lead to an extinction burst.) When Megan would overreact, the overreaction would be followed by fused catastrophic thinking on Loretta's part. Loretta continued to have thoughts that something terrible would happen to Megan, or that Megan would hate her if she continued setting limits in keeping with her new committed actions. Cognitive defusion transformed the functions of these scary thoughts so that instead of being filled with dread when having thoughts of Megan dying or going to prison, Loretta could respond to them as simply thoughts that, although a little scary, were not paralyzing. Loretta made the important observations that many of her stories about a catastrophic future were only thoughts, and that she was more likely to influence Megan's actions by modifying her own behavior than by engaging in yet more attempts at persuasion.

# Contact with the Present Moment and Committed Action

Ellen Langer noted that "mindlessness limits our control by preventing us from making intelligent choices" (1989, p. 50). Contact with the present moment means increasing attention to the here and now rather than letting the mind engage in wandering in the past or trying to imagine the future. In rumination about the past and worry about the future, the present moment is lost (Wilson, 2008). Present-moment awareness can facilitate committed action in a couple of key ways: by increasing awareness of opportunities for committed action in the present moment, and by helping clients more accurately track what happens as they engage in committed action.

Consider Jalen, a high school sophomore. His pediatrician recommended therapy after observing symptoms of anxiety and stress during Jalen's physical. In his first session, Jalen immediately acknowledged that he worries—about getting a girlfriend, earning good grades, getting admitted to a good college, making the varsity football team, having student loan debts when he finishes college, failing to get a good job someday, disappointing his mother, ending up like his "no-good father"—and the list goes on. Jalen is a good student, yet his teachers have frequently reported that he's an underachiever given his intelligence. He said he was hesitant to try out for the football team, because he was afraid that people would laugh at him if he failed. He also reported that he wants to go to college but wondered whether there was any point to studying when he imagined himself being rejected by desirable colleges or unable to afford the tuition. He didn't have many friends, which he attributed to being shy, and he noted that it wasn't worth the effort to make friends, since they would eventually reject him. He also struggled with insomnia and said this was because he was always thinking about everything. Then, when he was overly tired and worried, he found it difficult to exercise, socialize, or complete his homework assignments and often tried to avoid his worries by playing video games. Almost all of his worries were about events in the relatively distant future, and they kept him feeling anxious and hesitant to try new things.

When the therapist invited Jalen to practice mindful breathing, he was reluctant at first and said, "It seems weird." When the therapist challenged him to see what his experience was, rather than what his mind might tell him about mindfulness practice, Jalen agreed to try it and to practice it at home daily. He found that it helped him sleep better and approach his stress in a more mindful and relaxed way. (In ACT, relaxation isn't the primary aim of mindfulness practice, and increased relaxation is fairly common.) As Jalen experienced these benefits, he became willing to expand his mindfulness practice, so his clinician taught him additional mindfulness exercises, such as Tuning In to Your Body (Ciarrochi, Harris, & Bailey, 2014, p. 24). With continued practice, Jalen soon found that after completing a mindfulness exercise, he could more easily shift his attention away from his worries to engage in the present moment. He also noticed that when he was less worried about the future and more firmly grounded in the present, he was more likely to complete committed actions, including studying, exercising, and spending time with his friends. An additional benefit was that he enjoyed these and other activities more when he focused on what he was doing in the moment, rather than fixating on how his present-moment outcomes might be linked to future outcomes, such as getting into a desirable college or making the football team.

Jalen's experience demonstrates how an inordinate focus on the future can interfere with committed action in the present moment. An excessive focus on the past, especially in the form of rumination, can have the same effect. As an example, imagine a client who ruminates about having lost her house due to extended unemployment. She will be more effective at engaging in committed actions aimed at finding a new job if she focuses instead on what she can do in the present moment. It can sometimes be useful to process the past, especially when developing creative hopelessness and conducting defusion exercises; people can always learn lessons about effectiveness by examining their past choices. However, committed action takes place in the present moment, whereas rumination about the past increases fusion and avoidance and usually hinders committed action.

Often, clients present with symptoms of both depression and worry, with a focus on both the past and future that can get in the way of committed action. This was the case for Gina, who presented for treatment of dysthymia. She had just retired and said, "I want to be happy for the 20 years or so that I have left, instead of being miserable all of the time." Gina appeared to have an enviable life. She was happily married, had good relationships with her adult children and her grandchildren, had no health problems, was rather wealthy, and had many friends and hobbies. Yet she complained that she felt unhappy most of the time and frequently worried about unimportant matters. She typically began her therapy sessions by berating herself for failing to complete tasks she had assigned herself during the previous week, such as organizing her pantry, planting flowers, or taking gently used items to a local charity. When she described her week, she almost always mentioned that she had participated in some activity that she'd enjoyed less than she thought she would, or complained that she'd made plans to attend a social event and wasn't looking forward to it.

Closer exploration of her behavior suggested that she was frequently focused on the past or future and rarely tuned in to the present moment. For example, she berated herself in the present moment about actions she hadn't completed in the recent past, and even when she did accomplish tasks, she berated herself for failing to attend to them more promptly or thoroughly. And when she planned a future social activity, such as going to a party or a concert, she focused ahead of time on mildly unpleasant things that could occur as part of the event, such as getting stuck in traffic, encountering crowds, experiencing bad weather, or getting lost. Then, when the time eventually came to attend the event, her focus still wasn't in the here and now; instead, she tended to compare the event to similar past events or to think about what she could be doing if she were at home, or how complicated it would be to leave the event to go home.

Gina's clinician used the experiential exercise Take Your Mind for a Walk (Hayes, Strosahl, et al., 2012, p. 259) to illustrate that the mind is an annoying chatterbox that can be difficult to ignore. Gina learned to use mindfulness to notice her thoughts as if they were written on signs being carried by marchers in a parade (Hayes, Strosahl, et al., 2012, pp. 255–258), which helped her increase her focus on the present moment and let go of verbal content that might draw her into the past or future. As Gina's ability to stay in contact with the present moment broadened into her life more generally, she found that she was able to mindfully either complete tasks or choose to forgo them because they weren't a genuine priority. Of course, mindfulness isn't magic, and Gina's mind continued to chatter about the past and feared future events, often quite frequently. However, when she practiced mindfulness skills on a regular basis, she was much more likely to be engaged in the present and make choices about committed action based on what the present moment afforded.

By the way, as you were reading about Gina's case, if you had the thought that defusion would be helpful, you were correct. Defusion and contact with the present moment go hand in hand. (All of the six core processes have facilitative relationships.) When Gina focused on the present moment, she had a greater ability to catch fusion with content that got in the way of committed action—thoughts like, *This task will be boring,* and *I won't be able to find parking near the concert, so maybe I shouldn't go.* While focused on the here and now, these thoughts were depotentiated. This combination of present-moment awareness and defusion allowed Gina to engage in committed action more frequently and also increased her enjoyment of those actions.

# Self-as-Context and Committed Action

Self-as-context, sometimes called self-as-perspective or the observing self, is also closely related to mindfulness, as this sense of self can only be contacted in the present moment. Self-as-context is undoubtedly the most difficult of the core ACT processes to talk about, due to its transcendent and abstract nature. It's described as transcendent because it has no verbal content or form. Instead, it's more akin to the locus or place where one's experience unfolds. This core process can be difficult to discuss with clients and therefore is better experienced through metaphors, such as The Sky and the Weather (Harris, 2009, p. 175), in which the observing self is like the sky, and thoughts and feelings are like the changing weather that crosses the sky. In a turbulent thunderstorm or during a placid sunny afternoon, the weather patterns continue to change over time, but they do not damage or change the sky. The sky simply is the context for the weather. This metaphor is applied to the self in ACT. Experiential exercises such as the Observer exercise (Hayes, Strosahl, et al., 2012, pp. 233–237) can facilitate clients in experiencing self-as-context. From this perspective, clients can build distinctions between themselves and their content, including thoughts, feelings, and sensations. In this way, self-as-context facilitates acceptance, defusion, contact with the present moment, and committed action.

Consider Sanjay, who came to therapy for treatment of depression and management of chronic pain. He'd been diagnosed with rheumatoid arthritis a few years earlier, and his symptoms of depression began soon after the effects of the disease on his hands and fingers forced him to stop working as a dentist. Sanjay loved his work and had been accustomed to working long days. He was also athletic and feared he would soon have to curtail his physical activity. He had two young children and felt sad that his relationship with them was deteriorating as his pain increased; he was frequently irritable and felt disengaged, whereas he'd previously been highly involved in his children's lives. Before his pain and depression became so severe, he'd spent most evenings helping his kids with their homework or taking them to soccer games and violin recitals. He also felt bored because he now had so much time on his hands—most of which he spent reading dentistry journals and surfing the Internet. With his wife's encouragement, he finally agreed to seek psychological help.

His therapist soon found that Sanjay, like many people with chronic pain, had a hard time pacing himself. He tended to avoid pain by minimizing his activity, but on days when his pain level was lower, he tended to do too much, paying the price the next day with increased pain, and creating a vicious cycle of pain and pain avoidance. It became clear that Sanjay was fused with his pain and the stories he told himself about it: that pain made his life unbearable, and that he must avoid the pain. He was also fused with depression and viewed it as the cause of his problems, as evidenced by statements like, "The depression keeps me from doing more," and "I can't live my life as long as I feel this way."

Sanjay's therapist turned to self-as-context work, because Sanjay was so focused on disruption of important roles such as his roles as a dentist, athlete, and father, and because Sanjay frequently spoke of his rheumatoid arthritis as if it defined him. Because self-as-context is so hard to describe verbally, his therapist used the *classroom metaphor* and *the prince and the beggar metaphor* (described in Stoddard and Afari, 2014, pp. 120 & 122). Nevertheless, Sanjay tried to understand self-as-context conceptually, so his therapist turned to the more experiential Observer exercise (Hayes, Strosahl, et al., 2012) to help Sanjay more directly experience the observing self. As she led Sanjay through the guided exercise, she invited him to notice his experience—his bodily sensations, memories, feelings, and thoughts—and to also notice the person noticing those experiences. As called for in this exercise, she also asked him to notice—at the level of experience, not verbally—that although he has bodily sensations, he is not his bodily sensations, and although he has thoughts, he is not his thoughts, and so on, to get a glimpse of self-as-context.

Guided exercises such as the Observer exercise and its variants zero in on the experience of self-as-context, rather than verbal descriptions of it. As mentioned, self-as-context necessarily requires contact with the present moment, and it also facilitates defusion. After Sanjay became familiar with self-as-context, his therapist varied the Observer exercise and invited Sanjay to notice that, at the level of experience, he has roles and he is not his roles, and he has pain and yet is not his pain. Sanjay found that this exercise increased his willingness to feel pain, and that when he was more willing to experience pain he was more likely to engage in committed action. He gradually began to engage with his children more often. As he became less unitarily attached to his role as a dentist, he explored new roles and volunteered to be a coordinator for his daughter's soccer team, joined the board of the community orchestra, and eventually found part-time work teaching a class at a local dental school. As his activity increased, his depression began to diminish, and he also developed a greater capacity to notice and defuse from depressive thoughts. Committed action, in the form of behavioral activation, was an important part of his recovery, and without self-as-context work, he might have remained unwilling to act.

Mark, the veteran discussed earlier, also found self-as-context work helpful for facilitating committed action. His therapist used the Observer exercise to help him experience that he is not his body, and that at the level of self-as-context, he is fundamentally whole, even though his body is no longer whole as it once was. At the level of self-as-context, everyone is whole, complete, and perfect. This work, along with acceptance and defusion, helped Mark to view himself as whole even with his limitations. He was more willing to go out into the world and accept what others offered him, including offers to assist him with simple tasks such as carrying packages or holding doors. He was also more open to receiving the kindness and compassion others extended toward him. Mark experienced that self-compassion increases both compassion for others and acceptance of compassion from others. From a place of self-compassion, Mark was more willing to engage in committed action instead of angrily isolating himself from the world and the possibility of possibility.

# Values and Committed Action

Working with the ACT processes of acceptance, defusion, contact with the present-moment, and self-as-context can help remove many obstacles to committed action. Yet before clients can engage in committed action, meaningful committed actions must be identified. This is where values work comes to the fore. Of all the core ACT processes, values clarification probably has the most direct link to committed action. Even so, our hope is that by this point in the chapter it's clear that all of the processes are essential to committed action.

As a reminder, values are chosen life directions, and values clarification is the process of identifying those directions. The metaphor of moving in a direction, such as going west, described earlier in the book, is frequently used to help clients contact the understanding that, like traveling west, living their values is an ongoing pursuit in which no end point is ever reached. Examples include lifelong engagement in learning, being a loving and supportive partner, or taking care of one's health. Notice that unlike specific goals such as finishing a class, celebrating a wedding anniversary, or running a marathon, one can never finish or complete a value.

Additionally, although goals are by definition things a person hasn't yet attained and therefore are unavailable in the present, opportunities for valued action are always available. In ACT, committed actions are described as being in the service of one's values. For example, the committed actions of reading nonfiction books, learning a new skill, watching the Discovery Channel, or keeping up with current events might be the committed actions of a person who values a lifelong engagement in learning. Similarly, visiting difficult in-laws or cooking dinner while a spouse works on an important project might be committed actions in the service of the value of being a supportive partner. Thus, being clear about one's values is essential to identifying meaningful committed actions. It also bolsters willingness to engage in difficult actions.

Consider Alan, a married man with two children, who in his first session said, "I drink too much, but I don't want to quit drinking; I hope you can help me cut down on my drinking." He reported that he'd started drinking as a young teenager, and that his father, uncle, and two of his brothers were also heavy drinkers. He wanted his therapist to understand that although he acknowledged that he drank too much, he didn't regard himself to be an alcoholic like his father. When his therapist asked him to describe his alcohol use, he reported that he drank almost every day, consuming four to eight beers most evenings and more on weekends. He worked as a supervisor in a large factory and described alcohol as an important part of his social life, which included going to a bar with colleagues after work and socializing with his wife and other couples on most weekends. He also said, "I work hard for my family, and I've earned a few drinks after a hard day's work." He was emphatic that he never missed work or arrived late because of drinking, and he specifically noted that he never hit his children or wife while drinking, as his father had done.

After building rapport, when his therapist asked Alan if his drinking ever caused problems, he acknowledged that he frequently went to work with a hangover and was probably less productive on those days. He also said he was more likely to argue with his wife while drinking or hungover, and that he left many household chores unfinished, or did them poorly, once he started drinking. He also said, "I'm probably not the greatest dad when I'm drinking," and recounted a few instances when he ignored or yelled at his children after drinking. When the therapist asked Alan what made him decide to enter treatment, he acknowledged that he only considered treatment after his boss recommended that he do something about his drinking. He seemed to be ashamed that his drinking was apparent to his boss, and because he hoped to advance within the company, he was concerned that his drinking was affecting his performance at work.

Nevertheless, Alan was able to describe many reasons why he wanted to continue drinking and didn't see alcohol use as much of an obstacle to achieving goals that were important to him. Because this attitude seemed to indicate a disconnect between his values and actions, the therapist invited Alan to participate in a values clarification exercise that involved identifying his desired outcomes in several domains of life. After Alan elaborated some of his values, he completed the Valued Living Questionnaire (VLQ; Wilson, 2008, pp. 232–233).

A simpler version of the VLQ-2, discussed in chapter 3, the VLQ asks respondents to rate the importance of 10 life domains on a scale of 1 to 10, and then to rate how consistent their behavior has been with regard to each value during the previous week, also using a scale of 1 to 10. The VLQ and other such measures of values consistency are useful for highlighting discrepancies between one's actions and one's values. When a domain is rated high in importance and behavior in that domain is rated as low, there are two likely explanations: either the importance rating doesn't reflect the actual importance of that domain to the individual, or the individual's behavior isn't currently consistent with his values. For instance, if a person assigns a rating of 8 to spirituality, indicating that it's very important, yet seldom engages in behaviors related to spirituality, such as attending religious services, praying, reading spiritual texts, or donating time or money to spiritual endeavors, the individual may decide that perhaps spirituality isn't very important to him after all and adjust his importance rating. Alternatively, he may decide to increase his participation in spiritual activities in order to bring his behavior in alignment with his values. In the latter case, it will be helpful to first explore the obstacles to bringing behavior in line with his values. This will help him be more effective as he engages in committed actions in the service of his values. In general, the higher the discrepancy between the importance of a value and the consistency of behaviors related to it, the more likely it is that the person faces significant obstacles to committed action that need to be addressed.

Returning to Alan, he was startled by the discrepancies apparent in the results of his VLQ. Alan assigned high ratings—from 8 to 10—to the domains of work, marriage, parenting, social life, and physical self-care. However, his highest consistency rating in those domains was 4 out of 10. Working together, Alan and his therapist engaged in more values clarification in order to identify appropriate committed actions that could improve his consistency ratings. After brainstorming on this topic, they'd identified dozens of behaviors, simple and difficult, that he could perform in order to move in the direction for his values. For example, to better reflect his values in regard to his marriage, he could compliment his wife more, do more chores, go out on date nights, cook dinner on the weekends, and display more physical affection. In the domain of work, he identified talking with his colleagues more often, encouraging junior colleagues to ask questions, displaying a more positive attitude at work, and being more willing to volunteer for overtime work. He also generated substantial lists of actions that could improve his behavioral consistency in relation to his values in the domains of parenting, social life, and physical self-care.

When Alan's therapist asked him to consider how his alcohol use might influence his effectiveness in carrying out these committed actions, Alan was shocked to discover that it interfered with almost all of the committed actions he'd identified. For example, when he began drinking after arriving home from work, he didn't feel like engaging with his children, and he was more likely to insult his wife than compliment her. When he went to work with a hangover, his mood was surly, he didn't fully engage with his colleagues, and he would usually be disinclined to volunteer for overtime because at the end of the workday he wanted to go to a bar or go home and drink. This exercise made it impossible for Alan to ignore the effects alcohol was having on his behavior, and he seemed truly shocked that his alcohol use, rather than lack of time, was the biggest obstacle to committed action. Based upon this realization, he was willing to experiment with staying sober for two weeks. After one week, he noticed that he was much more likely to engage in committed action. He also noticed that his wife and children seemed to be happier with him and that he felt more engaged with his colleagues.

Values and committed action are so deeply intertwined that values clarification is almost always an essential part of identifying committed actions, building willingness to carry them out, and identifying and overcoming obstacles. This is abundantly clear from some of the case histories described above. Gina might use her values regarding health to build motivation for weight loss. Loretta might identify certain committed actions as helping Megan, rather than harming her, if she views those actions through the lens of her values related to parenting. Mark might be more willing to risk rejection if he contacts how important relationships are to him. Jalen might be more engaged at school if he examines his values related to learning. The relationship between values and committed action is so important that lack of clarity about values might itself be an obstacle to committed action to be overcome. Ultimately, values clarification is essential for increasing engagement in committed action.

# Committed Action and…Committed Action

Perhaps it's stating the obvious, but there are instances in which promoting the process of committed action is what's needed to help clients tackle committed action. Small committed actions may be undertaken in preparation for larger committed actions, and small committed actions are always a part of larger patterns of committed action. Furthermore, committed action can support all of the other core ACT processes, and in some cases may initiate growth in other ACT processes.

Consider Caleb, who was working while attending graduate school and wanted to dedicate more time to studying. In order to do so, he first carried out several smaller actions that helped him to free up time for studying. For one, he committed to taking the train to work instead of driving so he could study while riding the train. Taking the train meant he had to get up at least 30 minutes earlier each day, so Caleb committed to doing that. To facilitate waking up earlier, he decided to commit to going to bed earlier, which he did. And going to bed earlier meant watching less TV at night, which he also committed to.

Embarking on new patterns of committed action often requires engaging in many new behaviors. Taking baby steps can reduce fear and avoidance associated with taking larger steps. Returning to Michelle, who wanted to lose weight, she might want to take on several major steps in order to lose weight, such as trying a low-carb diet, and joining a gym so she could lift weights and swim. Initially, she found it difficult to simply start the diet and begin a regimen of weightlifting, so she identified smaller committed actions she could engage in to help her take these larger steps. For example, she read about various approaches to low-carb eating, and then she stocked her pantry with some new low-carb choices. She also researched gyms near her home and workplace, including their hours and costs, and visited several likely prospects to decide which seemed like the best fit for her. She also read the book *The Weight Escape* (Ciarrochi, Harris, & Bailey, 2014) to learn more about using acceptance-based approaches to weight loss. These steps helped Michelle get closer to the new eating and exercise habits she wanted to establish by ensuring that she had what she needed to successfully engage in committed action, and the reinforcing success of committed action can create momentum to continue the commitment.

As mentioned, committed actions can also initiate other core ACT processes, and vice versa. When Jason went out with friends while worrying about Serena, he was engaging in committed action and acceptance. When Loretta put money in her savings account while having thoughts that she should use the money to pay Megan's bills, she was engaging in committed action and defusion. When Alan completed the VLQ, doing so was a committed action aimed at identifying his values. The components of the ACT model all have mutual and facilitative relationships, and in the next chapter we will discuss how these processes can be used to assist ACT therapists themselves.

## Summary

This chapter has provided an overview of how all six of ACT's core processes can be used to support committed action and increase the effectiveness of the ACT model of behavior change. Each component can directly support strengthening committed action, and development in the area of committed action can bolster the other five components. In chapter 7, we'll explore how the ACT model supports committed action from the ACT therapist's point of view, as well.

# Addressing Obstacles to Committed Action on the Part of the Therapist

The work of committed action in therapy can require boldness and focused attention on the part of therapists, at least until clients build up enough forward momentum to keep themselves going through contact with reinforcing natural contingencies. Occasionally, therapists may be fortunate to have highly motivated clients who know what they need and want, in which case the therapist's job is simply to support them and nudge them in those valued directions. Most therapists can manage this kind of situation without much effort—the steps are clear, and the client follows through and makes progress.

However, the vast majority of clinical situations require revisiting values and committed action multiple times during therapy as the therapist and client work together to experiment and determine what does and doesn't work to help the client move in valued directions. Through a larger set of processes, fusion and pliance (behavior based on a history of reinforcement for following rules) are gradually stripped away, and experiential avoidance is reduced to allow for more effective action. Of course, commitment and psychological flexibility on the part of the client are essential for successful committed action in practice. However, commitment is also required on the part of the therapist.

## Therapist Obstacles to Facilitating Committed Action

Some therapists may be less comfortable with an approach to therapy that's explicitly directed toward committed action in an ongoing way, perhaps because of their style or personality. This can be the case for therapists whose training and supervision were within a traditional humanistic, person-centered model, a relational model, or a psychodynamic or psychoanalytic model. Such therapists may be less inclined to be directive in guiding clients toward committed action, or may feel that they're pushing clients too much by bringing a consistent, explicit focus on orienting clients toward explicit future actions. Therapists with such backgrounds might feel that it's their job to be with their clients wherever they are emotionally, and assume that clients will choose behavioral goals on their own when they're ready. When therapists are uncomfortable with a new approach for any reason, including not being sure how to apply it, they may return to using previous therapy approaches, which can create an inconsistent experience for clients. Furthermore, the ACT approach inherently includes creating space for sitting with difficult emotions (through mindfulness and self-as-context) and not rushing to help clients change how they're feeling (instead using acceptance and defusion). However, when the timing is appropriate, ACT therapists work with clients to help them set specific goals and behavioral targets. It is a "both-and" approach, not an "either-or" approach. It would be incorrect to label ACT as an experiential approach primarily focused on acceptance of emotions, just as it would be to label it a purely behavioral approach focused on goal setting and action. Both things are true and can be true concurrently across and within sessions.

In some circumstances, therapists may feel that focusing on committed action isn't the compassionate thing to do in the moment. For example, this can happen when clients are going through a difficult time and already seem to be facing too many challenges in life. Misinterpretation of the committed action process can add to this problem if therapists think committed action goals have to be herculean in order to be meaningful. However, even in times of great stress and difficulty, clients can still engage in small committed actions. For example, a client who wants to pursue her values related to physical health can still squeeze in a five-minute walk per day or do 10 push-ups. In fact, taking some sort of values-based action, even in the face of adversity, can be very satisfying and can help to demonstrate that the reasons that we give for not moving forward are often illusory. It isn't the therapist's job to assume that the client can't take on an additional responsibility or a new opportunity for growth. It's also important for therapists to remember that the goal of therapy is not to reach a specific outcome as quickly as possible, but to help clients build larger and larger patterns of effective behavior that are in alignment with their values. If committed action plans haven't been successful, perhaps the chosen goals have been too large or otherwise not immediately attainable. Similarly, lack of apparent success in attaining specific goals can also be a signal that it would be helpful to break those commitments down into smaller actions that will still move the client in valued directions. Larger committed actions aren't inherently more meaningful than modest actions. This is a reminder that is important not just for the client, but also for the therapist.

Other obstacles can arise due to a lack of mindful therapeutic timing. For example, some therapists may find themselves jumping ahead to committed action too rapidly in an attempt to quickly solve an issue, rather than being present with all that might be needed in a given moment. This often arises from genuine eagerness to improve the client's well-being and an acute sense of how much pain the client is currently experiencing. The therapist may think she's identified exactly what would be helpful and wish to facilitate it. However, if clients take on committed action work before they can reliably exercise sufficient willingness and defusion skills, before their values have been fully explored, or primarily as a result of pliance, their efforts have a high probability of failing. Therefore, in order to undertake committed action work effectively, therapists must be in tune with the client's current capacities.

Then, when working toward committed action, it can also be just as important to preemptively explore the client's likely emotional and cognitive barriers to following through as it is to choose desired target behaviors. An optimistic therapist who garners a commitment from a client may sometimes neglect to fully explore client reluctance regarding that commitment. This can happen because the therapist simply doesn't think to explore barriers, because the client seems so determined to complete a committed action, or because the therapist thinks there isn't enough time in the session to explore the potential reasons why the client might not follow through. A therapist may also overtly choose not to discuss the client's thoughts about potential barriers because of a perception that the client is already overly fused with a story about why changes aren't possible and a concern that this this story will be reinforced if the client takes this as an opportunity to bring it up again. In all of these cases, however, the choice not to spend time addressing potential barriers leaves clients unprepared and at a disadvantage when those barriers arise.

Finally, the process of committed action can be actively misused if the therapist is feeling increasingly frustrated in listening to a client's fused story about current circumstances and how there's nothing the client can do to change things. The therapist may then push committed action prematurely in an attempt to shift the client from fusion with a victim role to becoming more active in pursuing values-based actions. ("Well, since there's nothing you can do to alter what happened in the past, what can you do to change your situation here and now?") Such a shift in focus can be an appropriate direction if it's a transparent move that the therapist does alongside the client and with the client's engagement and permission. However, if it's done as part of a covert agenda to change the subject or transform the story for the client, it may come across as invalidating or disingenuous, or as the therapist not hearing or recognizing what the client needs.

# Therapist Obstacles to Practicing Committed Action

In order to fully engage with the treatment process, ACT therapists must also practice their own committed action before, during, and after treatment sessions. For starters, therapists generally need to spend time preparing before sessions. For experienced ACT therapists, this may simply mean reviewing their notes from the previous session and refreshing their memory about the behavioral assignments the client agreed to complete before the upcoming session. However, for therapists who are new to ACT, significantly more preparation time may be needed. For example, therapists in training may need to prepare by reading ACT texts to understand how to sequence and implement treatment tasks, or by watching videos to see exemplars of ACT implementation using different therapeutic styles. Or they may need to practice delivering ACT metaphors and exercises out loud so they'll be prepared to do so effectively with the client.

One potential obstacle to engaging in this level of effort is therapists' perception that they don't have enough time in their day-to-day lives to do substantial amounts of learning and preparation on an ongoing basis or for any one given client. And it's possible that this is true. Therapists are often generous, dedicated people who are very engaged in meaningful activities in their lives—both professionally and personally. However, it's important not to use this "reason" on a regular basis. One of the meaningful activities in the life of a dedicated therapist is providing competent psychotherapy that alleviates the suffering of others and facilitates their ability to move their lives forward. To that end, therapists may need to mindfully prioritize their own valued activities in a way that allows them to devote sufficient attention to preparation for therapy. Preparation and learning are not distractions in the life of a therapist; they are an integral part of the life and work of a therapist.

Of course, despite any amount of training and preparation, ACT therapists may sometimes feel stuck regarding how to effectively move a given client toward committed action. In these cases, it may be helpful for the therapist to share this feeling of "stuckness" directly with the client; perhaps an open discussion will identify new entry points into committed action. In addition, this can be validating for clients, as they see they aren't the only ones feeling stuck. When handled skillfully, such an interaction can lead to increased connection in the therapeutic relationship. If, despite sufficient training and preparation, and despite engaging the client directly, the therapist still feels stuck, it may be time to engage in peer consultation or formal clinical supervision in order to identify and address the barriers, including learning some new ways of addressing them.

The therapist's own well-being outside of the therapy room can also affect his ability to fully engage the process of committed action with clients. For example, if a therapist is struggling in areas of life in which he isn't acting in alignment with his own values, he may be inclined to avoid in-session conversations about committed action and fail to fully explore his clients' lack of follow-through on committed action. Alternatively, if a therapist is feeling like he has been falling short in important ways recently, he may overidentify with clients' experiences of being a fallible human being and therefore choose not to push them to do something he can't do consistently himself, for fear of being hypocritical, or out of misguided compassion.

All of these challenges can be heightened for therapists who are experiencing professional burnout, or feeling tired, listless, or disconnected from the meaning of the work. In such situations, conventional wisdom would suggest practicing self-care, getting enough rest, and spending time on relationships and activities outside of work. And while an ACT approach would support these healthy choices as appropriate, it wouldn't necessarily encourage therapists to back away from stressful or difficult work situations. Of course, if there are structural or logistical problems in the work environment that can be addressed with practical problem solving, that should happen. However, therapists experiencing burnout might also be productively challenged to reconnect with what's important to them personally and professionally about the work so they can regain a sense of meaning and vitality in conducting ACT. Through a combination of self-care, practical problem solving, and values clarification and recommitment, burned-out therapists can hopefully find a better balance in attending to both their own needs and those of their clients.

# Recognizing Therapist Barriers to Committed Action Work

To avoid the pitfalls of ineffective engagement in and facilitation of committed action, therapists must practice mindful awareness of their own private events in the context of specific clinical interactions and relationships. All therapists have, at times, had the experience of looking at their schedule for the day and feeling less than enthusiastic about spending time with a particular client. In these moments, therapists can ask themselves, "What are my sticky thoughts regarding this client?" Here are some thoughts that may sound familiar:

- *She's already dealing with enough right now without me adding more for her to work on.*

- *I know he probably won't follow through anyway.*

- *This is so uncomfortable.*

- *We talk about the same thing every week, and she just refuses to do anything about it.*

- *It's not fair to him to ask him to do this.*

- *She probably won't be successful in this situation, even if she tries. The circumstances are just too complicated and out of her control.*

- *I can't figure out how to get him unstuck so that he'll listen to my suggestions.*

Having these kinds of sticky thoughts may be a signal that the therapist is fused with thoughts about the client or the process, rather than simply tracking what's likely

101

to be effective and being willing to experiment with the client to find out what will work.

Other potential signs that the therapist may be functioning as an obstacle to committed action work are if the client seems to be frustrated with the therapist for pushing toward commitment or the client demonstrates counterpliance (in other words, repeatedly choosing to do the opposite of a socially expected rule, or the opposite of what the therapist suggests). This may indicate that there's a disconnect between where the client is and where the therapist thinks the client is. It may also indicate that the therapist is moving things in the direction of her own values rather than the client's. Likewise, sometimes therapists may have the sense that they are more invested and interested in a particular action or in making change than the client is. It may even initially seem like a specific goal is based on the client's values; however, if after several trials the client has made little or no progress, it may be time to reassess whether the client committed to that goal out of pliance or wanting to please the therapist, rather than as a reflection of the client's freely chosen values. Pliance-driven goal setting can happen without the therapist noticing it, sometimes because the goal so naturally comports with what the therapist wants for the client that the therapist doesn't thoughtfully question it or sufficiently explore it.

## A Clinical Example

Let's look at a case example showing how the therapist and, more specifically, pliance can pose a barrier to client committed action. The client is a 27-year-old military veteran, Nicholas, who has just been honorably discharged from the US Marine Corps and has been in treatment for depression and post-traumatic symptoms for two months. During the process of values clarification and goal setting, Nicholas said that he wanted to pursue education beyond his high school equivalency certificate. As a child, he had been diagnosed with a mild learning disability, and school had always been difficult for him, but he said that he wanted to overcome this barrier and get a college degree. After further exploration of his values around education, he enthusiastically set a goal of registering for an initial class at his local community college.

But week after week, he came back to session without following through on his commitment. The therapist hypothesized that avoidance of discomfort related to returning to school and potential academic failure was presenting an obstacle, so she conducted several experiential exercises with Nicholas in which she asked him to get in touch with the feelings evoked by the idea of returning to school. She specifically asked him to identify what showed up when he imagined registering for the course, and to be fully present with those feelings without pushing them away or trying to change them. At the end of the session, Nicholas reported a renewed intention to follow through with his commitment. However, to the therapist's dismay, Nicholas was a no-show for session the following week, which concerned the therapist, because the class registration deadline was closing very soon. When he finally returned to therapy two weeks later, Nicholas reported that he hadn't gotten any closer to following through with the plan.

Eventually, out of frustration, the therapist candidly said, "It's like you don't really want to go to college. That's all I can determine from the choices you've been making." Although said more out of frustration than keen therapeutic insight, this comment gave Nicholas an opening to talk about what was truly going on for him, and he shared that he had realized over the past few weeks that he truly didn't want to go to college. What he had actually been experiencing were romantic feelings toward the therapist. He believed that because she had an advanced degree, she would never be willing to date someone without a college degree. So if he was going to have any chance with her, he thought, he needed to go back to school. The therapist was caught completely off guard by this revelation, because it had never occurred to her that he would have set a goal for himself that wasn't actually important to him.

The therapist had, to her credit, explored potential barriers to commitment, but only those that left intact the initial assumption that Nicholas really did value going back to school. A thorough and collaborative functional analysis might have more quickly unearthed that pliance, and specifically an effort to please the therapist herself, was underlying the stated goal. However, pliance in itself obviously wasn't sufficiently powerful to motivate Nicholas to follow through. Following through with this challenging goal would have happened only if it was something truly valued by the client. Once all of this rich material was on the table (and after the therapist dealt appropriately and compassionately with the issue of romantic attraction), Nicholas and his therapist were able to productively reengage in a values assessment and identify behavioral targets that were more personally meaningful to him. Not surprisingly, he was much quicker to follow through on these new committed actions. The problem wasn't that he didn't have committed action skills in his repertoire; it was that they were being targeted in a direction he didn't genuinely value.

# Overcoming Barriers to the Therapist's Own Committed Action

At the most basic level, the therapist's job in the work of committed action is the same as the client's: be present, open up, and focus on engaging in values-based action. The criterion for determining whether a given therapeutic move is the right one for a specific client at a particular time is workability. Just as therapists might ask clients, "And how is that working for you?" they should also ask themselves this question during stuck points in the therapeutic process. For example, if a therapist is hesitating to push her client to make clearly stated behavioral commitments, she might ask herself if pulling back is actually saving the client from anything. Does that approach help the client to get closer to his values and goals? In other words, it's important for therapists to notice whether choosing not to challenge a client to work on committed action is actually in the service of the client's needs or is more about allowing for experiential avoidance on the part of either the therapist or the client.

Therapists who are struggling with such issues might consider whether they're costing clients anything by giving them a pass on following through with commitments. These costs could take many forms: the cost of additional sessions, the loss of opportunities for the client to move forward, or the client missing out on building confidence by setting a goal and following through with it—to name a few. That said, sometimes delaying can be the most effective thing to do; however, such a choice should be guided by a functional analysis of what will best serve the client, not by what comes most easily in the moment. When in doubt about whether to push on committed action, one option is to discuss the decision with the client. Together, therapist and client can then fully and nonjudgmentally explore the options. There isn't a right answer in such situations; what's important is to openly consider the function of a variety of answers as part of the decision-making process.

At times, therapists may not fully engage in committed action work because they feel frustrated or discouraged by a client's lack of progress on previous goals and actions. In such cases, it may be useful to first focus on identifying any related thoughts the therapist may be fusing with, and then practice standard defusion skills with them. Afterward, the therapist may be able to more openly notice what emotions have been arising and move toward acceptance of difficult private experiences rather than trying to reduce or change them. This may also be a useful time to explore the client's values again and clarify whether the stated goals are actually the client's, or whether they've been unduly, if unintentionally, shaped by the therapist's ideas or values. After practicing mindfulness and defusion, therapists may be in a better position to use their clinical skills to note subtle cues that indicate how genuinely important a valued direction is to a client. If there is a strong therapeutic relationship, the therapist can also choose to nonjudgmentally bring up her own frustration with the client to see if this modeling of openness might facilitate a more candid discussion of barriers to moving forward. Often, the therapist will find that the client is equally frustrated (or even more so!), and this becomes an experience through which the dyad can connect.

# Building the Therapist's Committed Action Skills

It can be argued that therapists can better facilitate acquisition and application of behaviors and skills if they already have those behaviors and skills in their own repertoire, in large part because they may be able to more accurately describe, shape, and coach the target behaviors for someone else. Within ACT, this point is most often made in relation to mindfulness and acceptance skills, which are less concrete. However, we believe that this axiom is just as relevant to committed action skills. In fact, gaining an experiential understanding of ACT is usually part of the process of learning the approach, and that includes engaging in activities related to values clarification and committed action. After all, can a therapist who hasn't actively worked to take steps in a valued direction that has been neglected for years really know what he's asking a very stuck client to do when working together to choose committed actions in domains that have long been neglected or abandoned?

This is one of those areas where it's helpful for both therapist and client to be aware that they're together in the same boat. Everyone has had the experience of wanting to do something differently or take a step forward, but not making that change, even when staying in the same place, is painful. Furthermore, when things are going smoothly in therapists' lives, or if they become emotionally disconnected during therapy, they may sometimes lose contact with the experience of what it's like to struggle with taking important valued actions or avoid doing so. Therapists are well advised to ensure that they maintain an experiential sensitivity to the experience of committing to change, so that they can share the perspective of the client more effectively while facilitating action. When the therapist consistently works on building her own "committed action muscle," she will be better able to serve as a commitment personal trainer to her clients.

Finally, it has been argued that successful commitment depends on willingness, because values are often interrelated with difficult internal experiences, and successfully engaging with difficult internal experiences requires willingness (Luoma et al., 2007). Ongoing committed action requires change, versatility, and persistence. If therapists actively take opportunities in their own lives to engage in committed actions even in the face of personally challenging circumstances, they will broaden their own repertoire and better be able to coach clients in applying committed action skills in a variety of situations.

# Exercise: Committed Action Refresher

If you frequently find yourself wondering why clients can't follow through with their commitments, it may be helpful to review your own behavior in regard to committed action.

1.  Start by identifying a behavior that's something that you really struggle with and have been trying to change for some time. Identify something you'd really like to work on because it's important to you.

2.  Spend a few minutes writing about your struggle and why it's been hard to follow through. See how many barriers you can identify. You don't have to share what you write with anyone else, so really dig deep and explore the details of what's gotten in the way.

3.  Spend a few minutes writing about the value that underlies the desired behavior change. Go into detail about how you would like to see yourself behaving in this area. Why do you choose to make this important?

4.  Spend a few minutes outlining in writing your commitment for the next week. Be as specific as possible. How will you move toward this goal, even if in a very small way?

5.  What barriers do you anticipate might get in the way, and how will you work through those barriers? (Hint: If the barriers are emotional, apply willingness and acceptance. If the barriers are cognitive, apply defusion. And if the barriers are practical, apply problem-solving skills and break the goal down into smaller committed action steps.) Spend a few minutes writing about this.

6.  Work on executing the committed action over the next week, practicing mindfulness to help you learn more about your personal barriers to following through, as well as about what facilitates you in engaging in committed action. You may find that writing weekly about your progress or lack thereof in accomplishing your commitment is illustrative not only of what you need to work on, but also of some of the complex (and mundane) barriers that get in the way.

The goal of this exercise is to gain a refreshed, personal experience of what it's like to commit to a personally relevant goal, so that when you ask clients to engage in similar processes, you do so more from a stance of shared experience. This exercise can also help you generate hypotheses about barriers that may be getting in the way of clients' committed actions—although it's always important to remember that everyone's experience is different. Therefore, use your own experience to approach such conversations in a compassionate way, without making assumptions about clients' experiences. Such conversations generally go best if the therapeutic relationship allows the client to openly disagree with your suggestions and interpretations and to share her own understanding of what hampered or facilitated her committed actions.

# The Therapeutic Relationship as the Context for Committed Action

At times, it can be extremely powerful for therapists to actively model and demonstrate committed action in session. One way to do this is to be on the lookout for a stuck point in the therapeutic process or the therapeutic relationship and then openly talk with the client about the therapist's own experience of feeling stuck (or disappointed, or sad, and so on). After nonjudgmentally describing the situation, the therapist can then work on identifying instances when the precipitating circumstance arises in session and openly noticing whatever shows up for him in those moments. Then he can talk through the choice point he's encountering and model in real time how to choose an action in line with one's values in the face of a difficult moment or situation.

For example, imagine a therapist who's had a very hectic day at work so far, who didn't sleep well the previous night because his daughter was sick, and who feels like he's coming down with a head cold. He realizes about five minutes into a session that he's distracted by his own mental and physical experiences and not paying very close attention to what his client is saying. In the context of a strong therapeutic relationship, he might say: "I'm sorry. I have to pause the conversation here for a moment. I'm just noticing that I'm not at my best today. I didn't sleep well and have had such a chaotic day that I haven't even fully gotten into the room so that I can be present with you and what you need today. *And*, what's important to me is to make good use of our time together and really focus on this moment and listening carefully to you. If it's okay with you, I'd like it if we could do a brief mindfulness activity together first. And then, when we come back to what you were talking about, my commitment is to stay present in the moment with you. And when I inevitably find myself getting distracted by my own busy mind or tired body, I commit to noticing that, taking a deep breath, and then coming back to our work together."

A therapeutic move like this might be considered unusual by many therapists, who might fear that disclosing their personal limitations might reduce their clients' confidence in them. However, within ACT, therapists establish early on that they are just as human and fallible as anyone else. By describing his experience nonjudgmentally and openly and directly committing to an ongoing course of action defined by his values, the therapist in that scenario turns what could have been an unsatisfying therapy session for both parties into an opportunity to model mindfulness, willingness, and committed action.

The same type of process can also be implemented without explicitly making the client aware that the therapist is engaging in this level of mindful, ongoing committed action. Consider a therapist who realizes that she stops listening actively to a client every time he starts talking, yet again, about how his mother deprived him as a child. She can make a personal commitment to notice when she starts to check out and to use that as a cue to practice mindfulness of the client's words and compassion for the pain of that child 30 years ago. Or consider a therapist who experiences frustration with a client who frequently responds with "yes, but…" to the therapist's suggestions. She can make a commitment that when she starts feeling that familiar frustration, she'll practice a moment of mindful breathing before choosing what to say next. Even when these committed actions are happening behind the scenes, they can potentially benefit the therapy because they're sharpening the therapist's own committed action skills.

# Therapist Barriers to Effective Use of Homework

Homework is an area where both clients and therapists can struggle with committed action. Yet behavioral assignments to be completed between therapy sessions are an essential strategy for supporting acquisition of skills in the real world. In the absence of specific plans for applying new behaviors in real life, clients' commitment to use the skills discussed and practiced in therapy can easily fade. Therefore, an important component of committed action work is collaborating with clients to choose homework assignments for the week. When clients don't have a specific target, they are much less likely to be successful in following through on values-oriented commitments. However, even when the potential utility of agreeing on homework assignments is apparent, following through with homework assignments is much easier said than done, often for both client and therapist. In this section, we'll focus on therapist barriers to committed action in regard to homework.

One potential model for homework in therapy might go like this:

1. The client and therapist collaboratively identify behavioral targets to be met by the client before the next session or within a specific time period.

2. The client and therapist identify potential barriers to committed action that are likely to arise and could get in the way of accomplishing the target behaviors, and they develop strategies to address those barriers in the service of successful committed action.

3. The client makes a commitment to follow through with the identified behavioral targets.

4. The client does (or does not) follow through with the planned behaviors.

5. The therapist follows up in the next session to determine whether the client successfully accomplished the homework assignment.

6. If the client followed through, the therapist works to ensure client awareness of and contact with the natural contingencies of the behavior. Or if the client didn't follow through or did so only partially, the therapist helps the client assess what the barriers were, and together, they make a plan to overcome those barriers in the future.

Sometimes barriers arise in the form of simple logistical issues. The fifth step in the preceding model of homework calls for the therapist to follow up and in subsequent sessions to determine whether clients completed homework assignments. This is easiest to do when both therapist and client note the same list of committed action goals at the end of session, so both have a record of what the client committed to. This can facilitate follow-up and ensure accuracy. In addition, written targets can provide a clear prompt for clients to remember what they agreed to do throughout the week and could also provide motivation to act in accordance with the written goals.

Although the responsibility for actually engaging in the committed action rests with the client, the therapist also has a key role to play in this process, and not all therapists may be comfortable in that role. Some therapists are uncomfortable with having a predetermined session structure that sets aside time for follow-up on the last session's homework and discussion of committed action goals the client might choose for the coming week. For such therapists, it can be helpful to remember that the goal-setting process is intended to be self-directed by the client, even if the therapist initiates that part of the discussion. So whenever possible, the client is the one generating the goals, and if the targets advance the client's values, then this process is in the direct interest of the client and is, therefore, person-centered. For most therapists, this would be a valued approach, making discussion of and follow-up on homework a values-based committed action for the therapist. Another aspect of this approach that may tie into therapist values is that when goal setting is undertaken collaboratively, the process can provide an opportunity for the therapist to demonstrate support and strengthen the therapeutic relationship. However, even with this knowledge, it can be difficult for the therapist to reliably follow through with homework-related activities in each session. It is important not to view setting aside time for homework as taking away from the work of therapy, but rather focusing time toward supporting the client in moving forward.

Another potential barrier arises when therapists themselves, just like many clients, have negative associations with the concept of homework. Such therapists may be reluctant to engage in a process in which they feel they would be (or would be perceived to be) an authority figure setting expectations and consequences for someone else. In this case, defusion can be especially useful, allowing the therapist to gain some perspective and distance from negatively evaluated labels or descriptors associated with facilitating homework. It can also be helpful to simply use language that may be more workable and have fewer connotations than "homework"—such as "goals," "commitments," "targets," "plans," or "action steps." If being in this type of more directive role is consistently aversive (and at times avoided) by the therapist, professional consultation with a colleague or supervisor focused on this issue may be helpful.

Finally, it is important to remember that these committed actions are chosen by the client, and only the client is responsible for their execution. Homework is about extending the work of therapy into the client's life, and is not a reflection on the therapist or the success of therapy. The therapist does not provide the contingencies for whether or not the commitment is completed—life does! Thus, the therapist can remain truly agnostic as to what the outcome is.

There are also many "reasons" that therapists might not follow up on homework assignments. They might get caught up in the natural flow of a session and not want to interrupt it to raise the topic of homework. They may feel that it's more important to go with what seems to be the client's priority on a given day or decide that it's more germane to address an immediate stressor or crisis in the client's life. Although all of these may be perfectly valid choices in specific situations, it's also possible that a functional analysis of the choice not to follow up on homework would reveal that it was related to experiential avoidance or fusion with negative evaluations related to the process, including considerations about how it might make the client or therapist feel. Specifically, therapists may be avoiding discomfort associated with asking about homework when clients are likely to say that they didn't complete it—especially if this has happened multiple times previously. Such situations can be uncomfortable in several ways. First, most therapists go into the mental health profession because they want to help people experience less pain and suffering. However, helping people hold themselves accountable to their own commitments doesn't always lead to feeling good in the short term (for therapist or client). Second, when the therapist is consistently the one asking for an update on how the homework went, it can put the therapist in a frame of coordination with an authority figure (in the mind of either the client or the therapist), which can interfere with the mutuality of the therapeutic relationship in ACT. This dynamic is heightened in situations where clients frequently fail to follow through. Although these therapist responses are understandable in context, if therapists repeatedly fail to follow up on mutually established behavioral commitments, it can cause ruptures in the therapeutic relationship as the client has less and less of an idea of what to expect. If this pattern persists over time, it can also reduce the likelihood that clients will effectively engage in future homework assignments.

For therapists who have difficulty consistently following up on homework, this provides an excellent opportunity to practice and overtly demonstrate their own committed action skills, either on their own or as an overt process shared with the client. Either way, they can begin by writing down or stating out loud their intention to follow up consistently on homework assignments. They can then identify barriers that have gotten in the way of doing so in the past and see if it could be helpful to practice willingness, defusion, mindfulness, or problem-solving skills in regard to these barriers. Finally, with permission from clients, they might work on arranging the environment to promote following through on this commitment, such as by raising the topic of homework in a consistent and timely way each session (for example, within the first five minutes) or by posting a note in the therapy room to serve as a reminder.

# Therapist Committed Action During Exposure Therapy

Exposure, a key component of many treatment approaches, is a powerful therapeutic tool for many reasons, including the fact that it provides a great opportunity not only to practice willingness but also to mindfully observe barriers to action as they arise.

This allows the therapist to actively model and coach new skills in the moment, often in the natural, *in vivo* environment in which they will ultimately be needed. Exposure involves a healthy dose of commitment on the client's part, and often the therapist's part as well. As discussed in earlier chapters, the goal of exposure within an ACT model is to help clients develop a broader and more flexible behavioral repertoire in the presence of challenging internal and external events. By its very nature, exposure often evokes difficult or unwanted private experiences for clients. However, it can also be quite difficult for therapists to see their clients in distress during the process of exposure.

An effective ACT-based exposure therapist will help clients learn to approach exposures and the related private events with a sense of curiosity and vital engagement—something that may require significant committed action on the therapist's part. For example, for some clinical presentations, the process of exposure requires that therapists make contact with difficult or potentially disgust-inducing stimuli, while still overtly modeling willingness and committed action (for example, facilitating in vivo exposure for contamination-focused obsessive-compulsive disorder). Therapists in such situations can benefit from using their own committed action skills to ensure that they're remaining present with the challenging content and aren't ending exposures early or skipping steps in a hierarchy due to a sense that the experience is too difficult, painful, or unpleasant for either the client or the therapist.

# Maintaining Committed Action in the Face of Slips and Relapses

Earlier in this chapter, we discussed the importance of not moving too quickly into committed action, before the client is prepared to do so successfully. However, even when all of ACT's other core processes have been covered, and client and therapist are in full agreement that the client is ready to commit to a specific course of action, it's almost inevitable that the path forward won't be direct and linear. Slips, missteps, and relapses are common; they are part of the growth process and to be expected. If change were easy, clients probably would have already taken the necessary actions, with no need to seek or remain in therapy. Therefore, therapists must be ready to provide nonjudgmental responses to slips or relapses into old, problematic behaviors. It's understandable that therapists might see relapses as a disappointment or a failure; however, these experiences actually provide an opportunity for therapists to model the approach to committed action that they're trying to instill in clients, wherein slips and relapses are seen as natural steps in the process, and the focus is on returning to the path of committed action. Furthermore, these detours provide therapists with an opportunity to highlight the dialectic of letting go of a specific outcome while still committing to active engagement in values-based living.

Consider a client struggling with long-term substance use problems. When setting up homework assignments, there should be an open acknowledgment that the goal is not to achieve immediate "success" and freedom from this long-standing problem. Instead, the focus would be on developing larger and more flexible patterns of behavior over time. So even if the client freely suggests behavioral targets for the week and commits to their execution, it can be useful for the therapist to proactively say something along these lines: "I'll be following up on this next week, and I'll be very interested to hear how it goes. But I want you to know that I'm here for you regardless of how this turns out. Hopefully you'll see for yourself that I won't just be enthusiastic if you're able to accomplish this goal to call a friend or go for a jog in the evening when you experience those cravings. If you come in here next week and tell me that you didn't meet your goal, I'll be equally enthusiastic about working with you to identify the barriers that got in the way. I'm here for you either way. We'll assess the results of these experiments together, in the spirit of moving your life and your values forward in a way that you can sustain over time, not just accomplishing a specific goal of abstinence." If the therapist can keep this framework in mind, it can help with approaching any of the potential outcomes in a more defused and accepting way.

By laying this foundation of openness to the client's experience, the therapist may prevent an unnecessary break from therapy if the client makes choices that don't reflect his values and stated goals. Having this sort of open conversation ahead of time can help inoculate the client from the self-judgment and resulting avoidance that would otherwise have probably occurred if things didn't go according to plan. It might seem paradoxical that the act of establishing that commitments aren't always successfully executed can improve the speed with which they are more reliably implemented. However, this isn't an attempt to use "reverse psychology" with an intent to provoke an opposite response. Rather, seasoned ACT therapists know, from years of direct and observed experience, that sticking with a commitment over time can be difficult. By openly planning for barriers and inconsistency, therapists can arm their clients with the tools they need to engage in long-term committed action.

## Questions for Reflection on Therapist Commitment

- How do I feel about regularly bringing commitment into the therapeutic process?

- Are there times when I avoid guiding or challenging my clients to commit to their next valued steps?

- What experiential practices can I bring to the committed action process, so that it is not all based on verbal formulations?

- Are there specific clients with whom I have a more difficult time working on committed action?

- Are there areas of my own life where I have struggled with commitment? What can I learn from these experiences that will help my therapeutic approach?

- What is one thing that I can commit to doing differently in session in order to facilitate committed action more effectively?

- Do I have trouble following through with any aspects of my own in-session committed actions related to homework or exposure therapy?

# Summary

Barriers to committed action can arise for therapists, just as they can for clients. And sometimes therapist behaviors may even present a barrier to effective committed action work in session. In order to overcome these barriers, therapists must be willing to openly acknowledge their role in the process and evaluate when their own avoidance, fusion, and divergence from a focus on client values may be getting in the way of facilitating committed action work. By approaching these barriers nondefensively, and sometimes even talking openly with clients about them, therapists can model an approach to effective committed action that includes working constructively with the barriers that arise in the process. Encountering barriers does not demonstrate a failure in committed action; it is the approach to overcoming these barriers that allows for the deepest practice of the processes that are inherent to committed action. Now that we have fully explored the role of committed action and ways to facilitate commitment and overcome barriers for both the client and therapist, in chapter 8 we will turn to an exploration of common evidence-based psychotherapies, which will help prepare us to describe how committed action interventions can be effectively incorporated into treatments beyond ACT.

# Reviewing Evidence-Based Psychotherapies

The effective application of ACT incorporates behavior therapy as well as other evidence-based treatments. Practical implementations of ACT frequently integrate additional empirically supported approaches. ACT also functions as a supplement to other workable behavior change strategies. ACT provides a foundational context for the psychotherapies that work, and attempts to strengthen and enhance the process and outcomes of those approaches. This integrative approach allows experienced therapists who are new to ACT to continue using many of the interventions in their toolbox while supplementing those approaches with acceptance, defusion, values, and mindfulness within a functional contextual framework. ACT therapists frequently blend in other treatments, such as exposure, flooding, and behavioral activation, which work for reducing suffering and improving quality of life. Throughout the earlier chapters of this book, we discussed the basics of contextual behavioral science, the assumptions of functional contextualism, and the introductory ideas of acceptance and commitment therapy in a way that shows the inclusiveness of ACT. The foundational ideas promoted in this book thus far provide the framework for therapists to build and maintain a scientifically supported practice while aiming to reduce suffering and improve quality of living for their clients. This chapter will help widen the scope of how ACT can be used toward that intention through its resonance with other evidence-based approaches.

## Considering Evidence-Based Psychotherapies

The field of behavioral health has an extensive literature focused on evidence-based psychotherapies (EBPs). In some domains, these treatments are referred to as empirically supported treatments (ESTs; Chambless & Hollon, 1998) or research-supported psychological treatments (RSPTs). For the sake of simplicity, this chapter will refer to all of these efficacious approaches as evidence-based psychotherapies, or EBPs. At the present time, there are 80 therapies on the American Psychological Association Division 12 Society of Clinical Psychology list, and five of them are specifically ACT-based. The goal of this chapter is to briefly discuss the effective interventions found on the Division 12 list, and highlight our interpretation that many of those components can fit into ACT as committed actions.

Covering all 75 of the other research-supported psychological treatments is beyond the scope of this book. This chapter provides a very brief précis introducing the major EBPs that have been shown to efficaciously address various diagnoses. As mentioned briefly in chapter 2, there is a significant and complementary amount of overlap between existing EBPs and the committed action processes of ACT. In figure 3, notice that the list of empirically supported treatments for different clinically relevant concerns are depicted as overlapping with ACT's committed action process. ACT leverages treatments that work.

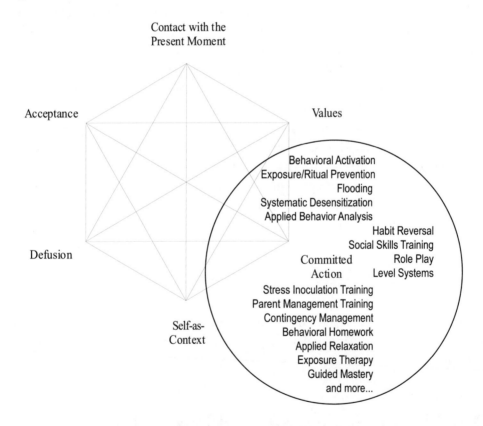

**Figure 3.** Visualizing the overlap between evidence-based psychotherapies and committed action

The aim of this chapter is to provide a primer on how evidence-based treatments provide treatment-relevant committed action steps for the acceptance and commitment therapy model. The following descriptions provide the link between reliable therapeutic implementations and an ACT approach. This list is not exhaustive, and for the sake of brevity—and because ACT therapists are typically dedicated to effective evidence-based practice—this chapter will only focus on the interventions that have "strong research support." Responsible therapists will seek out further education about the EBPs prior to putting them to use.

Keep in mind, not all of the other 75 treatment approaches are "ACT consistent," but contextual behavioral scientists can make the case that if these other therapies are shown to be helpful, their outcomes can likely be analyzed from a functional contextual perspective, and the effective components of all those therapies can be potentially blended into an ACT intervention. For instance, rational emotive behavior therapy (REBT) is on the Division 12 list as a moderately supported treatment, and REBT typically uses cognitive disputation techniques, which is at theoretical odds with ACT's defusion approach. Blackledge, Moran, and Ellis (2009) argue that the REBT disputation methods can be analyzed meaningfully through the lens of relational frame theory, and the REBT approach can be useful for clinical endeavors. Some components of REBT (such as cognitive disputation) can be incorporated in ACT; however, they will be implemented for purposes different from the REBT approach by a therapist using the ACT conceptualization. Simply because some of the other techniques on the Division 12 list might be perceived as inconsistent with the ACT approach does not mean they are not worthwhile when conceptualized through the lens of functional contextualism and relational frame theory.

Taking this perspective a step further, when looking at the APA Division 12 list of EBPs, you can see treatments rooted in psychodynamic theory. If you were to ask most therapists whether a psychodynamic approach is likely to be consistent with a behavioral approach to psychotherapy, it is reasonable to assume that the most frequent answer would be that those are two very disparate approaches to treatment. However, therapies on the EBP list have been tested to influence important dependent variables, and their outcomes have been consistently replicated. It is incumbent on the applied contextual behavioral scientist to look for the efficacious mechanisms of change from any relevant sources and see if they can be woven into the ACT case conceptualization, especially as committed actions. Even if there is a history of disagreement and conflict with other therapeutic approaches, ACT therapists are not required (or recommended) to avoid all of those potentially good ideas. Rather, therapists should contact the present moment, be guided by their values, and commit to being psychologically flexible as is needed in the treatment room by utilizing empirically supported approaches that have a strong likelihood of being helpful to clients, no matter where they originated. A flexible therapist willing to look beyond theoretical differences while embracing functional analysis and data-based interventions will have a greater likelihood of reducing the suffering of clients.

ACT therapists also have to demonstrate flexibility when working with language and the literature related to the organization of evidence-based treatments. Prior to moving forward with the list of evidence-based treatments, it is important to understand that the American Psychological Association uses the DSM diagnostic approach to discuss the clinically relevant concerns. In chapter 4, we were critical of the formal approach of the medical-model-inspired DSM and highlighted how the functional approach is important for applying the ACT model for changing committed actions. There is an additional concern with using the DSM within the ACT model. ACT is a *transdiagnostic* approach, meaning it primarily addresses aspects of the human condition that undergird suffering more broadly, rather than looking at the client's behaviors as falling into psychiatric diagnoses.

ACT therapists and other behavioral scientists (Mansell, Harvey, Watkins, & Shafran, 2009; Nolen-Hoeksema & Watkins, 2011) emphasize the usefulness of a transdiagnostic approach instead of a syndromal classification system for several reasons. Clinicians and researchers often identify significant levels of comorbidity among psychological disorders when using the DSM nosology (Kessler, Chiu, Demler, & Walters, 2005), suggesting there may be a common foundation to many clinically relevant concerns, rather than there being such a large number of diagnostic categories that just happen to occur together. In addition, research has shown that clinicians can offer similar therapeutic approaches for different disorders (Harvey, Watkins, Mansell, & Shafran, 2004). Further, when one clinically relevant concern is treated, it can also lead to improvements in a comorbid disorder that has not been directly treated (Borkovec, Abel, & Newman, 1995).

For several of these reasons, there is a growing trend among behavioral scientists to think about clinical issues from a functional approach, rather than a structural categorization system of diagnoses as if the behavioral concerns were discrete illnesses. At the same time, behavioral scientists must also recognize that the current context of clinical psychological treatment embraces the DSM nosology, and that a system of categorization cannot practically be ignored. Finding the balance between the conventionally accepted language of the DSM and the transdiagnostic, functional contextual way of thinking will require flexibility from the ACT clinician. In order to maintain a link to mainstream clinical psychology, and because it is often prudent and workable to maintain the broad, conventional way of talking about clinical issues when selecting appropriate treatments, this chapter will follow the APA Division 12 use of the DSM's diagnostic approach to identifying evidence-based psychotherapies.

# Exploring Evidence-Based Psychotherapies

In the late 20th century, there was a clamoring for evidence for the effectiveness of the psychological treatments that mental health practitioners were using. Third-party payors, patient advocates, and behavioral scientists were interested in making sure that interventions were efficient and successful for reducing suffering and improving quality of living. Responsible applied scientists wanted to reduce quackery that could be found in psychotherapy, and start to sharpen the clinician's focus on how to improve therapeutic outcomes. The world's largest psychological organization, the American Psychological Association, had its clinical division, the Society for Clinical Psychology, investigate and promote the ideas of evidence-based psychotherapies. The Society of Clinical Psychology created a website (www.div12.org) listing these EBPs, and this collection of practices sets the context for this chapter.

## Attention Deficit Hyperactivity Disorder (Adults)

According to the Society of Clinical Psychology's list, there is strong research support for applying cognitive behavioral therapy (CBT) techniques to attention deficit hyperactivity disorder (ADHD) for adults. The list very explicitly says that the "[c]omponents of CBT for ADHD include psychoeducation, training in organization, planning and time management, problem solving skills, and techniques for reducing distractivity and increasing attention span." These components are remarkably ACT-consistent, and each one of them can be perceived as a committed action. Planning one's day, keeping a calendar, and reorganizing one's living environment to be less distracting are all things that a client can measurably perform. In addition, the techniques for increasing attention span can be found in contact with the present moment exercises. Research "suggests that interventions that increase mindfulness might improve symptoms of ADHD" (Smalley, Loo, Hale, Shrestha, McGough, Flook, & Reise, 2009, p. 1). Inviting the client struggling with ADHD to begin a mindfulness practice can assist with contacting the present moment, as well as enhancing acceptance, defusion, and self-as-context skills, and that mindfulness practice can be regarded as a new, clinically useful committed action.

A client seeking treatment for ADHD can be assisted with this ACT approach, especially if the therapist is blending the aforementioned techniques into treatment in the committed action domain of the hexagon. When performing these EBP techniques, and conducting psychoeducation with the client—especially when asking the client to keep a calendar and use certain skills to accelerate better time management—the client might resist. That is also where the other five domains in ACT can supplement the therapy. For instance, the client might have the following obstacles for improvement, and ACT can assist:

- *"I don't feel like keeping a calendar!"*

  The client's declaration of her feelings, likes, and dislikes can be discussed with an acceptance approach. These feelings don't have to impede following through on this portion of the treatment plan. The therapist could also discuss defusing from such a thought to encourage the client to simply notice her problematic relational framing, and not get governed by such language events.

- *"But I'm A.D.D.! I can't follow these instructions!"*

   This relational framing can engender psychological inflexibility, and perhaps the concept of self-as-context can be brought into therapy at this point. The ACT approach suggests people not self-identify as their diagnosis, which can greatly limit the breadth of actions available to them, but instead to simply experience the difficulties related to the clinically relevant concerns while making effective choices.

- *"Organizing my life will be too hard!"*

   In the presence of this language, the therapist can highlight the importance of values and vital life choices. In addition, this might be a good time to work through creative hopelessness exercises, and ask how well such a verbalization has been working for the client in terms of her life goals.

There are myriad ways that a client might vocalize relational framing that influence resistance to the committed actions suggested in a treatment plan. The ACT therapist will use the other five domains in the therapy to influence those language concerns so the client becomes more mindful and aware of her relational framing, while leveraging the effective power of relational frames to increase values-based motivation.

The Society of Clinical Psychology's website also says that the CBT approach for treating ADHD uses "cognitive restructuring, particularly around situations that cause distress." This is where an ACT case conceptualization might depart from the typical EBP. Because defusion and cognitive restructuring are disparate approaches for clients to deal with distressing thoughts—and some research (Deacon et al., 2011) suggests that both approaches are worthy—using defusion for those thoughts, along with interpreting the rest of the behavioral interventions as committed actions in the ACT treatment for ADHD, may be a useful combination. Cognitive restructuring aims to change the form of the thinking (relational framing), while defusion aims to change the function of thinking (relational framing). The CBT approach attempts to change the thoughts affiliated with the distressing situations by challenging unhelpful, irrational, or unverified beliefs, and encourages the client to reframe those thoughts to be clearer, rational, and empirically based. ACT does not attempt to change what the client is thinking, but how the client is relating to what he is thinking. The ACT clinician teaches the client to simply notice that he is having certain thoughts while following through on committed actions that will help him with the ADHD concern.

## Bipolar Disorder

Mania and depression, the characteristics of bipolar disorder, both require treatment, and there is differing research support for the treatments related to both of these concerns. For mania, there is strong research support for Psychoeducation and Systematic Care. Regarding depression, there is strong research support for Family-Focused Therapy. Each of these treatment approaches can be complemented by ACT tools.

When considering treatment for mania, the Psychoeducation approach provides information about the disorder to the client and focuses on improving psychopharmacological treatment adherence. Many of these psychoeducation sessions occur within group formats. Essentially, this treatment—in order for it to be effective—requires the client to engage in the committed action of attending group sessions and taking the prescribed medication. The Systematic Care intervention capitalizes on psychoeducation, and also uses a level-system where different professionals, such as a nursing care coordinator and psychiatrist, attend to the client during scheduled appointments. Systematic Care has a "Life Goals Program" that is run in a group format "to provide support in achieving occupational and social goals. Participants also create personal self-management plans detailing coping strategies" (American Psychological Association website, 2017). Those goals from the Life Goals Program are the kind of tasks ACT therapists would want to focus on within the committed action domain, and can also be construed as SMART goals. Acceptance and commitment therapy's other five domains can be used as a supplement to Systematic Care. When the client declares, "I don't want to follow through on all these therapeutic goals," the ACT clinician makes sure to do a values-clarification exercise to assist with the lack of motivation, and teaches defusion to be applied with those types of thoughts. Self-as-context is taught to help the client reduce identification as a "manic person" and engage in acceptance and mindfulness so the client can "urge surf" (Marlatt, 1994) when dealing with feelings and thoughts related to initiating impulsive actions. (While urge surfing is typically discussed when talking about substance misuse, the ACT transdiagnostic approach will use the tools that will help out with urges if they are functionally called for, no matter what the "diagnosis.") Utilizing the approaches coming from Psychoeducation and Systematic Care in the treatment of bipolar disorder is one way that ACT therapists can make sure they have additional strong research support for their interventions.

Additional strong research support for treating bipolar disorder is provided for addressing depression with Family Focused Therapy (FFT). Family members are given psychoeducation and instructions about medication adherence. They are also taught about coping responses and addressing early warning signs of problematic symptoms. The therapist discusses how dysfunctional family interactions and expressed emotions can often exacerbate bipolar disorder symptoms. Instructions for how to most effectively interact with the client are also given. Of course, this is the area where committed action is required. Both for the family and the client, coping skills, functional social skills, and appropriate communication all require overt behaviors that can be conceptualized as committed actions. When there is interpersonal struggle, the ACT therapist is going to highlight how acceptance, defusion, value directedness, and mindfulness can assist, but "the rubber hits the road" in FFT when the family members treat each other kindly and communicate well, even in the presence of heightened symptoms and stressors. The other ACT domains serve to support those specified FFT objectives as committed actions.

During a course of FFT, the ACT therapist will certainly teach acceptance, defusion, self-as-context, mindfulness, and values work to the primary client dealing with bipolar disorder, and it will be just as important to teach those skills to the family members. ACT is not just for clinically relevant concerns, but also helps with the more universal aspects of the human condition, such as dealing with emotions when there is interpersonal stress. For instance, during an FFT session, suppose the overbearing father tells his son who has bipolar disorder, "Snap out of it! I created such a good lifestyle for you growing up! You don't have to be so miserable!" When that happens, the ACT clinician will not only implement the psychoeducation piece of FFT by teaching the father about the nature of the mood disorder, but also highlight the circular nature of the father-son conflict: the more the father criticizes the son, the more likely he will act in a depressed manner. The therapist could use this as a platform for discussing acceptance, not just for the son and his mood disorder symptoms, but for the other family members and their judgmental thinking, as well. The father could also be assisted with defusing from his angry thinking, and clarifying his parenting values in order to help him stay motivated to treat his son kindly, even (and especially) in the presence of his anger and judgmental thoughts. Mindfulness skills can also be used to support the father's committed action to speak compassionately to his son. All six of the ACT skills can be used to increase psychological flexibility in order to supplement the progress of Family Focused Therapy. In summary, there are three strongly supported ESTs for bipolar disorder. ACT therapists can explore these treatment approaches, looking for the components that address objective, measurable responses, and leverage those portions of the treatments to become committed actions as seen through the ACT conceptualization.

## Borderline Personality Disorder

Dialectical behavior therapy (DBT) has strong research support for treating borderline personality disorder (BPD). ACT and DBT are "fellow travelers" as mindfulness- and acceptance-based behavior therapies. Both come from the behavioral tradition, are empirically supported treatments, and utilize a mindfulness-based approach to help the client accept private events while engaging in practical change. Given the robust research behind DBT for borderline personality disorder, it makes sense for ACT therapists to learn DBT as an additional approach to the therapeutic repertoire. Although there is a paucity of research on the combination of ACT and DBT, some ACT therapists will say they do "ACTified DBT" with their clients who are diagnosed with BPD.

In this situation, one can conceptualize applying ACT principles to help clients engage in the committed actions called for in DBT.

Very succinctly, DBT has four modules:

**1) Mindfulness:** DBT therapists encourage clients to nonjudgmentally observe their private events, and develop a "Teflon mind" so that certain thoughts do not become "sticky" throughout the day. The "Wise Mind" is a term used in DBT to discuss each person's ability to find balance between her reasoning skills and her emotions and make sensible choices.

**2) Distress tolerance:** This module is an outgrowth of mindfulness by teaching the client to experience—without judgment or evaluation—her own self and her life situations and get through difficult moments. Once the client is skillful at tolerating her distress, she is in a better position to use her Wise Mind to make choices through her actions, instead of being governed by difficult emotions and thoughts that are often related to BPD. The Wise Mind is affiliated with the mindfulness aspects discussed in ACT, and can assist with distress tolerance. In addition, the DBT distress tolerance intervention includes the acronym ACCEPTS (Linehan, 1993):

- Activities—Engage in positive activities you enjoy.

- Contribute—Help other people or your community.

- Comparisons—Compare yourself to less fortunate people or to how you used to be when you were in a worse state.

- Emotions—Cause yourself to feel something different by provoking your sense of humor or happiness with corresponding activities.

- Push away—Put your situation on the back burner for a while. Put something else temporarily first in your mind.

- Thoughts—Force your mind to think about something else.

- Sensations—Do something that has an intense feeling other than what you are feeling, like a cold shower or a spicy candy.

Notice that some of the verbs leading to measurable responses in this acronymic advice, such as "use activities" and "help others" can be looked at as committed responses. Some of the other advice seems ACT-inconsistent, such as "cause yourself to feel something different," and "force your mind to think about something else." DBT is similar in many ways to ACT, but also dissimilar when using those kinds of emotional control strategies. An ACT therapist is less likely to encourage someone to "force your mind to think about something else," because such a strategy may backfire. The emotionally loaded, self-denigrating thoughts someone experiences are difficult to stop, and when the person fails to think of something else or distract herself from that thought, that failure becomes something else to be upset about. Instead of changing the thought to a different thought, the ACT therapist would suggest the client utilize defusion efforts with those thoughts. Further research is required to determine whether distraction or acceptance and defusion are the most workable approaches to help individuals with problematic private events related to BPD. In either case, both ACT and DBT are committed to working with the client to practice whatever strategies would be most functional and helpful in a given moment of distress.

**3) Emotional regulation:** Because people with BPD often demonstrate intense and labile emotions, DBT suggests developing skills that can help adjust their feelings, such as:

- Identifying emotions and obstacles to changing them

- Increasing positive emotional events

- Increasing mindfulness practice

- Applying distress tolerance techniques

- Taking opposite actions

These are specific committed actions detailed in most empirically supported treatments in one way or another, and in the DBT context, the therapist can utilize mindfulness skills to support each one of them. At first glance, an ACT novice might consider emotional regulation to be inconsistent with the model; however, emotional regulation skills *can be used* in ACT. While it is true that some emotional change strategies backfire, and ACT typically teaches acceptance of emotions, if the emotional change strategy *is workable*, doesn't exacerbate the concern in the long haul, and doesn't contradict the client's values, it is fine to use this strategy. At its core, ACT is concerned with what works, not adhering to a certain dogma. For a simple nonclinical example, if a person knows she gets cranky when hungry, and she is about to enter a sensitive meeting at the workplace with a dissatisfied customer, it would be perfectly fine for her to have a healthy snack so that she can maintain her composure in the meeting. That is an emotional control strategy, and it is workable, healthy, and in line with the person's values. Therapeutically, if the client is dealing with erratic mood swings, applying workable, healthy emotional regulation strategies may assist in dealing with those clinically relevant concerns in an effective way. In the aforementioned bulleted list, DBT suggests "identifying," "increasing," "applying," and "taking…actions," as alternatives to erratic or self-destructive action, and they can all be performed as committed actions within an ACT case conceptualization to supplement the therapy.

For example, a DBT therapist might suggest a client try taking a bath when overwhelmed and mindfully use this as an emotion regulation strategy. This could be looked at as a committed action for the client and might need to be supplemented by the rest of the ACT model in order to fully execute this skill. The client might think, *Taking a bath is stupid, simplistic advice. I'm not going to do something so immature. I have real problems.* And the clinician performing "ACTified DBT" could teach the client to utilize defusion and work on mindfully noticing such a judgmental, angry thought. Taking a bath can be recontextualized as a values-based behavior if the therapeutic dyad does a values clarification exercise in session. While committing to turning on the faucet for the tub, the person might feel emotions related to sadness, inferiority, and anger, and the ACT therapist could discuss how feelings are natural and not always under a person's control, and even in the presence of those emotions, they can be accepted while stepping into the bath. This would be a worthwhile time to discuss the dialectic of sometimes accepting some things as they are, and sometimes making a commitment to change them. The ACT and DBT message would be highlighted when the client makes a commitment to engaging in emotion regulation, and the discussion of the dialectic between acceptance and commitment could be impactful on the client's unstable behaviors.

**4) Interpersonal effectiveness:** Interpersonal problem solving and social skills training are inherent parts of DBT. The client learns socially appropriate assertiveness skills in order to deal with interpersonal stress and better facilitate her own ability to get her needs met by others. In order to help the client acquire what she desires through direct communication, the following process is used, summarized by the acronym DEAR MAN (Linehan, 1993):

- Describe the situation.

- Express why this is a concern and related feelings.

- Assert yourself by clearly asking for what you want.

- Reinforce your position by offering a positive consequence if successful.

- Mindful of the situation by focusing on desired outcomes and ignoring distractions.

- Appear confident even if you don't feel confident.

- Negotiate with people and come to a comfortable compromise.

Once again, these applications of DBT are mostly discussed as measurable action steps that the client can take in order to deal with challenging social situations, and each of the DEAR MAN steps can be supported by the ACT approach when conceptualizing them as individual committed actions. For example, when the clinician suggests that the client appear confident even if she doesn't feel confident, the clinician is talking about being purposeful with actions, and not impeded by emotions. The first complete book about ACT (Hayes et al., 1999) discusses the etymology of the word "confidence," and emphasizes that a confident behavior is done with faith (*con*-means "with" and–*fidence* means "faith"). The therapist could move the discussion about interpersonal effectiveness toward acting confidently in a social exchange, or, in other words, acting with faith in yourself while talking to someone else. The client could strengthen that approach by highlighting the usefulness of acceptance of nervousness or anger when in an interpersonal dialogue, being mindful of any negative self-talk, and remaining value-directed in the social exchange. The root of confident actions is found in psychological flexibility. ACT and DBT have a great deal of overlap and are generally highly consistent with one another. When DBT calls for behavior change and related exercises, those activities can be looked at as committed actions by the ACT therapist, and supported by the other five domains in the traditional ACT model.

## Chronic or Persistent Pain

According to Hooper and Larsson (2015), chronic pain is the most researched clinically relevant concern for ACT applications, and the interventions include performing measurable behaviors. For these interventions to be maximally effective, the actions are done in a committed manner supported by mindfulness, acceptance, and defusion, and with an emphasis on values. The APA list of evidence-based treatments for pain are parsed out by three specific diagnoses: fibromyalgia, chronic lower back pain, and chronic headache.

### FIBROMYALGIA

The APA list suggests treating fibromyalgia with cognitive behavioral therapy, and advises that the approach can specifically target the symptom domains related to fibromyalgia. The CBT approach includes education, symptom self-management (for example, regulating fatigue, promoting sleep hygiene, scheduling pleasant activity, and performing relaxation techniques), and lifestyle change (for example, long-term stress management, goal-setting, improving communication, and problem-solving). Very specifically, the empirically supported treatment list says that "in order to better learn and integrate skills into one's lifestyle, CBT relies upon self-monitoring, skill rehearsal, and social reinforcement," which is the framework of helping someone turn lifestyle changes into committed actions. These interventions are not exclusive to CBT, and can be managed using the ACT approach.

## CHRONIC LOWER BACK PAIN

Behavior therapy and CBT are the evidence-based approaches for chronic lower back pain (CLBP). Division 12 summarizes those treatments by summarizing that they include "reinforcement of adaptive responding, use of quotas and goals for gradual return of functioning" (APA Division 12, 2016). ACT therapists working with CLBP specifically have those tools in their wheelhouse. Division 12 goes on to say that the client will benefit from progressive muscle relaxation, learning coping skills, skill rehearsal, and self-monitoring. Building up willingness to do the interventions and engage in physical activity, even in the presence of pain and difficult emotions, can support all of these treatment components. Acceptance, mindfulness, and being motivated by personal values can strengthen the client's resolve to engage in the treatment as a committed action.

## CHRONIC HEADACHE

When clients are presented with stressors, they may have autonomic nervous system responses, such as change in blood flow, heart rate, muscle tension, and brainwave patterns. These reactions may be temporarily functional, but such stress responses may lead to chronic headaches in the long run. Teaching clients to engage in relaxation responses can ease these physical stress reactions and reduce the likelihood of chronic headaches. The EBPs for this condition ask the client to commit to "progressive muscle relaxation, visual imagery, and mindfulness meditation" (American Psychological Association, 2016). Participation in biofeedback is also part of the evidence-based treatment package, and engaging in all of these treatment modalities can be viewed from the lens of committed action.

Consider a client who works as a real estate agent in Chicago. The significant stress from her job contributes to experiencing chronic headaches. She sees her family doctor for help, and the doctor conducts a "soft handoff" to the ACT therapist who works in that health clinic providing integrated behavioral health services. The ACT therapist reviews the medical advice from the physician, and suggests that the client pick up a mindfulness practice and attend weekly biofeedback sessions to address the headaches. The busy real estate agent responds, "No! I don't have enough time to just sit around navel-gazing. And I don't think it's such a good use of my time to come to therapy and put pads all over my body." Of course, psychoeducation is in order at this point. In addition, talking about what is meaningful and vital in her life could start setting up some personal, values-based motivation to commit to doing the mindfulness exercises and the biofeedback work, even if she perceives them as odd and a waste of time. The ACT model can supplement the general physical health interventions by making sure clients see the value in the treatment (or at least that they are willing to try them to see for themselves whether there is any value), stay motivated to do the exercises, and regularly engage in these committed actions.

## Depression

There are several treatments listed in the Division 12 list of supported interventions for depression, and six of those treatments have strong research support for treatment of the condition: 1) Behavioral Activation, 2) Cognitive Therapy, 3) Self-Management/Self-Control Therapy, 4) Problem-Solving Therapy, 5) Interpersonal Therapy, and 6) Cognitive Behavioral Analysis System of Psychotherapy.

As the closest complement to ACT, Behavioral Activation (BA) embodies committed action in practice. The APA website describes the therapy as attempting to "increase the patient's contact with sources of reward by helping them get more active and, in so doing, improving one's life context…specifically [by] identifying values that will guide the selection of activities" (American Psychological Association, 2016). BA is obviously related to getting the person acting differently and engaging in new and more diverse behaviors so that he can encounter more appetitive experiences that could reinforce behavioral change. The modality is an invitation to engage in new, life-affirming committed actions. Such an approach can be supported by the rest of the ACT model, especially by utilizing a values clarification exercise. When inviting a client to activate his behavior in order to disrupt the immediately reinforcing, downward spiral of the impoverished depressive repertoire, and increasing flexibility while doing so, BA would be most effective if the "new" behaviors are in line with the client's values. When BA is implemented with purposeful and meaningful motivations, there are already "built in" reinforcers to the new actions, and that could increase the likelihood that a new, less depressed repertoire will form. As mentioned in chapter 5, Nietzsche wrote, "If we have our own why in life, we can bear any how" (1895, p. 3). The ACT therapist can utilize values authorship to assist the client in figuring out the *whys* in life, so the client can utilize BA to figure out *how* to move forward in that direction and how to be mindful of private events that might impede behavioral change.

Cognitive Therapy is also strongly research-supported, and although some of the procedures in CT are—at face value—inconsistent with the ACT approach, CT does also call for behavioral change, as well. The disputational portion of the therapy challenges the patient's inaccurate beliefs that he is unlovable, helpless, incompetent, and worthless. An ACT therapist would not necessarily try to change the form of the client's beliefs, but would instead use defusion to alter the function of those beliefs. CT and ACT would similarly assign new actions as behavioral homework to support the therapy outcomes, and those would be instances of committed action.

Self-Control Therapy consists of three phases that can all be perceived as committed actions. Phase one requests that the client engage in self-monitoring by recording her mood and the contextual variables that influence mood states. Phase two focuses on setting attainable goals and teaching the client how to follow through on the behaviors to achieve those goals. Phase three guides the client to develop a self-reinforcement repertoire to ensure that the new goals are attained and that the progress is maintained. Self-control therapy is a guide to committed action steps in order to address depression, and if each of these phases were plugged into the ACT model, the therapist could leverage mindfulness, values clarification, acceptance, defusion, and perspective-taking to support the approach.

Problem-Solving Therapy (PST) teaches clients a step-by-step approach for dealing with life's challenges. Essentially, clients learn how to identify problems, develop realistic solutions, choose the most workable of the different solutions, implement the plan, and evaluate the outcome. This very pragmatic approach comprises measurable behaviors that can be fitted very easily into the ACT model as committed actions.

Interpersonal Therapy (IPT) is rooted in the idea that personal relationships are at the core of psychological suffering, and strives to improve the client's communication skills with significant others in order to improve mood. IPT focuses on four areas of social functioning that could be problematic: complicated bereavement, role disputes, role transitions, and interpersonal deficits. IPT targets the client's "ability to assert his or her needs and wishes in interpersonal encounters…[and] to encourage taking appropriate social risks" as measurable responses for committed action (Markowitz & Weissman, 2004, p. 137).

Cognitive Behavioral Analysis System of Psychotherapy (CBASP) teaches "situational analysis," so the client can perceive how his behavior is affecting other people, including the therapist. CBASP also teaches clients how to "generate empathic behavior with the therapist and others" (cbasp.org, 2017). Keeping with the theme of all of the aforementioned treatments for depression, these components of CBASP can be blended into an ACT case conceptualization as committed actions. For instance, CBASP uses a significant amount of homework to be discussed in session, and research suggests that homework compliance positively predicts successful outcomes in therapy (Kazantzis, Whittington, & Dattilio, 2010). A therapist can conceptualize the homework assignments as committed actions. If the client is not performing the homework—and thereby having a deleterious impact on his own therapeutic outcomes—then the therapist can assess which of the five other skills on the traditional hexagon model need to be strengthened and applied in order to shore up the commitment to do the homework. If the client says, "I just don't feel like doing the homework," then acceptance can be highlighted in therapy. If the client says, "But I don't understand the purpose of these homework challenges," then psychoeducation and values authorship can be brought into the room. If client says, "I'm just not one of those people who fills out thought records during the day," this is a solid time to bring up self-as-context, and mindful defusion from such self-as-content thinking.

# Eating Disorders

The Division 12 list shows that there are multiple EBPs for the different types of eating disorders. Both bulimia nervosa and anorexia nervosa have worthwhile treatment approaches, and the ACT model can supplement these therapeutic endeavors.

## BULIMIA NERVOSA

According to the EBP list, "CBT has the strongest scientific evidence of all the tested psychological treatments for bulimia nervosa" (American Psychological Association, 2016). Like most CBTs, the first phase is about psychoeducation, and then the clinician and client work on identifying precipitants to binge-purge events, and attempt to set up abstinence from this cycle and prevent future relapse. Such refraining from bingeing and purging can be considered a commitment. As discussed in chapter 3, it is helpful for the clinician and the client to understand the antecedents of the behavior, in order to set up a change in committed actions, and the EBP list supports this idea.

Interpersonal Therapy is also on the EBP list for treating bulimia, and—as in the treatment of depression—focuses on complicated bereavement, role disputes, role transitions, and interpersonal deficits. These four target behaviors can be conceptualized as having great relevance to committed action. For instance, people with disordered eating typically have difficulties making or sustaining relationships, and this failure can lead to social isolation. Addressing interpersonal defects can be done as a committed action when the therapist asks the client to engage in a role-play exercise to strengthen skillful interactions. The therapist can ask the client to practice her newly trained social skills with other people in the local mall or supermarket as an exposure exercise. This kind of exercise challenges the client to engage in an action in the direction of her values even in the presence of her nervousness and negative thinking. In this way, addressing the interpersonal deficits can be looked at as a committed action.

Addressing how the client's role is changing in the world—as is apt to happen in adolescence—may also require newly learned behaviors. Interpersonal Therapy's approach to role disputes and role transitions can be conceptualized as entailing a focus on committed actions, and these core elements can be supplemented by weaving acceptance, defusion, values, and mindfulness into the approach. Keep in mind, the research also suggests that CBT is "significantly more rapid in engendering improvement in patients with bulimia nervosa than IPT," (Agras, Walsh, Fairburn, Wilson, & Kraemer, 2000), and those behavior therapy interventions should be considered first when preparing a treatment plan for this eating disorder. The research-based psychological treatments that utilize ACT may have added benefit, and research about the combination is an important future direction.

## ANOREXIA NERVOSA

Family-Based Treatment for anorexia nervosa sets up treatment objectives that will require significant committed action for clinical success. This approach is an extension of the Maudsley model that helps the client with refeeding and weight restoration, taking control of healthy eating, and becoming responsible for engaging in mature, adolescent relationships and activities. At one point, the family is asked to have a family meal. This will include weighing the client, preparing and serving the food together, and encouraging siblings to be supportive during this process. During the family meal, the parents may ask the client to eat more food than she is originally prepared to eat. The ACT approach to this therapeutic endeavor may include reviewing values-based motivation and mindfulness skills. The values-based motivation is not just for the client to declare why she will eat a healthy meal, but also for the family members to declare their motivation for acting kindly during the meal. Then, all participants stay aware of their values during mealtime. Mindfulness skills can also assist the participants with that values awareness, help them defuse from self-denigrating or judgmental thinking, and accept the emotions that are provoked during the exercise.

## *Generalized Anxiety Disorder*

The research-supported psychological treatment for generalized anxiety disorder (GAD), according to Division 12's list, is Cognitive and Behavioral Therapies for Generalized Anxiety Disorder. This broad set of approaches refers to a collection of techniques that can be functionally selected and performed as committed actions from an ACT point of view. There are specific behavioral techniques, such as exposure to anxiety-provoking situations that fit hand-in-glove with the lower right-hand corner of the ACT hexagon. According to the Division 12 website, "[t]he purpose of these exposures is to help the person learn that her feared outcomes do not come true, and to experience a reduction in anxiety over time." However, when these exposures are used to treat GAD in the ACT framework, the primary measure is *not* to prove that the worries are untrue or to reduce anxiety. Essentially, ACT will utilize the intervention steps that work, but reformulate the conceptualization. The goal of ACT is not to make the client feel *better*, but to *feel* better. In other words, the clinician will have the client come in full contact with the worries and anxieties without trying to control them. The invitation is to experience them for what they are: natural emotions. It is the attempt to try to *not* feel the feeling that can often exacerbate the problem. The ACT conceptualization will create exposure opportunities to give the client the experience of engaging in value-directed actions in the presence of anxiety. The client is experiencing the private events that were previously avoided. In the long run, the anxiety sensations may be counterconditioned, and occur less intensely and less frequently, but that is *not* the major aim of the approach. The client may be asked to schedule specific "worry time," participate in pleasurable activities, and engage in relaxation training. Each one of these can be considered committed actions when treating GAD with ACT.

## Insomnia

According to the APA Division 12 list, there are five evidence-based psychotherapy treatment protocols for insomnia: 1) cognitive behavioral therapy, 2) stimulus control therapy, 3) relaxation training, 4) sleep restriction therapy, and 5) paradoxical intention. Cognitive Behavioral Therapy for Insomnia (CBT-I) actually combines portions of all these evidence approaches into one treatment package.

Stimulus control therapy instructs the client to go to bed only when tired, limit activities in bed to sleep and sex, get out of bed at the same time every morning, and get out of bed if not asleep in 10 minutes. These could be difficult actions to do, and all will require solid commitment. A sleep-deprived client could find it significantly aversive to get out of bed in the middle of the night when he is feeling exhausted but still not sleeping after 10 minutes. When electing to teach the client about stimulus control activities, the ACT therapist will also teach acceptance of the aggravation and irritation that ensues when getting out from under the warm blankets and venturing into other parts of the darkened living quarters. The clinician can teach defusing from thoughts such as, *This is the worst! I demand more sleep! My life sucks!* and coupling that process with mindfulness practices to simply perceive those thoughts in that moment as neutral events that do not have to control behavior. The therapist would caution about the potential of those fused thoughts turning into rumination, which could potentially lead to further insomnia. When the client engages in the stimulus control treatment and grouses, "Why the heck do I have to do this nonsense in the middle of the night?" the ACT clinician can teach the client to respond with a values clarification response. During therapy, the dyad can discuss the concept that stimulus control can lead to a healthier lifestyle that might aid in following through on commitments affiliated with occupational, parenting, or social values, for instance.

Relaxation training is a set of practices that clients perform as bedtime approaches— including progressive muscle relaxation practices, meditations, and guided imagery exercises. For this approach to work, the client must commit to doing these exercises on a regular basis. Sleep restriction therapy suggests the client go to bed only when sufficiently tired, and not take naps during the day. As in stimulus control therapy, acceptance, defusion, and values could play a strong role in following through on these techniques in a reliable way over time. The client's emotions or cognitions related to the therapy itself might impede him from doing the relaxation exercises at night or the sleep restriction during the day, and acceptance and defusion could assist in helping him commit to the treatment plan.

## Obsessive-Compulsive Disorder

Exposure and response prevention (E/RP) is an effective treatment modality for individuals with obsessive-compulsive disorder (OCD). The client is asked to confront his obsessive fears and not engage in his compulsive escape response. For example, a client like Miguel can be diagnosed with OCD and have obsessions about his hands getting contaminated when touching objects in his environment, and then compulsively wash his hands to escape from those fears. The therapist could use E/RP and request that the client start touching doorknobs, handrails, and light switches in public areas. Such committed actions will expose him to his fears and will likely provoke his anxiety. The client would be instructed not to wash his hands, and to notice his subsequent feeling of anxiety and his thoughts about contamination in the presence of those provocative stimuli. Given that this therapy is purposefully anxiety provoking, the client will be required to engage in a committed action during the exposure and also when resisting engagement in the compulsive responses.

E/RP is traditionally conceptualized as an approach to reduce anxiety responses through counterconditioning. ACT for OCD does not only use exposure exercises for the benefit of reducing anxiety through counterconditioning, but also supplements the therapy by creating opportunities to engage in broader psychologically flexible committed actions in the direction of chosen values. If the client struggles with contamination obsessions, the clinician may encourage shaking hands with strangers at the mall—not just to get used to being in contact with feared stimuli to diminish their impact, but to expand the client's values-inspired repertoire for engaging in socially appropriate committed actions, whether or not the client is in the presence of anxiety. The outcome of the therapy is being able to engage in the process of meaningful behavior, not just symptom reduction.

## Panic Disorder

Similar to OCD treatment, the treatment of panic disorder calls for exposure. The EBP list includes cognitive behavioral therapy, and the behavioral portion invites clients to contact anxiety-provoking stimuli and learn to be present with the experience. In vivo exposure challenges the client to contact the real-life conditioned stimuli that elicit the panic experience and also contact the discriminative stimuli that evoke an avoidance repertoire.

For example, if the client is panicky about driving over a bridge, the in vivo exposure exercise would be to drive over the bridge while feeling that level of anxiety. The therapist might frontload that therapeutic endeavor by first starting with interoceptive exposure, which would be an office-based exercise that involves having the client experience bodily sensations similar to panic. This can be accomplished through exercises such as inviting the client to sit in an office chair and then spinning it around and rocking it back and forth. This traditional office-based behavior therapy exposure move not only attempts to countercondition the client's reactions to the interoceptive experiences, but also builds up a willingness to have those feelings in a safe environment. Such a process could assist the client with being willing to have such private experiences during an in vivo exposure outside of the office over time. The ACT model can wrap around these exercises in order to shore up willingness and values-based motivation to complete these anxiety-provoking tasks. Whether working with the office-based or in vivo exposure, the client might "not feel like" doing the exercises. It is incumbent on the therapist to assess the obstacles. If the client says, "It is too difficult for me to do something like that," the ACT therapist could invite the client to apply her mindfulness skills to notice and defuse from such a verbalization. If the client protests that the sensations are too overwhelming, the client could be encouraged to apply acceptance skills to such interoceptive experiences. "If you're not willing to have it, you've got it" is an oft-used phrase in ACT, especially when talking about anxiety issues. In other words, the more a person attempts to get rid of an emotion or sensation, the stickier it becomes. This kind of discussion related to the client's experiential avoidance during exposure exercises might assist in the commitment required to make the EBP approach effective.

## Post-Traumatic Stress Disorder

Five psychological treatments have strong research support for post-traumatic stress disorder (PTSD): 1) Prolonged Exposure, 2) Eye Movement Desensitization and Reprocessing, 3) Cognitive Processing Therapy, 4) Present-Centered Therapy, 5) and Seeking Safety.

Prolonged Exposure (PE) begins with imaginal exposures that challenge the client to remember the traumatic memory in great detail and discuss the event with the clinician while revisiting the emotional experience. After multiple trials of imaginal exposure, the client is challenged to engage in in vivo exposures in order to confront relevant trauma-related stimuli in the environment. The fact that the therapy explicitly calls for getting into contact with "anxiety-provoking events" already sets the context for using ACT as a supplement for PE. Evoking emotions that are experienced as aversive by the client can lead to avoidance of such a treatment approach in some cases. The ACT therapist will enhance the EBP by weaving mindfulness into the treatment plan to help the client have a different perspective on the anxiety, while also encouraging the exposure to be a values-based choice so the client is more willing to commit to following through with multiple iterations of making contact with the difficult experience.

Eye Movement Desensitization and Reprocessing (EMDR) also involves an exposure method while pairing eye movements in order to process the traumatic memories.

The data suggest that the approach is effective, and the treatment is controversial because the eye movement component may be superfluous. Some critics suggest that it is simply an exposure method. Either way, as with prolonged exposure, EMDR requires contacting the memories and sensations related to the trauma, and such an approach can be supported with acceptance, defusion, and mindfulness training from the ACT model. If the client responds skeptically to the eye movements, perhaps the clinician can invite the client to defuse from the thoughts that might be influencing him to resist the therapy and ask if he can be willing to try the treatment to see for himself whether or not it will work. If the client complains, "I am not the kind of person to do that kind of treatment," the clinician may bring in self-as-context exercises to help the client reduce the influence of attachment to a conceptualized self that may be impeding participating in empirically supported treatments.

Cognitive Processing Therapy, Present-Centered Therapy, and Seeking Safety treatments do not rely significantly on exposure methods and also have strong research support for the treatment of PTSD. Cognitive Processing Therapy focuses on the effects that the trauma had on the survivor's belief system about self, others, and the world. Present-Centered Therapy attempts to alter the problematic behaviors the client is currently engaging in, provides psychoeducation about the impact of trauma, and teaches problem-solving strategies focused on present-day issues. Seeking Safety is also a present-focused therapy designed to help clients attain a sense of safety in relationships, their thinking, and their behavior. This therapy includes a component that trains the client to develop coping skills for dealing with challenges related to PTSD as well as substance misuse. All of these talk therapies are likely to invite clients to change some aspect of their lifestyle, habits, or avoidance repertoires. Even though exposure and specific action changes are not explicitly discussed in these three approaches, a client can still commit to engaging in the therapy relationship and following up on any coping skills being taught.

## Schizophrenia and Other Severe Mental Illnesses

There are seven therapeutic approaches identified that address severe mental illness (SMI): 1) Social Skills Training, 2) Cognitive Behavioral Therapy, 3) Assertive Community Treatment, 4) Family Psychoeducation, 5) Supported Employment, 6) Social Learning, and 7) Cognitive Remediation.

Social Skills Training (SST) is a behavior therapy approach to reinforce skills in communication, independent living, assertiveness training, and disease management, and often is conducted in a group format. The facilitators of the group break down each of these skills into discrete steps, teach the skills specifically, and then have the clients role-play to demonstrate that they have learned the skill. The facilitators then provide feedback to the clients, and continue with the process until clients are quite fluent with whatever procedure is being coached. This is a very straightforward behavior therapy approach and can certainly be viewed as a method of implementing therapeutic actions requiring commitment in order to build the skill to fluency.

Cognitive Behavioral Therapy for severe mental illness involves creating a solid therapeutic alliance, utilizing goal setting, and building the client's skills and strategies for symptom management. According to the EBP list, CBT utilizes "behavioral experiments/reality testing, self-monitoring, and coping skills training" (American Psychological Association, 2016). Because commitment is action in the direction of what is vital and meaningful, even in the presence of obstacles, these CBT techniques can easily be formulated into the ACT model as committed actions.

Assertive Community Treatment is an interdisciplinary approach providing a network of behavioral health professionals who endeavor to collaboratively help the client and give access to care around the clock. Social support, employment, housing, medication, and therapy are all a part of the treatment. Assertive Community Treatment essentially sets up a context for engaging with a number of therapeutic interventions that are also EBPs, and the client would benefit from committing to those integrated therapies, as well as participating in the Assertive Community Treatment milieu.

Family Psychoeducation requires committed actions from the client's relatives in order to support relationship harmony in the family. Because family members can have an important influence on the client's actions and feelings, they are taught better social skills, communication, and problem-solving techniques to use when with the client, so that their interactions do not exacerbate the clinically relevant concerns. Even though the therapy is not focused on the client, it may be useful to utilize acceptance and commitment therapy training for the family so that they can leverage the influence of values and mindfulness when interacting with the client, and committing to the more effective communication skills.

Supported Employment focuses on vocational rehabilitation—teaching the client valuable skills for occupational success and providing a context for leveraging such skills. Social Learning capitalizes on token economies to shape up appropriate repertoires. Both of these environmental milieus have been shown to be effective treatment modalities for SMI and set the occasion for clients to engage in important committed actions related to functional life skills and have them reinforced by fitting positive consequences.

Cognitive Remediation is an intervention designed to train the client in cognitive flexibility, working memory, and planning skills using an educational approach. The modality can use computer training or paper-and-pencil tasks. Research on incorporating ACT into this particular training scenario has not been investigated, but there is nascent research in the area blending ACT with education (Capel, 2012). Creating a scenario where cognitive remediation is supported by mindfulness and values-based motivation seems like a potentially worthy target for research.

## Social Phobia

Exposure therapy is the primary empirically supported treatment for social phobia. The Division 12 website lists cognitive behavioral therapy for the treatment of social phobia, and a meta-analysis (Feske & Chambless, 1995) has shown that a CBT package and exposure treatment alone are equally effective for social phobia. Treating social phobia can begin with imaginal exposure and progress to in vivo exposure. A fear hierarchy is developed from a list of anxiety-provoking situations, and the client is guided through these less-intense to more-intense scenarios in therapy. To help the client during these anxiety-provoking treatment exercises, as discussed with other exposure methods throughout this chapter, the therapist can supplement the endeavor with mindfulness of the private events while accepting and defusing from the content. Values authorship exercises may shore up the motivation for clients to expose themselves to these provocative stimuli so that psychological flexibility is increased and a behavioral repertoire is broadened in the presence of anxiety.

Classic social phobia exercises include asking strangers to talk in an elevator, giving someone a compliment, or asking someone for the time of day. Sometimes a therapist might request that the client do something more challenging, like asking strange questions to a cashier at a store, or hosting a party for lots of people. These challenges to the client are not just to countercondition anxiety responses, but to increase opportunities to engage in values-based action. Because of the anxiety-provoking nature of these interventions, they can be conceptualized as committed actions and can be supported by the other domains in the ACT model.

## Specific Phobias

Much like social phobia, specific phobias can also be treated by exposure, and the ACT model can similarly be woven into the treatment plan. In vivo exposure would have the client confront the feared stimuli that are associated with the phobic response. Graduated exposure would have the client purposefully come into contact with the anxiety-provoking situation starting with a less intense scenario, such as simply visualizing an event, and progressively intensifying the scenario. For example, if a person exhibits cynophobia (fear of dogs), the therapist might first talk about dogs, then have the client read a story about a dog, then watch a gentle movie about dogs, followed by a scary movie about dogs. The clinician may then challenge the client to pet a docile dog and eventually move up to visiting a kennel or a rescue shelter with multiple dogs that may seem less predictable.

Systematic desensitization can also be included in exposure treatment. In a systematic desensitization approach, the clinician similarly moves through the hierarchy, but also pairs each situation with practicing diaphragmatic breathing and progressive muscle relaxation to countercondition the anxiety response. Although the counterconditioning exercise could be perceived as experiential avoidance and emotional control, it is important to keep in mind that this attempt is not deleterious to the client's health or a life well-lived. If the counterconditioning, breathing, and muscle relaxation actually do reduce subjective units of distress, allow for more appropriate oxygenation of the blood, and set the occasion for successful behavior, then they can still be considered ACT-consistent. If the approach is especially used for broadening flexibility rather than exclusively symptom reduction, systematic desensitization is definitely a worthy tool for ACT clinicians to have in their repertoire.

Guided mastery is also on the EBP list, can be performed as a committed action supplemented by the ACT processes, and assists the client in building motivation and proficiency while progressively coming in contact with anxiety-provoking stimuli. When implementing guided mastery, a hierarchy is used, and therapeutic assistance is gradually withdrawn. Progressing through the intensifying steps leading to mastery requires significant commitment and focus, and the other five domains from the traditional ACT hexagon model can assist with practice as a committed action.

Participant modeling is a technique in which the therapist assists the client by demonstrating functional behavior in the presence of the feared stimuli, and additional techniques can be used to supplement the exposure methods. Sometimes, virtual reality is used to introduce the client to feared stimuli in a less threatening environment. Any "negative" reactions the client has during the introduction of the participant modeling or virtual reality can similarly be addressed with ACT strategies. In sum, all of these variants on exposure can be considered committed actions, and can be further supported by the other five domains in the ACT hexagon model.

## Substance and Alcohol Use Disorders

Substance use concerns can be focused on alcohol, smoking, cocaine, and mixed substances. Alcohol and mixed substance clinical issues do have a few strongly supported treatment approaches. Cocaine and smoking interventions have only modest research support. (Nevertheless, those treatments include similar behavior therapy approaches).

### ALCOHOL USE DISORDERS

Behavioral Couples Therapy (BCT) assumes that partner interactions can be triggers for problematic drinking, partners can positively reward not drinking, and reducing relationship distress can mitigate the potential for relapse. The clinician helps the partner identify cues for problematic drinking, develop sobriety contracts, and increase positive social interactions between the two individuals. Constructive communication and coping skills are also taught. If the BCT clinician wanted to assess if ACT can assist with the therapeutic outcomes, the behavioral skills could be blended into the model as committed actions for both the client and the partner.

## MIXED SUBSTANCE USE DISORDERS

There are three research-based psychological treatment categories that have strong support for mixed substance use issues: 1) Motivational Interviewing, Motivational Enhancement Therapy (MET) and MET plus CBT, 2) Prize-Based Contingency Management, and 3) Seeking Safety.

Motivational Interviewing (MI) is described on the APA Division 12 website as a "method for strengthening clients' motivation for and *commitment to* change" (American Psychological Association, 2016, italics added). MI therapists aim "to identify, evoke and strengthen client change talk" in order to help clients engage in committed actions. MET is an additional clinical style related to MI that helps the therapist motivate commitment to change, and it can be combined with CBT techniques leading to new behaviors. Given the overarching topic of increasing propensity to engage in functional behavior, MI is another "fellow traveler" with ACT and dovetails nicely with the committed action domain.

Prize-Based Contingency Management is developed from fundamental behavioral science applications. At its core, it develops committed actions by monitoring target behaviors and using tangible positive reinforcers to increase the likelihood of that response in similar situations. For instance, clients are given prizes for clean urine samples and attendance at therapy. The prizes alone, which are usually quite modest, are not likely enough to keep the client from partaking in drug misuse. Using acceptance skills when an urge arises, and defusion skills when a rationalization for misuse becomes present, will also help the client engage in behaviors here-and-now, moment-by-moment so that a future-based prize can be earned.

Seeking Safety, which is tailored to comorbid substance use disorders and PTSD, focuses on teaching clients coping skills. There are different skills training modules in the treatment model, such as Healthy Relationships, Life Choices, and Commitment. Being motivated to use the skills in these models can be influenced by values clarification, and seeing the cues for action related to these modules can be assisted through contacting the present moment. Seeking Safety and Prize-Based Contingency Management both have components that evoke behavioral change, and the goals can be perceived as committed actions supplemented by the other areas in ACT.

# Summary

These 15 broad diagnostic categories set the context for this chapter's discussion of empirically supported psychotherapies. Acceptance and commitment therapy is a transdiagnostic approach, and still uses diagnostic categories for communication of clinical issues and suggestions for treatment modalities when that is appropriate. Each one of the successful treatment packages has some behavioral change agenda affiliated with the therapeutic plan. The committed action component in the ACT model can incorporate these treatment plan objectives with the aim of supporting that change with acceptance, self-as-context, defusion, values, and contacting the present moment. Keep in mind, this chapter is not suggesting that the ACT model underlies all treatment approaches. The principles and applications are simply transdiagnostic and can complement the therapies that have been shown to work. As a supplement, ACT is not aiming to replace other therapies, but to support what has been demonstrated to be effective. No therapy on the Division 12 list is perfect. Even the most effective therapies do not work for everyone with a given diagnosis, and even when successful, they do not completely eradicate a client's clinical issues. The EBPs can be enhanced with additional ACT components, and this chapter suggests that the EBPs can be utilized and strengthened with the ACT model. We also strongly endorse a research agenda that would more fully explore empirical evaluations of the effectiveness of blending these various therapeutic endeavors with ACT. Principles of combining ACT with other EBPs in a theoretically consistent way will be addressed more fully in chapter 9.

# CHAPTER 9

# Blending Evidence-Based Approaches with ACT

The evidence-based psychotherapies described in chapter 8 can be integrated with ACT with ease in many cases—so much so that it might appear to the beginner that "anything and everything is ACT." It would not be unusual to observe a seasoned ACT therapist using interventions borrowed from other approaches such as family systems therapy, Gestalt therapy, behavior modification, self-compassion training, or dialectical behavior therapy—and all within the treatment of a single client and within the six core ACT processes. The observations that ACT therapists use many different types of interventions was apparent in the results of a survey comparing clinicians who use so-called "third wave" therapies such as ACT to clinicians who use second wave approaches such as Beckian cognitive therapy. The investigators found that third wave therapists used a greater number of techniques and were more technically eclectic with regard to the types of techniques they used (Brown, Gaudiano, & Miller, 2011). In a similar vein, McCracken and Vowles (2014, p. 181) explain that psychological flexibility is integrative by its very nature and, "it is this core functional contextual framework that allows within ACT more routes toward healthy functioning: one where methods can seek to reduce the intensity or frequency of psychological experiences such as pain, fear, or sadness, if this achieves improved functioning, and another where methods seek to reduce the influence these experiences exert over behavior without necessarily reducing their intensity or frequency." Thus, technical eclecticism is built into the ACT model, and the bulk of this chapter will be dedicated to illustrating how the clinician might integrate evidence-based interventions into ACT.

ACT is pragmatic, and at the level of technique, a wide range of clinical approaches are acceptable and even desirable in ACT, so long as they are all theoretically coherent within the functional contextual framework of ACT and will help the client attain desired clinical outcomes. Theoretical coherence implies that the process of integrating evidence-based practices into ACT is not haphazard; a growing body of research provides the clinician with guidance on when integrated treatment might be advisable and how to implement integrated treatment. Two broad approaches to integrating ACT with other interventions are using transdiagnostic case formulation and treatment planning, and using specific integrated treatment protocols.

# ACT and Transdiagnostic Treatment Planning

Many clients arrive at treatment with multiple problems and meet criteria for more than one diagnosis. Thus, it has been recognized for decades that it is clinically useful to consider how to approach treatment in the context of a specific client reporting a specific constellation of symptoms, rather than approaching treatment in the narrower context of treating a single diagnosis (Persons, 1986). During the same time, the number of empirically supported treatments has been growing to such an extent that it is not practical for any one clinician to master the delivery of so many detailed treatment protocols. A transdiagnostic approach allows the clinician to approach treatment more broadly by using functional assessment to identify psychological problems and processes that contribute to psychopathology and then identify interventions or treatment modules that target those specific diagnoses or psychological processes, rather than relying on lengthy treatment protocols that focus on a single diagnosis (Frank & Davidson, 2014).

Transdiagnostic models may be wide-ranging, including interventions from a number of theoretical perspectives, or narrow, focusing on interventions from a single perspective such as the psychological flexibility model in ACT. One broad model is offered by Frank and Davidson's (2014) Transdiagnostic Road Map. In their model, the clinician is advised to first complete a thorough assessment aimed at understanding psychological mechanisms associated with the development and maintenance of psychological problems. Once such mechanisms are identified in collaboration with the client, a transdiagnostic formulation is developed that explains client problems in terms of psychological mechanisms, and identifies client strengths and potential obstacles to treatment. The clinician and client then identify treatment goals, and interventions are selected and implemented based on their ability to target the psychological mechanisms identified in the assessment and to aid the client in meeting treatment goals. The mechanisms identified by Frank and Davidson (2014) are derived from an extensive research literature and include vulnerability mechanisms that contribute to the development of psychopathology and response mechanisms that maintain problem behavior. Vulnerability mechanisms include neurophysiological predispositions, behavioral deficits, learned responses, pervasive beliefs, cognitive constructs such as anxiety sensitivity and fear of evaluation, and the multidimensional construct of distress tolerance. Response mechanisms include experiential avoidance, cognitive misappraisals, attentional focus, attributional bias, and repetitive negative thinking. Once mechanisms are identified and treatment goals are selected, the clinician can choose interventions.

Interventions in the transdiagnostic road map (Frank & Davidson, 2014) are categorized into four groups based on their functional properties. The first group is for interventions that enhance understanding and motivation, such as psychoeducation and values clarification. The second group is for interventions that facilitate stepping back from the problem, such as self-monitoring, mindfulness, and cognitive defusion. The third group of interventions is for core strategies for change, such as behavioral activation, cognitive restructuring, compassionate mind training, and emotion regulation. The fourth category is for adjunctive skills training for specific problems, such as progressive muscle relaxation, anger management, sleep management, and problem solving. Therapists select interventions based on which transdiagnostic mechanisms are identified in the assessment, client strengths and deficits, and client treatment goals. Any of the interventions might target one or more psychological mechanisms. The interventions are not necessarily theoretically coherent, and what they share is having solid empirical support. The clinician must carefully and creatively select interventions that make sense in the context of the client presenting complaints and goals.

ACT is well suited to a transdiagnostic approach to treatment, and ACT interventions are included in transdiagnostic approaches such as the Transdiagnostic Road Map described above. Modularizing treatment is another approach to transdiagnostic treatment. In modularized treatment, a lengthy treatment protocol is divided into components or modules that can stand alone in the treatment of specific problems. Research on modularizing treatment has shown promise. A modularized approach to ACT differs slightly from other transdiagnostic approaches in that interventions are selected based on a functional contextual approach to psychopathology, and based upon client psychological flexibility regardless of the diagnosis. Basing selection of modules on the psychological flexibility model allows the clinician flexibility in selecting appropriate interventions using modules based on the core ACT processes without relying on any one treatment protocol. Research suggests that clinicians rate modularized approaches as more effective than standard treatments, and they value the flexibility of transdiagnostic approaches because they allow for greater personalization of treatment (Villatte, Vilardaga, Villatte, Vilardaga, Atkins, & Hayes, 2016).

All of the core ACT processes are amenable to being modularized and to being integrated with other evidence-based interventions, and given the title and focus of this book, the case examples provided here will necessarily tilt toward instances of integrating evidence-based interventions with committed action. Integrating committed action with other interventions almost always means also integrating values clarification. Behavior change is rarely easy, and values clarification fuels willingness to engage in committed action with all of the accompanying discomfort. Committed action also happens to be the process in which integration with other interventions is most obvious (as highlighted throughout the previous chapter), as in many cases participating in an evidence-based intervention might itself be a committed action. For instance, when a client commits to participating in a skills training group, practicing exposure and ritual prevention, or engaging in behavioral activation, following through with the plan can require a full complement of committed action skills.

# Blending Committed Action with Other Core ACT Processes

Values clarification is closely linked to committed action, as the former is typically used to identify targets for the latter. Recent efforts to create therapy modules from the ACT core processes combine values clarification and committed action into a single treatment module (e.g., see Villatte at al., 2016). Ideally, a client interested in increasing action in the service of specific values will identify and execute committed actions that align behavior with chosen values. Values clarification and committed action go hand in hand when values clarification is used to build motivation to change behavior or, conversely, when behavior is analyzed to understand the values supporting it. Both processes can be important for increasing the success of other evidence-based interventions. For example, in an investigation of treatment of chronic pain, McCracken (2013) found that committed action, as measured by the *Committed Action Questionnaire* (CAQ) accounted for variance in social functioning, depression, mental health, and vitality in persons with chronic pain.

Acceptance and defusion can also be integrated with evidence-based interventions, and recent research suggests that acceptance-based interventions can build willingness for long-term behavior change (Forman, Butryn, Hoffman, & Herbert, 2009). Acceptance work can be integrated with other interventions and used to address avoidance that serves as a barrier to committed action. Acceptance work can also be used to increase willingness to participate in any intervention likely to be accompanied by feelings of distress, such as exposure and ritual prevention. Excellent examples of this type of integration can be found in Roemer and Orsillo's (2012) chapter on the use of acceptance-based interventions in the treatment of anxiety disorders, or Woods and Twohig's (2008) guide to using ACT-enhanced behavior therapy in the treatment of trichotillomania. While acceptance strategies can enhance willingness to experience unwanted feelings, cognitive defusion techniques can be used to address unhelpful thoughts that might function as obstacles to behavior change—such as when a client is fused with thoughts of being unable to execute a new behavior, or thoughts that something terrible might happen during exposure or other interventions. Acceptance and defusion are not isolated from the other ACT processes and are most usefully integrated with evidence-based interventions when integration facilitates values-consistent action.

Contact with the present moment and self-as-context work can also be used to enhance the effectiveness of evidence-based interventions. For instance, a client may use mindfulness skills to increase awareness of opportunities to practice new skills, and self-as-perspective work can help with identifying barriers to change. McCracken and Vowles (2014) considered the different core ACT processes and their relationship to other evidence-based interventions, and concluded that none of the core ACT processes must be used all of the time. They further suggest that acceptance and defusion techniques can be used selectively and according to client values to improve behavioral functioning. In contrast, they note that (p. 181), "Certainly both present-focused attention and self-as-observer extend the reach of ACT into emotional and cognitive processes, and values and committed action extend its reach into issues of motivation, positive behavioral regulation, and maintenance of behavior change."

It makes sense intuitively that a treatment that has psychological flexibility as its chief outcome would allow for the flexible integration of interventions that might enhance clients' psychological flexibility. And, this does not mean that any and all interventions can be usefully integrated into ACT. It is also important to be mindful that interventions integrated with ACT should be theoretically compatible with ACT. For instance, simplistically integrating cognitive defusion and cognitive restructuring might be problematic, as it would seem to present the client with conflicting messages that they can merely notice thoughts without trying to change them, and that changing negative thoughts is important (Bach & Moran, 2008). However, it is also possible to construct what might formally look like cognitive restructuring exercises in ways that are designed to fundamentally promote cognitive defusion.

Although it might go without saying, it is not only important that interventions integrated with ACT are compatible with ACT. It is also important that they are evidence-based. ACT has its roots in clinical behavior analysis (Hayes, Strosahl, et al., 2012). Successful clinical behavior analysis requires measurable variables. Techniques without an evidence base are tricky, as it is difficult to connect outcomes to the intervention. At the level of the individual client, measurable variables allow the clinician to evaluate the effectiveness of interventions and make flexible adjustments. Additionally, measurable variables are essential for a robust evidence base that allows scientist-practitioners to stay abreast of clinical research developments and trends.

Now we shall turn to some brief case examples illustrating how a therapist might integrate transdiagnostic interventions with ACT. While chapter 8 was organized by diagnostic category, the case examples below are organized by intervention used. The present volume is too short to be exhaustive, and instead of regarding the examples below as akin to a treatment manual, the examples below are more in the spirit of multiple exemplar instruction.

## ACT and Role-Play Activities

A chronic challenge to the effectiveness of evidence-based practices is client reluctance to engage in them. Many ACT interventions are utilized to increase acceptance of thoughts, feelings, and body sensations that clients are likely to avoid, and that interfere with willingness for committed action. The case of Loretta, introduced in chapter 6, illustrated how role play is used to facilitate willingness to engage in committed actions rather than avoiding them in the service of avoiding unwanted thoughts and feelings. Role-play activities can be usefully integrated into ACT as rehearsal for in vivo activities such as prolonged exposure as opportunities to practice new skills while feeling difficult feelings, or to practice acceptance when difficult feelings arise during a role-play activity. Role-play activities are exposure activities to the extent that the client contacts difficult thoughts and feelings while practicing new skills. Loretta wanted help in her relationship with her adult daughter. Loretta's daughter lived with her, was dependent on her for financial support, and struggled with substance use problems. Loretta had difficulty making requests of her daughter and saying no to her daughter's demands for money. In her therapy sessions, Loretta talked frequently about her frustration with her daughter and her desire that her daughter get a job and get treatment for her substance misuse. However, as much as she talked about these concerns, she rarely talked directly to her daughter about them, stating, "Talking about it won't do any good. We'll only end up fighting." Loretta cried a lot during therapy sessions and reported that she felt better at the end of each session; however, it was clear that although the emotional support of the therapist might make Loretta feel better temporarily, she wasn't changing her behavior outside of the treatment room and thus wasn't making any significant progress. Since she wasn't willing to talk to her daughter outside of the therapy room, the clinician decided to bring her daughter into the therapy room through role play to more directly address Loretta's avoidance of conflict. When the clinician asked Loretta to participate in a role-play activity with the therapist playing the role of daughter, Loretta readily agreed.

*Therapist:* (*in role of Loretta's daughter*) What is it now?

*Loretta:* I'm worried that you won't be able to live on your own without a job.

*Therapist:* (*in role of Loretta's daughter*) So, you want me to move out, is that it?

*Loretta:* No, I worry about your future.

*Therapist:* (*no longer in role of Loretta's daughter*) You're always on my case about something. Fine, I can just move out today. I'll start packing my things right now.

*Loretta:* No! No! (*Bursts into tears.*) You can stay as long as you need to.

*Therapist:* (*no longer in role of Loretta's daughter*) Tell me about your tears.

*Loretta:* If she moves out, then she'll have nowhere to go, and she'll be all alone, and she'll be homeless or worse.

*Therapist:*    Wow, no wonder a conversation with her is difficult. You're not just talking about getting a job. You're talking about her very life being at stake.

The role-play activity created an opening for exploration of fused content, and as she became less fused with feared outcomes, Loretta became more willing to consider the possibility of talking to her daughter directly.

After some defusion and acceptance work, Loretta established talking to her daughter as a committed action in the service of values related to parenting and honesty in her relationships. However, for each of the next two weeks, she planned to talk to her daughter and then reported in the next session that she had "chickened out." Role-play activities were again a useful intervention for helping Loretta make progress with regard to committed action.

*Loretta:*    If you want to continue living here you need to contribute to cleaning and maintaining the household.

*Therapist:*    *(in role of Loretta's daughter)* You are always on my case!

*Loretta:*    No, I can't do this. I get too upset when she is mad at me.

*Therapist:*    *(no longer in role of Loretta's daughter)* Tell me about those upset feelings.

*Loretta:*    I feel all shaky and I'm like nervous and mad at the same time.

*Therapist:*    Yes, that makes sense when someone is yelling at you. And could you continue talking even while feeling those feelings?

*Loretta:*    I don't know. Why are you asking me to have all these difficult conversations?

*Therapist:*    You identified having a clean home as something that is important to you…

*Loretta:*    I know. I know.

*Therapist:*    Let's try again.

*Loretta:*    If you want to continue living here you need to contribute to cleaning and maintaining the household.

*Therapist:*    *(in role of Loretta's daughter)* You are always on my case!

*Loretta:*    I like having a clean house, and I'd like you to stop leaving cigarette butts in the yard and driveway, and put your dishes in the dishwasher.

They continued to engage in role-play activities in which the clinician played the role of Loretta's daughter, and others in which Loretta played the role of her daughter and the clinician played the role of Loretta. This work allowed Loretta to rehearse what she wanted to say and increased her willingness to have the conversation even in the presence of her fear and anger. It also allowed her to more compassionately take the perspective of her daughter, rather than staying fused with her story about her daughter's motivations. She eventually began to engage in the committed actions of sharing her feelings with her daughter, and although there was certainly continued tension between them at times, Loretta's worst fears were not realized.

## ACT with Exposure and Ritual Prevention

Exposure can be integrated with committed action in the treatment of all anxiety disorders. Additionally, exposure and response prevention for OCD is one approach that can be enhanced by the addition of ACT. The results of a recent meta-analysis indicate that approximately 19 percent of those participating in E/RP and 30 percent of those receiving E/RP and antidepressant medication dropped out of treatment prematurely (Öst, Havnen, Hansen, & Kvale, 2015). There is some suggestion that ACT may be helpful for reducing attrition. The following example illustrates this application.

Logan, 15, arrived to his treatment intake session accompanied by his parents. His parents were informed consumers and reported that, having read about its efficacy, they were interested in Exposure and Response Prevention to treat his OCD. However, Logan was resistant to the idea of E/RP. He talked about his checking behaviors, and he reported that he wanted to change his behavior. At the same time, he refused to continue the treatment session when any type of exposure was introduced.

The form of Logan's checking behaviors varied, and his obsession was that he might inadvertently harm someone. When he spent the night at a friend's house, he could not sleep, because he kept having the thought that his medication might fall out of its bottle and then be eaten by his friend's dog or baby sister. He spent the night checking his pill bottle to make sure it was tightly closed, and counted the pills to make sure none were missing. (Ironically, the pill bottle contained medication he took to treat symptoms of OCD.) While at school, he feared that he did not properly put away a blowtorch he had used in his shop class earlier in the day, and he was suspended from school after he broke into the shop room in order to make sure he had properly shut off all of the equipment. Logan dropped out of his driver's education class after he began having thoughts that he had run over a pedestrian. He felt that dropping out of driver's ed was his only option, because the instructor would not allow him to return to verify that he had not hurt anyone.

Logan's parents accommodated his checking behavior by purchasing smart appliances that either shut off automatically or that Logan could check remotely from his cell phone. At times, even these accommodations were insufficient to prevent checking, as Logan might fear that the automatic shut-off switch did not function properly, and someone might be hurt despite his best efforts. Logan was frequently late to school because of his checking behavior, and, although he tried to hide his behavior from others, his peers found him difficult or odd.

Logan acknowledged that his obsessions were irrational, yet he was convinced that he was completely unable to resist the compulsion to check; at other times, he was convinced that others might be harmed if he were prevented from checking. This information suggested that cognitive defusion might help Logan relate to these catastrophic thoughts differently and reduce thought-action fusion. To some extent, Logan was willing to participate in cognitive defusion exercises merely because it did not entail exposure (yet), and as he became somewhat less fused with his thoughts, his willingness to consider E/RP increased. Values clarification was introduced to help Logan contact values and the costs of avoidance.

*Therapist:*    I want you to imagine you could wave a magic wand and make your problems go away. What would you be doing if you were no longer worried about harming other people?

*Logan:*    That would be great! I could sleep later and get to school on time, because I wouldn't be checking. I could stop thinking of excuses for why I keep doing weird things because I wouldn't do them anymore. And I could get my driver's license.

*Therapist:*    It sounds like there are many things that are important to you.

*Logan:*    Yes, and this stupid OCD won't go away like magic.

*Therapist:*    Well, there might be another way.

*Logan:*    You're talking about exposure again.

*Therapist:*    What if it were possible to have difficult thoughts and do what is important to you at the same time?

*Logan:*    I don't think it is possible.

*Therapist:*    Are you willing to find out?

Logan's introduction to exposure was graduated. He began by creating a hierarchy of target behaviors. Although defusion increased his willingness, he was still unsure if he was willing to be exposed to obsessions combined with refraining from compulsive checking. However, he was willing to engage in imaginal exposure. Imaginal exposure allowed him to strengthen cognitive defusion skills while he imagined himself leaving a power tool plugged in and without a safety lock engaged, or dropping a bottle of pills on the floor and being unable to retrieve them. Logan's treatment also illustrates how ACT processes cannot always be neatly compartmentalized. Whenever Logan participated in imaginal exposure, he had the opportunity to practice acceptance of distressing thoughts and feelings, as well as defusion from negative thoughts.

The use of imaginal exposure to introduce exposure and response prevention to Logan ensured that his willingness stayed high and allowed him to build acceptance and defusion skills before beginning more difficult in vivo exposure tasks. When full exposure and response prevention processes were eventually introduced, Logan felt more confident that he would be able to use acceptance and defusion to successfully contact obsessive thoughts without engaging in compulsive checking, and values clarification increased his willingness to engage in the committed action of participation in E/RP.

E/RP is regarded as the "gold standard" among evidence-based treatments for OCD and related problems. Interestingly, a recent study showed ACT to be effective for treatment of OCD without including E/RP (Twohig, Hayes, Plumb, Pruitt, Collins, Hazlett-Stevens, & Woidneck, 2010). In this treatment study, values clarification and committed action were used to identify committed actions unrelated to exposure to obsessions. In their procedure, exposure was related to engaging in committed actions related to values rather than exposure to obsessive thought content. Whether engaging in committed action in the service of reducing compulsions or increasing other valued actions, values clarification and committed action can be useful in the treatment of OCD.

Values clarification and committed action are relevant for building willingness to engage in exposure with children as well as with adults (see Coyne, McHugh, & Martinez, 2011). Olivia, age 9, was seen for treatment of social anxiety after her teacher reported that Olivia would rarely speak to her classmates and would shake her head "no" when asked to answer a question in the classroom. She would, however, speak to her teacher in private. Olivia's therapist wanted to use exposure exercises in the treatment clinic by having Olivia engage in simple social interactions with members of the office staff or other therapists. The tasks included greeting people with a simple "hello" and progressed to asking and answering questions such as, "What is your favorite color?" Olivia was initially unwilling to engage in exposure. She was verbally agreeable, yet when she encountered the target, she would smile and would not speak. Olivia's therapist decided to do a values clarification exercise, and Olivia was able to identify values of being brave and making her parents proud of her. She was more willing to engage in exposure over time when she was reminded of her values. Her therapist and parents praised her for her courage. Values clarification facilitated her willingness to engage in behavioral activation initially. The natural consequences of social interaction—namely, engagement—maintained her willingness to increase social interaction in the clinic and in her classroom. Values clarification is a useful intervention for building willingness to engage in other interventions.

ACT modules on acceptance and defusion skills or values and committed action can be effectively integrated into transdiagnostic treatments for anxiety disorders. And consulting the literature can be helpful in preparing to do so. For example, Villatte and colleagues (2016) found that values and committed action modules were useful in the treatment of generalized anxiety, and that in the treatment of PTSD, values and committed action were more helpful after several sessions of acceptance and defusion. Even as you are reading these words, research on integrating ACT with other interventions is ongoing.

## ACT and Behavioral Activation

Behavioral Activation (BA) is a treatment for depression that emphasizes having patients get more involved in their own lives through behavioral tasks such scheduling, engaging in, and rating the enjoyment of activities. Further, BA can be effectively delivered by clinicians with differing theoretical orientations (Martell, et al., 2013). ACT and BA are a good combination, as the core ACT processes can be used to identify and build motivation for engaging in committed actions. Like ACT, Behavioral Activation is a functional contextual approach to treatment in which the contingencies that maintain depressive behavior are explored, and behavior is explored in relation to the environmental context of the specific client. Recent approaches to BA also explore the role of behavioral avoidance in maintaining depressive behavior. Specifically, it is hypothesized that depressed individuals often experience negative events, and aversive consequences such as negative feelings states are escaped or avoided by behavior deactivation that results in more depressive symptoms and more avoidance behaviors (Hopko, Ryba, McIndoo, & File, 2015). Also like ACT, while earlier versions of Behavioral Activation did not include values clarification, revised versions stress the importance of values clarification to enhancing treatment outcomes (Lejuez, Hopko, Acierno, Daughters, & Pagoto, 2011).

BA is typically conducted in eight to 10 sessions. Treatment begins with assessment, exploring the functions of depressed behavior and consequences of behavior change. Clients complete weekly self-monitoring to measure baseline behavior and aid in identifying potential target behaviors. Values assessment is conducted, and values-congruent behavioral goals are identified. Patients then collaboratively create a hierarchy of goals from easiest to most difficult and set weekly and final behavioral goals. In subsequent sessions, patients review goals and identify new goals based on the success or difficulty with prior goals (Hopko, et al., 2015). The functional contextual approach to BA along with values assessment and goal setting within BA make it amenable to integration with ACT.

While second wave treatments for depression emphasized selection of pleasurable activities as behavioral goals that were presumed to be helpful in themselves for ameliorating depressive symptoms, in third wave therapies, behavioral goals may be pleasant (such as socializing with a friend or eating ice cream) or unpleasant (such as cleaning the kitchen or paying bills). Behavioral goals are selected if they are positively reinforcing to the specific client based on behavioral assessment and values clarification (Turner & Leach, 2012). The case of Doris will be used to explore integration of ACT and BA.

Doris became depressed following the death of her husband of 45 years, and she was prescribed antidepressant medication. Nearly two years later, her primary care physician referred her for psychotherapy after Doris reported that she still felt depressed and asked for an increase in the dosage of the medication. At intake, Doris reported that she spent much of the day in her home watching news, talk shows, and old movies on television. When the clinician inquired about how her activity today differed from her activity when her husband was alive, she reported, "We always went out; we went to dinner parties almost every week, and we liked dancing, golfing, and boating." When asked about the possibility of doing any of these activities today, Doris stated, "No one wants to invite a widow to a dinner party," "I won't dance without my dance partner," and "Boating was never my thing; my husband loved it, and I went along because I loved him." Behavioral Activation can be helpful for treating bereaved individuals presenting with symptoms of depression or post-traumatic stress (Papa, Sewell, Garrison-Diehn, & Rummel, 2013), and given Doris's depressive symptoms and low level of activity, it seemed that Behavioral Activation might be a useful approach.

Though Doris was skeptical when the clinician introduced Behavioral Activation, she reluctantly agreed to give it a try. During assessment, she reported that she did not enjoy herself when she interacted with others, believed that others did not want to be around her because she was sad and no longer had a partner, and felt upset when activities she used to enjoy evoked memories of her husband. A functional assessment suggested that, through inactivity, she was avoiding aversive feeling states, and avoiding upsetting others—or at least she *believed* she was avoiding upsetting others. Although it took a while for Doris to fully engage in the conversation, values clarification allowed Doris to connect her actions to her values and to recognize that since her husband's untimely death, she had abandoned many activities that had previously accorded with her values. After the loss of a spouse, it can be difficult to separate the participation in activities with one's partner from other values. For instance, a person who values eating healthfully may find it difficult to identify cooking healthy meals as a value separate from a long history of cooking meals for her husband. Doris's therapist was able to use values clarification to help Doris identify what was important to her.

*Therapist:* On the one hand, you've said that you can't imagine a life without your husband, and on the other hand, you made it here. What brought you here?

*Doris:* My doctor said it might be helpful, and she didn't want to give me more medication.

*Therapist:* Okay, so it sounds like taking care of your health is important to you.

*Doris:*       Yes, it is. And two of my friends also said that therapy might be helpful.

*Therapist:*   Tell me about these friends.

*Doris:*       Karen is a neighbor, and Beth and I have been friends since grade school. They keep calling, and I feel bad when I don't answer the phone, or when I decline their invitations to go out.

*Therapist:*   It sounds like friendship is important to you.

*Doris:*       Yes, I have many good friends.

It is said that you "value with your feet." The therapist was able to gently move Doris to identify her values by answering questions about her behavior. Once she examined her values, she was able to connect both old and new actions to them. For instance, when she discussed her values related to friendship and family, she noted that she used to frequently call and visit with various relatives and friends in order to check on their well-being, share news, and spend time together. She noted that being physically active had been an important part of taking care of her health, and that pastimes such as golf and dancing allowed her to simultaneously engage in healthful activities and socialize with people she cared about.

Doris was able to identify several potential target behaviors, such as calling her best friend, son, or favorite aunt; inviting a friend out for coffee; visiting the pro shop at the golf course; and so on. She agreed to start small and engage in two specific activities during the next week. When Doris returned to her next session, she guiltily reported that she had not engaged in either of the behaviors. The clinician explored obstacles to behavior activation with Doris by asking questions such as, "What happens when you think about visiting your friends?" or "What happened the last time you went to your favorite coffee shop?" And it soon became clear that experiential avoidance was the primary barrier to action. Doris indicated that she did not want to talk with others about her husband or about how much she missed him, and she did not want to visit places that reminded her of him, such as the golf course or their favorite coffee shop. The clinician responded with more work on acceptance of grief and sadness, cognitive defusion, and values clarification. Doris was eventually able to acknowledge—not just logically, but also experientially—that the ACT truism that "if you are not willing to have it, then you've got it" applied to her. Doris was avoiding others in the service of avoiding memories and mourning, and despite her attempts to avoid others in the service of avoiding unwanted thoughts, feelings, and memories, she was in fact spending her time alone engaged in remembering and mourning.

As Doris recognized both the futility and the costs of avoidance, she became more willing to engage in behavioral activation. She selected activities that she had enjoyed in the past, such as joining a women's golf league and getting together with friends, and she tried new activities that she thought might interest her, such as attending a cooking class. Her mood began to improve as she increased her engagement. She eventually made plans to go to a dance—the one activity that she had resisted because of its association with her husband. During the therapy session the week after the dance, she began to cry and tearfully explained that she felt guilty because, "I was laughing and having a good time while my poor husband is dead." This revelation led her therapist to initiate more defusion and acceptance work, and Doris gradually accepted that she could cherish the memory of her husband and also form new memories during life without him. She eventually began to notice that she was having more of what she described as "happy memories" and said, "Now I smile when I think of him at least as often as I cry when I think of him."

## ACT and Skills Training

Skills training is another evidence-based therapeutic component that can be usefully integrated with ACT. Juan, a 24-year-old first generation Mexican American who lives with his parents and grandparents, presented for treatment of social anxiety and depressed mood. He said that he decided to begin treatment because he did not like the side effects of the many medications he had tried, and he noted that, "I want to have a girlfriend—I have to get over this so I can ask girls out." Juan was a relatively informed consumer. He had read a little bit about the treatment of social anxiety, and he was anticipating that he would be asked to engage in exposure. He worked with his therapist to develop a hierarchy of social interactions, ranking them from least to most difficult. For example, easier activities included having a short conversation with a cashier at the grocery store or an elderly neighbor, and difficult activities included talking to a young woman that he found attractive or talking to a group of three or more same aged peers. Juan also participated in role-play activities with his therapist, and it soon became clear that he had poor social skills, and that this skills deficit interfered with his ability to connect with others. Specifically, although he was able to initiate a conversation with relative ease, he had difficulty keeping a conversation going for very long without becoming awkward. Juan had immigrated to the United States at the age of 8, and he reported that when he first began school, Spanish was his first language. For that first year, he was often teased by other children because of his poor English skills. Juan noted that his father most likely also had social anxiety, and his mother did not learn English for many years; thus, his parents had not modeled effective social interaction skills for him. Because social skills training can enhance the effectiveness of treatment for social anxiety disorder (Herbert, Gaudiano, Rheingold, Myers, Dalrymple, & Nolan, 2005), Juan's therapist recommended it as an adjunct to exposure.

Though Juan had been a willing participant in exposure and role-play activities, he balked at his therapist's suggestion that he join a social skills training group, stating, "No way am I going to look like an idiot in front of a whole group of people." Getting

Juan to agree to attend a social skills training group required the therapist's full ACT repertoire. Juan was fused with thoughts and images of being teased by others, and these thoughts were based largely on rumination about events long past. Acceptance, defusion, and present moment work helped Juan approach his thoughts about the past differently; he was able to notice his thoughts as mere thoughts, and his previous experience with exposure was used to build acceptance. That is, Juan became more confident that it would be okay if he felt anxious in a new social setting. Mindfulness and self-as-context exercises helped Juan to stay present with his experience and be less "in his head." Juan continued to resist, and the therapist returned to values clarification. Values clarification was easy in the early stages of treatment. As noted above, Juan was an informed consumer and his values around friendship and romantic relationships motivated him for treatment. The therapist used the following dialogue to link those values to the committed action of joining a skills training group.

*Therapist:*   You've been working very hard to accept feelings of anxiety and practice having conversations with different people. You haven't done these activities because they are fun. What meaningful goals have made you willing to do these difficult activities?

*Juan:*   I like people, and I want to have friendships, and I want to have a girlfriend.

*Therapist:*   That's right; you're the kind of person that values getting to know others and being a good friend, *and* you value accepting difficult feelings in the service of getting closer to your goals of having friends and girlfriends.

*Juan:*   I guess so; I want to conquer my fear and go out and be with other people like a man.

*Therapist:*   When you practiced talking to other people, like your neighbor and kids at school, did those activities move you closer to or further away from your goals?

*Juan:*   Closer, for sure.

*Therapist:*   When you think about going to a social skills training group, would doing that activity move you closer to or further away from what matters to you?

*Juan:*   Closer…but it would be hard.

*Therapist:*   And would avoiding activities that scare you move you closer to or further away from what matters to you?

*Juan:*   Further…I see what you are trying to do.

Juan agreed to join the next social skills training group. He scheduled a therapy session right before his first social skills training group, and his therapist also agreed to meet with him briefly after the group ended. Juan reported that he was very nervous before the group and during the first half of the meeting. He also said, "I realized that everyone there was just like me—feeling scared to be there. And all of a sudden it was like it was okay to be scared. I never wanted to look scared in front of people, but it was okay in that group." Juan reported ups and downs in the group, and Juan's performance during role-play activities indicated that his social skills were indeed improving over time.

Juan made a few mistakes during his skills training course; he skipped a group without telling the group leader in advance, and he asked a group member out on a date while the group was still meeting, which violated the group rules. When his therapist confronted him about these behaviors, he noted that he was ambivalent about being in the group. Cognitive defusion and values clarification helped build willingness to attend and participate fully without violating group norms. More importantly, he stayed with the group and developed enough skills to enhance the effectiveness of his social interactions outside of the group. The improvement was noticeable to Juan himself, and served to increase his willingness to take risks. Juan was making some progress before he began the social skills training group, and his participation in the group more than likely contributed to an enhancement in his positive treatment outcome.

The case example of Juan was presented to highlight the integration of skills training with ACT. However, Juan's positive treatment outcome depended on several evidence-based interventions, including skills training, exposure, homework, and behavioral activation. The example also illustrates the utility of skills training in ACT. Many therapy clients have skills deficits, and the ACT model of psychopathology suggests that skills deficits are best regarded within the committed action component of ACT (Bach & Moran, 2008). Like Juan, other clients may benefit from formal or informal skills training related to any number of behavioral deficits, such as learning medication management skills, parenting skills, skills related to vocational activities, or skills related to health management. Even ACT interventions themselves could entail skills training, as when a client learns mindfulness skills. In almost all cases, participating in skills training will be a committed action, and getting the client there may require interventions from all core processes of the ACT model.

## ACT and Habit Reversal Training

Habit Reversal Training (HRT) is a useful intervention for problems such as trichotillomania and skin picking. HRT is a behavioral treatment that involves detecting early signs of such problem behaviors and engaging in a competing response that is physically incompatible with the problem behavior—such as closing the hands into fists. ACT may be a helpful addition to HRT, because ACT addresses avoidance behaviors involved in maintaining behaviors such as hair pulling and skin picking, facilitates defusion from thoughts that maintain problematic behaviors, and builds motivation to engage in committed actions, such as out-of-session exercises and practice (Capriotti, Ely, Snorrason, & Woods, 2015). Integrated treatment protocols include standard HRT procedures along with ACT interventions. One such treatment is acceptance-enhanced behavior therapy (AEBT), which has been shown to be effective in the treatment of trichotillomania and skin picking (Flessner, Busch, Heideman, & Woods, 2008). The three components of HRT—awareness training, competing response training, and social support—are combined with ACT techniques and exercises.

Ashley complained of long-standing trichotillomania. She was not confident that treatment would be helpful, and she was feeling distressed by her appearance. Specifically, she had pulled out her eyebrows and eyelashes and had a large bald spot that she could no longer hide by carefully styling her hair; she was now wearing a wig. She initially stated that she was not bothered by her hair pulling behavior itself, and that if she could better control her appearance she probably would not have sought therapy. Ashley's therapist implemented AEBT.

Ashley was resistant to treatment, because her focused hair pulling had avoidant functions and she could not imagine tolerating or finding another way of coping with distress. Awareness training helped Ashley both to become more aware of automatic hair pulling and to notice thoughts and feelings that accompanied focused hair pulling. Acceptance interventions helped her to become more willing to learn and practice competing responses. However, Ashley balked at seeking social support. She was deeply ashamed of her behavior, and she did not want to share her struggle with others, no matter how close she perceived her relationship with her sister and her closest friends to be. There are many HRT procedures, and on the one hand, treatment progress might be made even if Ashley refused to engage in any one procedure. On the other hand, social support is important to more than successfully managing HRT.

Ashley engaged in values clarification to contact her values related to family, friendship, and social support. She became aware that she would want to help a friend who asked for her support, and she noticed that she would feel sympathy or empathy rather than antipathy toward a friend who asked for her help with a problem. Acceptance and defusion helped Ashley to contact her fear of rejection and reduce the level of entanglement with negative self-judgments.

Ashley initially made treatment progress using awareness training, stimulus control, alternative behaviors, and other behavior modification techniques alone (before she began seeking social support). And the addition of social support was followed by more behavior change. For example, Ashley increased her social engagement. She also reported that she felt less ashamed when she pulled her hair, and reduced shame was associated with reduced hair pulling. (Notice that this is yet another example of the adage, "If you are not willing to have it, then you've got it.") Once again, it is clear that most evidence-based interventions can be successfully integrated with ACT. When the rationale for integration is theoretically compatible with ACT, and the clinician is clear about how the combination of treatment approaches is best introduced and implemented, ACT will often be enhanced by the addition of evidence-based practices.

# Flexibly Integrating ACT and Other Evidence-Based Interventions

The case examples described above illustrate how some widely used evidence-based interventions might be integrated with ACT. That said, there is no single "cookbook" approach as to precisely how one might optimally combine interventions. Ideally, the clinician will have a sufficient repertoire with regard to ACT processes and other evidence-based interventions, and will regularly consult the clinical research literature so as to be able to implement any number of intervention combinations in a meaningful and theoretically consistent way. Over time, a clinician will increase his clinical repertoire through multiple exemplar training; a broad repertoire will increase opportunities for flexibility. The standard definition of psychological flexibility also applies to the clinician flexibly applying ACT. When the client is improving, persisting in the treatment strategy may be the most values-consistent choice, and when the client fails to improve or encounters obstacles to treatment, the flexible clinician can change course by implementing alternative evidence-based interventions until the client can move forward in identifying and overcoming barriers to acting in the service of her chosen values. Michelle's treatment exemplifies this type of flexibility.

Michelle, who was introduced in chapter 6, presented with binge eating disorder, morbid obesity, and multiple health problems. Over the course of her treatment, all of the core ACT processes and several additional evidence-based interventions were implemented in order for her to attain increased psychological flexibility. As you may recall, Michelle was looking for a quick and painless fix. She entered therapy requesting treatment that would allow her to lose weight rapidly and without cravings or discomfort.

The initial assessment suggested that Michelle used food to cope with negative emotions, and because, "if you're not willing to have it, then you've got it," when Michelle binged in order to avoid unwanted negative emotions, she invariably faced even more negative emotions after she binged; however, now the predominant emotion was shame about her binge rather than (or often in addition to) the feeling she was trying to avoid prior to the binge. Michelle had tried many different diets, and although she knew the calorie counts of many foods, she did not know much about nutrition. Consequently, her diabetes was poorly managed. Weight loss might appear to be a straightforward and measurable goal, yet the treatment needed to get there is not necessarily so straightforward. Over the course of her treatment, Michelle and her therapist used all of the core ACT processes, along with several additional evidence-based interventions.

Michelle approached treatment essentially saying to her therapist, "Tell me what to do and I will do it." Her therapist wanted her to get in the habit of taking a more active role in her self-care and thus assigned her homework of reading *The Weight Escape* (Ciarrochi, et al., 2014), a self-help book that uses ACT for weight loss. Michelle's resistance to doing this homework was explored, and she came to the realization that, "if I know everything about losing weight, then it will be my fault if I fail." This insight was very helpful in helping Michelle eventually move forward.

Values clarification was used to identify specific committed actions in the service of those values. As she participated in values clarification, Michelle recognized that weight loss would help her live in greater accordance with her values, and her willingness to engage in committed actions increased. Her therapist introduced skills training by having Michelle schedule appointments with an endocrinologist and with a nutritionist with a specialization in diabetes management. Specifically, Michelle learned about the appropriate diet for managing diabetes while losing weight, along with other health behaviors needed to effectively manage her diabetes. The specialists provided Michelle with written materials so that she could learn more on her own. Skills training gave Michelle tools to help her more effectively change her eating behaviors in the service of taking care of her health, and also served to increase her overall sense of self-efficacy.

Michelle reported difficulty resisting cravings when she felt bored, angry, or stressed. Cognitive defusion exercises were used to explore Michelle's thoughts about food and eating and to identify new ways of relating to her thoughts. Michelle reported that she had thoughts such as, "I deserve to have this [preferred food]," and after working on cognitive defusion skills, she began saying to herself, "I'm having the thought that I deserve this." This is one example of how a simple verbal convention allowed her to psychologically distance herself from thoughts and decrease cognitive fusion.

Acceptance work indicated where exposure might be helpful. Michelle reported that she found it difficult to be around food in situations such as going to a restaurant or party without "craving and giving in to temptation." She and her therapist collaborated to develop exposure exercises that would help her practice psychological flexibility and effectiveness in the presence of desired foods. Michelle created a hierarchy of risky food situations and would order a healthy item off the menu, noticing her thoughts, feelings, and bodily sensations as she observed alternative food choices as listed in the menu or on the plates of nearby patrons. She was able to acknowledge and accept feelings of craving, and thoughts that she wanted, deserved, or missed carbohydrate-laden entrees and sweet desserts, or that it wasn't fair that she didn't get to eat them anymore.

Weight loss is a necessarily slow process, and Michelle found that she was often thinking about the future, "when I'm thin," or berating herself for poor choices she made in the past. Present moment focus and self-as-perspective exercises helped Michelle to increase self-compassion and notice opportunities for positive reinforcement in the present. She also began to practice mindful eating, both as an exercise to increase present-moment focus generally and to increase her opportunities to enjoy the food she was eating.

After Michelle visited her parents for a weekend, she complained to her therapist that her mother and sister frequently attempted to sabotage her weight loss efforts, and she surmised that they behaved this way because, "they're fat too, and as long as I don't lose weight, they don't have to change—it's like I get to fail for all of us." Michelle then described a difficult weekend in which she found that her mother offered her sweets and fattening meals even after Michelle had told her mother about her new diet prior to her visit. Michelle also indicated that her mother and sister persisted in the behavior of offering her forbidden foods even after she asked them to stop and said that she was full. When her therapist asked how Michelle would like to plan for her next visit to her mother, she reported that she could not imagine confronting her mother "without crying or getting really mad." Michelle's therapist introduced assertiveness training skills and used role-play activities so Michelle could practice setting limits with her mother, sister, or others who might not respect her choices. After her next visit with her mother, Michelle reported that "we had a good conversation, and I got a little mad, but I didn't cry." More importantly, her mother respected her boundaries afterward, and her sister expressed her envy about Michelle's weight loss. "We had a good conversation about what I am trying to do." Michelle later noted that she believed the role-play activities were an essential part of preparing to effectively talk to family members.

Over the next two years, Michelle lost more than 100 pounds and reduced her dependency on insulin and her blood pressure improved. As she controlled her diet, she shifted the focus of her treatment to working on relationships. For most of her adult life, Michelle had few close friends and avoided dating. She surmised that she used weight as a way to keep others at a distance. As her health and mood improved, she became more interested in getting close to others and found that she felt significant anxiety in social situations, which she tried to avoid by "running away the minute someone tries to get close." Once again, she and her therapist relied on ACT and other evidence-based practices to facilitate the development and execution of relationship skills. Michelle participated in skills training using a dating skills program, she participated in role-play activities to practice new behaviors, and she was willing to engage in exposure as she made new friends and started to date. Along the way, she also relied on acceptance and defusion skills, mindfulness skills, and self-compassion, and all of her change endeavors required concerted committed action in the service of her chosen values.

# Summary

ACT can undoubtedly be conducted without significant reliance on other evidence-based practices, and many evidence-based interventions can be implemented without the introduction of core ACT processes. At the same time, we have found that a clinical repertoire that includes ACT as well as other evidence-based interventions affords the clinician more tools to assist clients in solving problems and developing greater psychological flexibility. Now that we've described how to combine ACT-based committed action practices with evidence-based treatments, in the next chapter, we'll bring everything in the book together in a series of extended case examples that illustrate many aspects of facilitating committed action in practice.

# CHAPTER 10

# Application of Committed Action: Case Examples

Throughout this text, we've provided various case examples to highlight specific processes and topics related to committed action. We've also discussed the role of evidence-based psychotherapies and how ACT, and specifically the process of committed action, can be integrated with them. In this chapter, we pull all of those pieces together with several extended case examples that demonstrate a more detailed application of committed action work with common presenting problems.

## Obsessive-Compulsive Disorder

Veronica, a 32-year-old devout Catholic woman who lived with her mother, sought psychotherapy for scrupulosity OCD. She reported having a high rate of obsessive blasphemous thoughts, and when she had private verbal events she judged to be sinful, she would compulsively punish herself. She said she couldn't control her irreverent thoughts, and she attempted to prove to herself that she was pious by decorating her house with Christian icons and portraits of the saints in an attempt to direct her thoughts with these adornments. Although she told herself that this ornamentation would make her a better Catholic, it actually made her blasphemous thoughts more likely, as seeing these images regularly set her up to have the automatic thoughts related to sacrilege. (This is similar to how the statement "Don't think of a pink elephant" evokes thinking of a pink elephant.)

When Veronica recognized that she had blasphemous thoughts as she walked around her house, she would atone for her sins by kneeling down facing a crucifix while placing her knees in two cigar boxes filled with unsharpened pencils. The ridges of the hexagon-shaped pencils would press into her kneecaps, causing significant pain, and she would then attempt to expiate her transgression by saying the rosary. She reported that this punishment had been meted out in her parochial school when she was young, and she believed she should engage in this behavior whenever she sinned. The duration of the rosary was approximately 20 minutes for her, and according to her self-monitoring worksheets, she completed that compulsion six to 17 times per day.

When Veronica confided in some of her fellow parishioners about what she was doing, they talked to their pastor about it. Her pastor called Veronica and suggested that she might have OCD and promised to accompany her when she sought professional help. That led to her first appointment with the therapist, an ACT clinician who excelled at empirically supported treatments.

During their first session, the therapist sketched out a treatment plan that included exposure and response prevention. However, prior to engaging in E/RP, the clinician wanted Veronica's pastor to weigh in on some of her spiritual concerns. Veronica brought a Bible to the session, and in regard to her blasphemous thoughts, she pointed to Matthew 5:28–30: *You have heard that it was said, "You shall not commit adultery." But I tell you that anyone who looks at a woman lustfully has already committed adultery with her in his heart. If your right eye causes you to stumble, gouge it out and throw it away. It is better for you to lose one part of your body than for your whole body to be thrown into hell. And if your right hand causes you to stumble, cut it off and throw it away. It is better for you to lose one part of your body than for your whole body to go into hell.*

Veronica was convinced that her thoughts were sins, and that beating up her body was what God wanted. The pastor countered with James 2:14–26, which addresses the distinction between thoughts or beliefs and deeds: *What good is it, my brothers and sisters, if someone claims to have faith but has no deeds? Can such faith save them? Suppose a brother or a sister is without clothes and daily food. If one of you says to them, "Go in peace; keep warm and well fed," but does nothing about their physical needs, what good is it? In the same way, faith by itself, if it is not accompanied by action, is dead…As the body without the spirit is dead, so faith without deeds is dead.*

The priest then said that while Veronica might believe she was being pious and faithful by punishing herself, her faith might be better demonstrated by overtly serving people in need. Veronica acknowledged that being of service to others was consistent with her values related to her religious beliefs and to who she wants to be as a person in general. Her priest thus suggested that instead of regularly isolating herself in her house and rotely saying her prayers, she might challenge herself to dedicate her free afternoons to working in the church's soup kitchen.

The therapist viewed this as a measurable committed action: an overt behavior in the service of Veronica's spiritual values, to be performed in the presence of the obstacle presented by her impious thoughts. Veronica agreed to work in the soup kitchen as a committed action at the rate of five times per week, with a duration of three hours per visit. She also agreed to show up for therapy every week, and keep a record of her behaviors.

During the first week, Veronica received significant social positive reinforcement from her churchgoing friends when they saw her volunteering, and when her pastor saw her serving the people who came in for a meal, he made sure to respond to her efforts with a smile and kind words. Because these were people she cared about, such responses served as reinforcers and increased the likelihood that she would continue to engage in the committed action of volunteering in the service of one of her most important values: "serving the Lord." However, during therapy, she complained that she was still beleaguered by irreverent thoughts and asked whether ACT could help her deal with those private events.

The therapist explained that the goal of ACT, and committed action in particular, is to help people expand to live life more flexibly and in greater alignment with their values, even in the presence of difficult thoughts and feelings. Even though Veronica could understand this logically, she still felt extremely uncomfortable with her irreverent thoughts. So even as she fulfilled her commitment to work in the soup kitchen, sometimes she still punished herself when she got home. Because Veronica was willing to engage in E/RP, the clinician created values-based exposure exercises that included challenges that would help Veronica build defusion skills while engaging in committed actions.

In one exercise, the clinician brought out some index cards and then asked permission to place the cards on Veronica's lap after he wrote on each one. When Veronica agreed, the clinician asked if they could play tic-tac-toe on the first card. She agreed, and when they were done, she allowed him to place the card on her lap. Then the clinician wrote some letters from the Greek alphabet on a card, and once again Veronica agreed to let him place the card on her lap. The intervention continued as set forth in the following dialogue:

*Therapist:*  Are you okay with those cards on your lap?

*Veronica:*  Sure.

*Therapist:*  On a scale of 0 to 100, where 0 is no distress and 100 is the most distress you can imagine, how are you feeling right now?

*Veronica:*  I don't know…like 15.

*Therapist:*  Okay. Can we do some more cards?

*Veronica:*  Sure, but now my distress is going up to 20! What are you going to do?

*Therapist:*  Nothing without your permission!

*Veronica:*  Fine, then. Let's do it.

Continuing with several more cards, the clinician scribbled, doodled, and wrote nonsense syllables on each and then placed it on Veronica's lap with her consent. She continued to report being fine with the process.

*Therapist:*  Why do you think that you're so relaxed with this?

*Veronica:*    I guess it's because they're just silly marks on the card.

*Therapist:*    What would you say is on your lap right now?

*Veronica:*    A bunch of index cards you wrote on.

*Therapist:*    Okay…go a bit further.

*Veronica:*    I suppose it's just lead and paper on my lap.

*Therapist:*    Hmm… Okay. It's actually graphite in my pencil right here, and could you go as far as to say that the paper is actually pulp?

*Veronica:*    Yeah. Paper is made of pulp. Sure.

*Therapist:*    How's your distress now?

*Veronica:*    Still at about 20.

*Therapist:*    Great. Can I put some more pulp and graphite on your lap?

*Veronica:*    I guess…

On the next card, the therapist wrote: *Jo sephs ho uld noth avem arri edtha thar lot.* Veronica looked at the card, looked blankly at the clinician, and again allowed him to place the card on her lap.

*Therapist:*    How's your distress?

*Veronica:*    Fine. Still at 20.

*Therapist:*    Great. Can I create another card?

*Veronica:*    I guess…

On the next card, the clinician wrote: *Joseph should not have married that harlot.* Veronica initially allowed him to place the card on her lap, but after reading what was written on it, she swatted all of the index cards on her lap onto the floor. The therapist found the previous card, picked it up, and held it out alongside the final card, and asked, "Why are you unwilling to be with this last card but willing to experience the previous one? Both are just pulp and graphite. Both have squiggles and lines. In fact, on both of these the graphite and pulp are almost identical. It's just that one card has a different amount of space between some of the squiggles than the other one. You were fine with the first one but refused to contact the second one. Both are simply squiggles and lines made of graphite and pulp. May I go ahead and place that last one on your lap? Can you notice it for what it is and not what your mind interprets it to be?" Veronica agreed to continue the exercise at that point, even in the presence of heightened distress and worries that she was being blasphemous. The therapist referred to these worries as mind chatter and encouraged her to continue to notice what came up as she sat with the cards and the symbols written on them.

The latter part of the exercise has a strong defusion component involved. Committed action is required to actually contact the anxiety-provoking stimuli, and given the strength of Veronica's obsessive thoughts, the therapist thought it would be helpful to promote defusion before presenting a highly challenging stimulus. The therapist could also challenge Veronica to mindfully be aware of the index cards without getting caught up in their content, and might also help her explore how being present with aversiveness can allow for more options in pursuing values-based actions. By the end of the session, she had committed to three small actions that were important to her and that she would practice doing, even in the presence of her challenging mind chatter. In other words, for Veronica to fully live in alignment with her value of serving her Lord, the therapist suggested that she may need to develop more willingness to experience uncomfortable feelings and sensations. In the end, the therapist was able to turn this exercise into an opportunity for Veronica to contact the present moment, accept uncomfortable thoughts and feelings, and defuse from "impious" content while committing to measurable, important behaviors that were consistent with her faith and values.

# Post-Traumatic Stress Disorder

John, a 42-year-old man, had served for 12 years in the Army National Guard, which he had joined for the extra pay and benefits, as well as to serve his community. He was deployed to Afghanistan for 13 months, serving as a convoy driver. During that time, he was exposed to a number of potentially traumatic events, including witnessing nearby Improvised Explosive Device (IED) detonations and seeing Iraqi civilians killed as they attempted to attack his base. However, when he presented for therapy and discussed these experiences, he was able to do so with an appropriate but not overwhelming level of affect. He said that his war experiences didn't impact him on a day-to-day basis, because he had received training to prepare him for these kinds of events, and he generally had known what he was getting into.

When asked why he was seeking therapy, he said that a year ago he'd been deployed within the United States to assist with recovery efforts after a catastrophic flood. During the two weeks of that assignment, he was responsible for humanitarian concerns (such as providing food, water, and tents) for people who had been displaced from their homes, and he also went door to door through several neighborhoods to determine whether there were any casualties. During the course of that effort, he personally found the bodies of 12 people who had died in their homes. He said he was still haunted by the sights and smells of the dead bodies he'd helped recover.

After a thorough assessment, John's therapist found that he met the full diagnostic criteria for PTSD related to the flood recovery efforts. The PTSD symptoms that were most troubling to him were nightmares, difficulty sleeping, and emotional numbness. Three of the bodies he'd found were children who were similar in age to his own children, and he reported that he was now having difficulty connecting with his children, because spending time with them triggered memories of the dead children's bodies. These memories led to intense feelings of sadness, which he quickly escaped either by drinking alcohol or by finding an excuse to get away from his children.

John's therapist provided him with two options for evidence-based approaches they could try to ease his PTSD symptoms: cognitive processing therapy and prolonged exposure therapy. Cognitive processing is a type of talk therapy that focuses on the effects of a trauma on a client's belief systems about himself, others, and the world, whereas prolonged exposure therapy focuses more on overcoming anxiety and avoidance through repeated imaginal and in vivo exposures to trauma cues. John chose to go with cognitive processing therapy, because he wasn't willing to do the repeated exposures necessary for prolonged exposure therapy. At the end of his first session, John agreed to the standard homework stipulated by cognitive processing therapy: working on writing an Impact Statement in which he was to explore what he thought it meant that he had experienced these events, and how the trauma had affected his beliefs about himself, others, and the world. However, he didn't bring the written impact statement in to his second session, and even after a lengthy discussion of the impact of the trauma during that session, he still didn't write down his reflections and bring them to his third session, nor did he start completing the A-B-C sheets, on which he was asked to identify an activating event, relevant beliefs or stuck points, and consequences during the week. John's therapist believed that this lack of follow-through reflected particularly entrenched avoidance that could benefit from supplementing the cognitive processing approach with ACT in order to overcome barriers that were preventing John from fully engaging with the work.

In the fourth session, John's therapist devoted the first half of the meeting to re-evaluating the overarching values that brought John to therapy. As part of this re-evaluation, they reviewed what John's avoidance had cost him in his relationships with his children and his wife, and in terms of his deteriorating job performance and waning commitment to his National Guard service. He felt an especially strong sense of loss about not spending quality time with his children anymore, so John's therapist led him in an experiential exploration of this. She asked John to remember a moment of connection he'd had with his children before ever being deployed for the flood recovery mission, and he identified an afternoon they'd spent together at the pool. She asked him to contact the sights, sounds, and other sensations associated with that moment as he had connected with his children emotionally and engaged in physical displays of affection as they played together. John started crying as he contacted the memory, and the therapist helped him slow down, rather than quickly moving away from that pain and sense of lost innocence. She asked him to sit with the memory for a few minutes without attaching new verbal content to it. Then she asked him to put words on his values related to being a caring father and asked, "What if doing this hard work between sessions could help you get closer to once again being able to give and receive love with your children on a regular basis?" John readily agreed that moving toward this value would be worth the discomfort of his therapy homework and committed to following through before the next session. John and his therapist continued with cognitive processing therapy after that, but with a modification in which they spent 10 to 15 minutes reconnecting to John's most important values at the beginning of each session. Engaging in this way allowed him to more openly practice willingness to the responses that were brought up both during therapy and between sessions.

# Sequelae of Child Sexual Abuse

Jill, a 53-year-old woman who works at home as a bookkeeper, sought therapy because of chronic emotional distress due to persistent feelings of emptiness and hollowness. When she arrived at her first session, she reported that during her childhood she'd been sexually abused by her father for several years, and that she'd been in and out of therapy for most of her adult life. She said that she had engaged in self-injury when she was in her 20s and 30s, but eventually stopped because she believed it wasn't working as a distraction anymore, and because people stared at the scars on her arms anytime she didn't wear long sleeves. She reported that she'd been diagnosed with PTSD, depression, and borderline personality disorder at different times in her life.

When the therapist asked Jill why she was coming for therapy again now, she said that she'd started drinking more over the past several months whenever she began to feel emotionally dysregulated or numb. Initially, she started drinking after work as a way of calming down after a stressful day. However, because she worked at home, there weren't clear boundaries on her workday, and she was starting to drink increasingly early—as early as 3:00 p.m. if she didn't have any business calls after that time. She'd finally decided it was a problem when she realized she was having trouble resisting pouring herself a glass of wine at lunch.

Jill's therapist felt it would be important to conduct a functional analysis of what was prompting and maintaining Jill's current drinking behavior. At first, Jill identified stress as the antecedent. However, further exploration of exactly when the drinking started becoming more problematic revealed that two major events during the past two months had probably contributed to her emotional dysregulation. First, she'd had a falling-out with her best friend over a trip they'd been planning, because Jill found out that her friend had purchased tickets to go on the trip with another friend instead. This left Jill feeling extremely angry, sad, and resentful, and as a result, Jill was spending an hour or two each day rereading old emails and texts to ensure that she was justified in feeling angry. Around that same time, Jill also found out that her father, from whom she'd been estranged for many years, had recently passed away. She said she still hated him and was glad he was dead, but that somehow his death had left her feeling emotionally numb in a way she hadn't experienced in a long time, and she didn't know how to manage that.

As Jill's therapist attempted to further explore how Jill's history of sexual abuse had affected her as an adult, Jill dissociated several times, and each time it took several minutes for her to fully return to the present moment. When asked about her dissociation, Jill reported that although she hadn't thought about it, she believed she'd also been dissociating at home sporadically over the past two months, because she sometimes lost time during the day. Further exploration revealed that these gaps of time seemed to co-occur with her feelings of numbness, and that they seemed to be associated with an increased likelihood of giving in to urges to drink in an effort to move away from the numbness, which was highly aversive to her.

Based on this functional analysis, Jill's therapist hypothesized that Jill had a skills deficit in terms of being able to stay in the moment in the presence of feelings of emptiness and numbness. Furthermore, several of her other exacerbated symptoms, including interpersonal sensitivity, emotional avoidance, and alcohol misuse (which was conceptualized as a self-harm behavior) were consistent with her previous diagnosis of borderline personality disorder. He suggested that it could be very useful for Jill to work through a series of distress tolerance skills from dialectical behavior therapy, which is designed for individuals diagnosed with borderline personality disorder, and grounding skills from seeking safety, a therapeutic approach that includes training in skills for coping with challenges related to both PTSD and substance misuse. He explained that these skills could increase Jill's ability to remain mindfully in the present moment, even when under stress. Jill said that she'd engaged in dialectical behavior therapy in the past and had found parts of it helpful, and said she was willing to try the approach the therapist outlined.

If you're familiar with the distress tolerance skills in dialectical behavior therapy and the grounding skills in seeking safety, you may wonder about incorporating them with ACT, given that they appear to promote avoidance, which would seem to be antithetical to an ACT approach. And indeed, some of these skills are sometimes applied in an avoidant sort of way. So as Jill's therapist introduced these skills, he was careful to point out this potential discrepancy, and then said that, as with many things in life, this wasn't a black-and-white issue in which acceptance is good and avoidance is bad. Then he presented an alternative view in which behaviors that move a person in valued directions (or that at least don't move the person in the opposite direction) can be considered to be effective, even if they're functionally avoidant in the short term. So, for Jill, using nonproblematic distraction skills such as watching a video, going for a walk, or running her hands under warm water may function as avoidance in the moment, but if they help her get through a difficult moment without drinking alcohol or dissociating, they would be considered effective in moving her toward her values over time.

Jill liked this approach and appreciated the idea that she could avoid how she was feeling at times. So she and her therapist worked together to find new, nonproblematic ways for Jill to cope with difficult emotional states while they worked toward the longer-term goal of helping her acquire the skills she would need to be able to mindfully accept and contact those same emotions in the future.

# Depression

James, age 45, had recently gone through a divorce and had partial custody of his 8-year-old daughter. He had been married since graduating from college and was now living alone for the first time in his life. He sought therapy nine months after the divorce and reported feelings of hopelessness and loneliness. Since the divorce, he had significantly reduced his activity level and had stopped socializing with friends and colleagues outside of work. He said it was too awkward to engage in the same sorts of social activities he used to enjoy, because now he was always the odd man out, without a spouse or partner, and because he was tired of fielding questions from concerned friends about how he was doing and when he was going to start dating again. For the most part, he'd stopped responding to texts or emails from friends asking him to get together, and he'd even quit going to the gym and hockey games, which he used to really enjoy. James told the therapist that he just wanted to get past this time in his life and expressed passive suicidality in which he hoped every night when he went to bed that he would not wake up in the morning.

Because of James's significantly reduced engagement in activities and how this coincided with his depression, his therapist thought he could benefit from behavioral activation. This approach was further supported by James's assertion that he really didn't want to talk about his ex-wife or the divorce. Behavioral activation would instead create a focus on changing his actions to overcome his depression, without requiring that he be willing to undertake deep emotional reflection. However, because James appeared to be relatively emotionally cut off as part of his depression, his therapist thought it would be useful to engage in a values clarification exercise before making specific behavioral activation commitments.

James's therapist guided him through a version of the classic ACT bull's-eye exercise (Lundgren et al., 2012), asking James to choose several life domains in which he had strong values, and then marking a bull's-eye diagram to indicate how closely his current actions aligned with his values in each of those domains. This exercise revealed a major discrepancy between James's values related to physical health, social relationships, and family relationships and his current actions in each of these areas. This baseline understanding gave James's therapist a touchstone to return to throughout the behavioral activation process, both when identifying committed action goals and in overcoming barriers to executing those actions. James and his therapist worked together to set multiple targets for behavioral activation, starting with small goals, and then reviewing his progress each week.

Over time, through a combination of increased physical activity and more consistent engagement in committed action, James started participating in activities he cared about on a regular basis again. His mood also began to improve, but at the end of treatment, James stated that what he cared about wasn't so much the level of his depressive symptoms, but that he wasn't just sitting around and allowing his feelings of loneliness to run his life anymore. He thought he might be willing to consider dating again sometime soon, and in the meantime, he was going to work on getting back in shape at the gym and enjoying watching his local hockey team again.

# Serious Mental Illness

Fred, age 25, had been diagnosed with schizophrenia at the age of 23. He'd been hospitalized five times in the past two years for his psychotic symptoms, as he, his psychiatrist, and his family worked to identify the medication regimen that was most helpful in reducing his positive symptoms (hallucinations, delusions, racing thoughts) to a less disruptive level. During those two years, Fred had regularly denied that he was having any problems, and he didn't think a diagnosis of schizophrenia fit him. As a result, he wasn't reliable about taking his medications and tried to get out of going to treatment appointments or case management meetings whenever possible. Because of his inconsistent follow-through, his progress hadn't been straightforward, and his problematic behaviors had contributed to increased stress and conflict within his family.

Finally, Fred agreed to try a combination of individual therapy and group social skills training, an approach that had been repeatedly recommended to him by his treatment team. His primary motivation was that his mother had told him that he couldn't continue to live with her if he didn't follow through with treatment, and he didn't know where else he could live. During Fred's first session with the new therapist, the therapist noted that Fred didn't appear to be actively psychotic; however, she felt that Fred was at risk of losing quite a bit of stability if he couldn't accept his current diagnosis and circumstances, and so she suggested that ACT would be an appropriate form of individual therapy to try as a starting point to complement the social skills training and medication management.

After describing the proposed treatment and obtaining Fred's consent, the therapist asked Fred how he thought he had gotten to this point and what his current major concerns were. Fred was able to give a fairly detailed report about how he started thinking that his neighbor was trying to poison him, and the behaviors that belief had led to. As he talked about the situation, he became more energized and highly focused on that line of thinking. With some redirection, he was able to acknowledge that the actions that he had taken as a result of his beliefs (such as spying on his neighbor and stealing his neighbor's mail) had gotten him in trouble, and that he was now in a situation where he might not be able to keep living with his family if he couldn't approach the situation in a different way.

Over the next two sessions, Fred's therapist worked with him in two parallel directions. First, she helped him explore his values: what was important to him and what he wanted his life to be about. For the past two years, several of Fred's treatment providers had fallen into the trap of "thinking small," encouraging Fred to take his medication and go to treatment but not providing him with hope that his life could be about much more than symptom management. In fact, this explained part of Fred's resistance to treatment thus far; he'd been unwilling to accept the diagnosis of schizophrenia, because it felt like if he did, he also had to accept that his life was going to be constricted to staying home, managing his symptoms, and trying not to upset others. And to a large extent, this had happened, leading to significant feelings of loneliness. Fred also wasn't totally convinced, even when he was taking his medications, that there wasn't something shady going on at his neighbor's house.

Based on all of this, Fred's therapist chose not to address treatment adherence head-on and instead focused on what Fred wanted his life to be about, including inquiring into what he had wanted two or three years ago, before his current problems started. Fred hadn't spent much time as an adult exploring what his hopes and desires were because he'd been a very young adult when his major symptoms developed, and because he now had a persistent sense that his life seemed to be getting smaller and smaller. After spending some time on values clarification, he was able to identify that he had always enjoyed spending time with his little brother, who was 10 years younger than him, but that over the past two years, he hadn't done much of that; instead, he'd been spending most of his time in his room, because he felt judged by his family and didn't want to be around them if they were thinking of him as crazy. He also talked about how he missed his job at a movie theater: he missed spending time with the friends he worked with there, and he missed getting to see the movies before anyone else. He also said that over the past year, he'd been sneaking beers out of the refrigerator whenever he could. Unfortunately, when he drank, he was more likely to start talking about his beliefs about the neighbor, and then his younger brother would start avoiding him because he didn't know what to do when Fred started talking that way.

After identifying several major values-based goals (spending time with his brother, working at the movie theater with his friends, being able to continue to live at home), Fred's therapist worked with him to determine whether Fred might see engaging in treatment (both psychosocial and medication treatments) as a way of taking action in the service of his values, rather than as something he had to do because he was "crazy." They explored these forms of committed action both as a way of contacting positive things that Fred wanted in his life (such as more quality time with his brother, and seeing whether he could get his job at the theater back), as well as avoiding the potential costs of his current way of living (such as potentially being kicked out of his mom's house, and being avoided by his brother).

Although Fred remained somewhat skeptical that things could get better, he was willing to make small commitments to treatment adherence over the next few weeks to see how things would go. Over the previous two years, he had learned that people became concerned and uncomfortable when he talked candidly about the thoughts he was having and the things that bothered him. However, as his therapist began to gain his trust, Fred started to share some of his concerns that his medications might actually be making his symptoms worse, and also shared his belief that only crazy people have to take meds. Fred eventually told his therapist that he was afraid he would never get better and that there would never be anything good about his life. Fred's therapist worked with him on defusing from the thoughts he was buying into around medications and his own self-stigma—mental content that wasn't helping him move forward. She also worked to help Fred experientially understand that his symptoms didn't make him "crazy," and that having negative thoughts about his neighbor wasn't the problem. She used an exercise in which she had him make a number of statements (such as "I can't raise my arm," and "I can't move across the room"), try as hard as he could to believe those statements were true, and then engage in the opposite behavior. Practicing this experientially helped Fred to see that it wasn't simply the thoughts that he had that led him to make problematic choices. Instead, his fusion with those thoughts and his belief that he had to act on them was what had been getting him into trouble.

As they continued their work together, Fred was able to make commitments not just to being compliant with his treatment, but also to actions that were more intrinsically reinforcing to him, like reaching out to the friends he'd worked with at the theater. He wanted to see if there was any way he could get his job back, but he was concerned that his former boss knew about his hospitalizations and wouldn't rehire him. Unfortunately, clients with psychotic disorders often face environmental, logistical, or social barriers that make it more difficult for them to take certain valued actions. So rather than focusing on the specific outcome (which couldn't be predicted anyway), Fred's therapist helped him frame the act of going to the theater and talking with his boss as an expression of his social and vocational values. That way, even if the outcome was disappointing, Fred could still experience some satisfaction for taking actions aimed at exploring the possibility of creating a more values-based life, rather than staying stuck.

# Extended Case: Bipolar Disorder

Alana, age 24, is single, has no children, and lives alone. She cofounded a tech start-up company in Houston and is friendly with her coworkers but seldom socializes outside of work. When she leaves the office, she typically spends her free time working on developing apps for her company. She's a talented programmer with a flair for innovative design. Recently, her work performance has been suffering due to her moods, which have ranged from occasional mania to deep depression. During one manic episode, Alana used a company credit card to make extravagant purchases, which she felt compelled to pay back with her own savings. More recently, she'd missed work for two weeks because, as she put it, she felt "too depressed to get out of bed." Her absence caused the company to miss an important deadline. Her colleagues knew that Alana's unique talents were essential to the success of the company, and they could also see that the fluctuations in her performance were having a negative impact on the company and its entrepreneurial vision. Her colleagues eventually gathered for an intervention and suggested that Alana visit a medical doctor because she was missing work so often and was sometimes acting erratically.

Alana agreed to seek help, and her primary care physician provisionally diagnosed her with bipolar I disorder and suggested that she start seeing a psychiatrist. Though resistant to the idea, she reluctantly went to the psychiatrist suggested by the primary care physician a few weeks later. The psychiatrist prescribed a mood stabilizer, and after Alana had been taking it for a few weeks, it seemed to be effective in reducing the wide mood fluctuations. However, during a routine follow-up session with her psychiatrist, Alana reported that she was considering quitting the medication because her company needed more of her creativity, and she missed the enhanced energy levels the mania had given her. Her psychiatrist responded by explaining that adhering to her medication regimen would help Alana meet her occupational goals more effectively in the long run, and suggested that she see a behavioral therapist for assistance in medication adherence and to help her with some of her other choices and habits. She sought a second opinion from her primary care physician, and he agreed that behavior therapy would be helpful for her.

During the first session with the behavior therapist, Alana agreed to participate in interpersonal and social rhythm therapy (IPSRT; Frank et al., 1994, 2005), an evidence-based therapy with modest research support for treatment of bipolar disorder (APA, 2016). IPSRT utilizes the interpersonal psychotherapy approach (IPT; Klerman, Weissman, Rounsaville, & Chevron, 1984) to reduce relationship conflicts and blends in behavioral techniques to help clients develop healthier social rhythms by creating improved daily routines and adhering to medication regimens. In addition, IPSRT attempts to modulate biological and psychosocial factors to decrease circadian and sleep-wake cycle vulnerabilities, improve functional repertoires, and manage the symptoms of bipolar disorder. These various components were introduced to Alana over the course of the next several sessions.

The interpersonal psychotherapy portion of IPSRT focuses on treating four areas of social functioning: role disputes (experiencing substantial relational conflict), role transition (going through an important life change), complicated bereavement (losing a significant relationship), and interpersonal deficits (having impoverished social skills).

Alana's therapist noticed that she was mostly struggling with a problematic role transition that arose when the start-up was founded. Alana went from being a computer science student in graduate school to taking a leadership role at a company aiming for international success in a burgeoning field. Alana wasn't used to people counting on her, or to the stress of the fast-paced world of entrepreneurialism. There was pressure from her teammates, the venture capitalists who'd invested in the company, and the company's competition. Most of all, Alana was putting a great deal of pressure on herself to be successful. Given this stressful role transition and Alana's sense that so much was dependent on her alone, the therapist leveraged IPT techniques by creating a solid treatment alliance, empathically engaging Alana during sessions and making sure she felt understood. Beyond the general expectation of building a strong therapeutic alliance in any therapy, these are all key aspects of IPT—and therefore IPSRT—and they're also helpful common factors in most psychotherapy approaches, including ACT.

Alana's therapist thought incorporating ACT into the IPSRT could be helpful, so he recommended to her that he weave in some ACT-based concepts. She agreed this could be helpful. For example, he brought in the concept of acceptance to help Alana deal with the stressful emotions accompanying her role transition. He also taught Alana that feeling "too depressed to get out of bed" is a private event one can willingly experience without acting on it—identifying several instances of other times she had had powerful thoughts or feelings that she hadn't followed. Furthermore, they explored how Alana's attempts to avoid her depression and other emotions related to her role transition issues might actually be exacerbating her uncomfortable emotions. The more Alana attempted to avoid the stressful experience of depression, the worse it became. The therapist suggested that even in the presence of difficult emotions related to her role transition, Alana could continue to engage in values-based actions.

This approach naturally led to an exploration of Alana's values. In the course of an ACT values clarification exercise, Alana realized that she was genuinely motivated by innovation and making the world a better place through her inventions. She articulated that her chosen values were related to advancing applications in technology so other people would benefit. Her therapist highlighted the dialectic between truly caring about following through on important, personally relevant values and the fact that engaging in such behaviors was likely to provoke uncomfortable emotions. He then suggested that Alana's values could dignify a goal of accepting her difficult emotions and make those choices meaningful. In addition, the therapist suggested that verbally articulating what was important to her in her life (her values) could change the context of her depressive feelings, even if the feelings didn't diminish.

Alana's therapist also taught her several mindfulness exercises (such as the "leaves on the stream" exercise) and asked her to experiment with a daily practice of contacting the present moment and accepting any sensations or emotions that arose during her practice. From the therapist's point of view, the purpose of the exercises was to increase Alana's psychological flexibility, help her be present with her emotions instead of countertherapeutically avoiding them, and facilitate engaging in values-based actions even in the presence of stress and tension. And in a very real sense, practicing mindfulness daily could help Alana learn how to make and keep commitments.

Although all of these approaches were somewhat helpful, Alana continued to report that the pressure of running the start-up was "too much to take." She also said that every time she was stymied by a programming issue, she berated herself for being stupid, which led her to give up on the task and ruminate on her pessimistic and depressive thoughts. After she acknowledged the strength of these thoughts, the therapist taught Alana several defusion techniques, highlighting that defusion is related to the mindfulness exercise they had been practicing of watching thoughts as if they were leaves floating down a stream. He pointed out that distancing herself from her thoughts wasn't just part of the mindfulness exercises she was doing in her daily practice, but also a skill applicable to the problematic role transition thoughts she was having throughout the day. Then he invited Alana to apply the three skills she was strengthening with her daily mindfulness practices—acceptance, contacting the present moment, and defusion—to her values-based committed actions related to work.

Alana said she could see the merit of this approach, so she and her therapist worked together collaboratively to develop measurable goals related to the IPSRT treatment plan, using her ACT skills to increase her commitment. They initially chose two clinically relevant actions: adhering to her medication regimen and following a healthy activity and sleep schedule. Alana's therapist conceptualized both of those clinically relevant behaviors as committed actions in the traditional ACT model and pulled from the rest of the model to support Alana in following through.

## Adhering to a Medication Regimen

Based on the literature, Alana's therapist believed that Alana could optimize her behavioral health by continuing to take her mood stabilizers as prescribed. They were part of the evidence-based therapy for bipolar disorder, and Alana did seem to benefit from pharmacotherapy. Unfortunately (but not unexpectedly), she continued to think that she'd be more creative and productive if she were to have mania experiences again. In response, the therapist revisited the defusion skills Alana had been using for her self-talk about being stupid and about the stress being too much to take, and guided her in applying those same defusion skills to her thoughts about discontinuing the medication. The therapist first normalized these private verbalizations by sharing firsthand accounts written by other individuals who had been diagnosed with bipolar disorder and had similar feelings about their medications. He also reminded Alana that she could simply notice that she's having those thoughts without acting on them, and he pointed her back to the mindfulness exercises they had been practicing together.

Based on the ACT model as well as Alana's direct experience, it was obvious that Alana could not control whether or not she would have those unhelpful thoughts. In fact, she experienced reinforcing consequences for some behaviors occurring during a manic phase, so it's reasonable her self-talk (relational framing) would influence her to seek out opportunities to gain from those manic experiences again. At the same time, Alana's therapist believed she might benefit from taking a broader perspective on her disorder. Her therapist aimed to help her recognize that if she went off medication, she might act so erratically during a manic episode that it would have a damaging impact on her company, and such damage could surpass whatever innovation she *might* create. In addition, she might also experience significant depression, which could actually reduce her productivity and harm her company even further.

The therapist also leveraged acceptance in regard to Alana's complaints that the medication was quashing the creativity she felt when manic. He revisited the concept they had worked on earlier, that acceptance is about actively allowing feelings to be present or absent, and continuing to act in a meaningful, purposeful manner. He asked Alana whether she could choose to predicate her choices on her values, rather than her feelings. Throughout therapy, whenever Alana referred to the presence or absence of emotions as obstacles to action, her therapist pointed out that her values around innovation and making the world a better place might help motivate her to get back to work, no matter what her feelings were.

On one occasion, Alana countered with the statement, "Fine, but I'll just accept the highs and the lows without the medication!" The therapist was able to understand the impulse behind this assertion, yet conceptualized this as a misunderstanding of how acceptance works in treatment. (For context, Hayes et al., 1999, define acceptance as "actively contacting psychological experiences, directly, fully without needless defense"; given the biological concomitants of bipolar disorder, and Alana's desire to engage in committed actions, perhaps taking the medication was a *needed defense*.) Based on that conceptualization, after acknowledging that he could understand where she was coming from, the therapist replied, "How workable is your strategy to simply accept your wide mood swings? Have you ever been able to demonstrate to yourself that you can accept your feelings and follow through in a consistent way on your values-based goals when you're markedly depressed, or even when you're in a manic phase? As far as I can tell, the medication assists you in reducing the intensity of your moods. Yes, we've been working together very well on acceptance, yet it isn't a panacea. It will be much easier for you to live with your mood fluctuations if they aren't varying so widely and intensely." This tack helped Alana agree to keep taking her medication for a while, albeit reluctantly.

Still, the topic came up again in a subsequent session, when Alana said, "Taking lithium just screams, 'I'm bipolar and something is wrong with me!' I don't want to have something wrong with me that makes me need to be medicated for the rest of my life." The therapist saw this as an ideal time to talk about self-as-context, suggesting: "What if you aren't 'bipolar?' You experience fluctuating moods due to a medical condition. You are not your disorder. You are simply you—a person here on this planet right now.

There are lots of ways you could label yourself. Consider saying 'I'm bipolar' the same way you might say 'I'm blonde' or 'I'm five-foot-seven.' Those are just things about your physicality, stuff that was given to you genetically. But none of those things defines you in entirety. The same goes with your emotions and your roles and your thoughts. You are not 'depressed,' or 'a programmer,' or 'a bad cofounder.'" Each time the therapist mentioned a label, he would gesture "scare quotes" with his fingers to emphasize that they were simply various words. The therapist continued, "You are simply you, and you have lots of different characteristics. Please consider caution with all your self-talk and judgments about yourself."

Alana retorted, "Okay, but when is this ever going to go away? These meds don't clear it up, like taking penicillin for pneumonia. This bipolar stuff is supposedly going to be with me forever!" That naturally led to a discussion about present-moment awareness. "You're correct that the medication won't change the fact that you experience the symptoms of this disorder, but staying on the medication will help you stabilize your moods as long as you're on it. They won't cure you, but they will help you in the present moment. And your life is *here, now.* You can only experience this moment. That's what the mindfulness exercises have been about: being in the present. Your worry and anger about how 'this stuff' is supposedly 'forever' is taking you out of the present moment and making you even more upset. And when you get more upset, it riles up your moods and influences you to shut down or act erratically. I understand your pain and I feel for you…and you're turning your pain into suffering by focusing on 'forever.' Let's work together to help you focus on *now,* because now is the only time you can do the things that you care about. If you want to live in the direction of your values, consider focusing on committing to actions that you can do now. One of those commitments can be doing your programming. Another commitment can be keeping yourself healthy with your medication."

As you can see, in these interactions, Alana's therapist walked her through defusion, acceptance, self-as-context, values, and contact with the present moment—all in the service of engaging in the committed action of taking her medication.

## Following a Healthy Activity and Sleep Schedule

Regarding Alana's second goal, following a healthy activity and sleep schedule, this strategy is critical for maintaining mood stability in bipolar disorder, and it's a key target of IPSRT's social rhythm component. Research suggests that there's a connection between daily routine disruptions and mood destabilization in bipolar disorder (Malkoff-Schwartz et al. 1998), so the behavioral component of IPSRT aims to stabilize circadian rhythms, and particularly to design sleep patterns that can help prevent manic episodes (Frank, Swartz, & Kupfer, 2000).

To that end, IPSRT clinicians utilize social zeitgeber theory (*zeitgeber* is German for "time giver" or "synchronizer" and in this context refers to environmental cues that affect biological rhythms). Therapists treating bipolar disorder can help clients attain greater harmony in their lives by encouraging them to pay close attention to zeitgebers and disciplining themselves to follow a regular schedule so there is less chaos in their lives.

In order to create more regularity in bipolar clients' schedules, IPSRT uses a self-report assessment called the Social Rhythm Metric, which is available in two versions: a nine-item version (SRM; Monk et al., 1990) and a five-item version (SRM-II; Monk et al., 1990). In the five-item version, clients record when they wake up, when they first have contact with another person, when they begin a significant valued activity, when they eat dinner, and when they go to bed. Alana's therapist requested that she complete the SRM-II every day, and asked her to generally attend to her zeitgebers more mindfully.

During her first week of tracking, Alana realized that she tended to start working early in the morning and often was still at it late at night. Because, as an entrepreneur, she didn't punch the clock, there was a great deal of variability in when she first had contact with another person (typically a coworker), and her dinnertime fluctuated chaotically from day to day. When Alana's therapist suggested that she adjust her routine to support her wellness, Alana resisted, saying, "But when you run a start-up, anything can happen. I have to be ready for lots of changes at all times of the day or night." The therapist employed techniques from interpersonal therapy to show his understanding, and also encouraged Alana to make some small changes, especially to her sleep schedule.

Her reply to this suggestion was similar: "I'd like to go to sleep at a regularly scheduled time, but I have a lot to do." It seemed that Alana was fused with thoughts about the demands on her time, so he responded with the classic Get Off Your Buts exercise (Zettle, 2007, pp. 178–179) to help Alana defuse from her rigid rule that being busy prevented her from engaging in good sleep hygiene: "Alana, I'm going to encourage you to say, 'I'd like to go to sleep at a regularly scheduled time, *and* I have a lot to do.' It's almost impossible to accomplish everything you have to do. Entrepreneurship and inventing are values to live by, again and again, not goals to complete...*and* you can still commit to sleeping well so that you're refreshed and less prone to mood shifts, which could really hurt your productivity in the long haul."

"Okay," Alana replied, "but—I mean, *and*—I am just not one of these goody-two-shoes that goes to bed early."

The therapist said, "This isn't about going to bed early. This is about gaining some regularity in your lifestyle...And we've talked about the problem of attaching your identity to particular labels about yourself. When you say stuff like 'I'm a programmer' or 'I'm depressed,' it limits your flexibility in following through on your values. The same goes for 'I am not a goody-two-shoes.' Resisting taking care of yourself because it doesn't fit with your self-concept may not serve you very well."

Alana responded, "The problem is, as soon as I put my head down on the pillow, I'll be thinking about everything I have to do the next day."

Again, Alana's therapist responded by reminding her of some of the ACT skills she'd been learning: "Then that would be a perfect time for you to practice the mindfulness skills that you've been working on. There's some research showing that mindfulness practices can assist with sleeping. You know about contacting the present moment. Practice it then. Notice those thoughts about the next day, and then bring yourself back to the here and now with your breathing. Link that set of mindful behaviors to your values. Remember what you care about in this world—your ideas and inventions—and see if you can commit to good sleep hygiene in the service of those things."

Alana retorted, "You're making this sound easy. This isn't going to be easy for me."

Her therapist replied in a way that's consistent with both IPSRT and ACT: "I'm not trying to imply that this is easy. I care for you, and I'm not denying your struggle. I'm simply inviting you to try out a new approach to your lifestyle. You've shared with me about your difficulties with your moods. You've described some behaviors that you're concerned about. I'm concerned too, and I want to help you. I'm suggesting you consider changing the rhythm of your day to assist you in following through on your values. Can you make some commitments to your health and to your own well-being? I really think that will serve you greatly—not only in dealing with the mood fluctuations, but also with your values related to your work."

Because bipolar disorder is a chronic behavioral health problem, Alana and her therapist are likely to engage in similar interactions time and time again. However, integrating ACT with IPSRT, and using that approach to help Alana comply with her medication regimen and maintain a more regular schedule could go a long way toward improving her quality of life over time.

# Questions for Therapist Reflection

- In the case studies above, which applications of committed action interventions did you find most creative? Most powerful?

- In which case study did you see an application of ACT to committed action that didn't fit with how you would have handled the case? How would you have approached the situation differently?

- Which of the cases did you think had the best fit with an ACT approach? Are there cases you have seen where ACT would not be applicable or enhance the treatment?

- What do you think that the addition of ACT to IPSRT brought to Alana's treatment? Are there areas that you think you would have approached with more or less emphasis?

# Summary

The cases in this chapter provide practical demonstrations that ACT can be used effectively with a wide variety of clinical presentations. Sometimes, ACT is appropriate as the primary approach to the presenting problems, while other times it is more effectively integrated with other evidence-based treatment approaches. Because ACT is a conceptually-guided treatment, rather than a collection of techniques, it has broad applicability to a wide variety of cases and can readily complement and enhance other treatments, including behavioral, cognitive behavioral, interpersonal, and even pharmacotherapy treatments. Chapter 11 will attempt to bring the key points of this book together in an overarching model, as has been demonstrated clinically with these cases.

# CHAPTER 11

# Bringing It All Together

It can be argued that committed action is the sine qua non for therapeutic change. When individuals come to therapy, it is because there is some aspect of their lives that is not working, and they are looking for assistance in finding ways to address their challenges, whether those challenges are perceived to be internal or external. Most therapeutic approaches will work to conceptualize the client's presenting problem and identify what skills the client needs to learn and what actions the client needs to take. From an ACT perspective, those skills and actions are driven by the client's values, and therapy is successful if the client is able to initiate and maintain committed actions that are necessary to move life forward toward those values. Through the course of ACT, clients may gain insight; however, insight just for the sake of insight is not seen as inherently valuable. The ACT model generally only sees therapy as a success when an individual is living better, which generally requires the ability to make and keep self-generated commitments. Thus, as stated at the beginning of this book, the authors wrote this book with three goals, for its readers to better facilitate committed action in their clinical contexts by:

1. developing and increasing a repertoire of interventions that build commitment;

2. enhancing and integrating other core ACT processes that assist with implementing committed action;

3. promoting behaviors that are in the service of client-identified values related to psychological flexibility.

Regardless of which of your values was served by reading this book, if you now have a better understanding of committed action and how to work with your clients in this domain, then this book has served its purpose.

# Exercise for reflection

- What were your primary goals for reading this book?

- How did you hope it would change or improve your clinical work?

- To what extent did you consider that you would be able to benefit from improving your personal application of committed action skills in your own life?

- What were two approaches or skills that you learned for the practical implementation of committed action interventions?

- What were two principles about the process of committed action that were relevant to your experience and improving your application of these skills?

- Which two evidence-based treatments or techniques that you already use will these skills be most useful to integrate with?

Although this book is ostensibly about committed action, committed action can only be facilitated effectively by implementing all of the processes in the hexaflex. All six of the processes entail and aid the others in moving away from avoidance and fusion and toward psychological flexibility. In order to be able to successfully implement and coach committed action within this model, the effective therapist needs to be facile with all of the ACT processes. Ironically, it may be useful for the reader to examine, after reading this book, which ACT process he sees as the least relevant to committed action and explore that process further.

Commitment is not just about setting a goal and assuming that one will automatically follow through. In fact, the follow-through rarely happens smoothly and predictably. For this reason, committed action can be among the most frustrating—as well as rewarding—of the ACT processes. The ACT therapist will likely need to bring to bear all of the ACT components and additional behavioral tools in order to deal with the challenges of committed action. Furthermore, the successful coaching of committed action requires not only ACT processes and skills, but also those of a number of other evidence-based treatments for specific presenting problems. ACT-based processes and committed action skills can often supplement the evidence-based practice approaches that lead to the desired and measurable outcomes sought by the client.

# Setting a Specific Commitment

A commitment is an intended action in the direction of what an individual cares about, even in the presence of obstacles. It is the work of ACT to facilitate both setting an effective commitment in line with the client's values and following through with that commitment, even when barriers are present. In order to facilitate the setting of meaningful, prioritized targets for commitment, it is important to conduct a thorough functional assessment to assist with appropriate, relevant, and achievable goal setting. The therapist who has a strong grasp of basic behavioral principles and the ability to conduct a thorough functional analysis will best be able to identify with the client what is reinforcing and maintaining aspects of the current situation, in order to inform the targets and commitments for future behaviors.

It is not enough to simply set and state a behavioral commitment. The utility of a given commitment can be understood only within an individual's current and historical context. Similar behavioral topographies can have very different functions depending on the client's history, values, and current circumstances. For example, a target that relates primarily to symptom reduction may be considered a great success for one client, and an avoidance move for another. The same goals for committed action may function very differently for different individuals, and at different times in the life of one individual. When taken from the abstract to the concrete, a goal of reducing calorie consumption can serve a very different function for someone who has recently been diagnosed at risk for diabetes versus for someone who was berated by her mother for her weight throughout her childhood and adolescence and has struggled with disordered eating as an adult.

Even for the former example, the function of a given committed action is also influenced by the values of an individual client—the motivations behind goal setting and attainment are not one-size-fits-all. The individual who is attempting to prevent the development of a chronic obesity-related illness may commit to eating fewer calories during the day because she is motivated by a value of self-care and promoting personal physical health, or because she is motivated by the importance of her family to her and wishes to see her granddaughter grow to adulthood. It is important that the therapist not make assumptions about what the guiding values behind a given commitment are; only by exploring and understanding what is important to this client in this moment will the therapist be best able to help shape the planned behaviors that can make the committed action successful.

Therapists may find a best practice to be shaping the target commitments to be as specific and measurable as possible. Commitments are generally most successful when they are focused on targets that are related to adding or increasing valued behaviors, not decreasing or stopping unwanted behaviors. This approach allows clients to focus on what they can be doing at any given moment, rather than emphasizing the inhibition of specific behaviors, which is much more difficult to implement and shape. It is clearer how to go about doing something than it is to plan for how to not do something. It is also important to assess in which contexts the target behavior does and does not occur, in order to discover whether the commitment has successfully generalized to the contexts where it would be most relevant. Not every commitment needs to be a grand proclamation of ultimate progress; small committed actions may be part of larger patterns of committed actions, and small actions may also help prepare the person for larger committed actions.

Thus, when working on goal-setting, it can be useful to keep in mind the characteristics of SMART goals (as described in chapter 2), which are specific, measurable, attainable, relevant, and time-bound. Creating goals that are specific and measurable is consistent with basic behavioral principles and the ACT definition of a goal: one must know what the goal specifically is and how one will know whether it has been accomplished in order for it to serve as a target for behavior. Within ACT, goals that are attainable and relevant take on a slightly different metric, because they are guided by a person's values. One can pick the smallest attainable goal that is consistent with a value, and it is by definition in accordance with the value—there is no requirement that a goal be any specific size in order to be meaningful. It simply has to align with a chosen value. Similarly, "relevant" in this context means that it comports with a person's values—that is all the relevance that is required. Finally, time-bound is simply another way of making a commitment specific and perhaps more likely to be acted upon.

It is essential that the therapist and client explore potential barriers to committed action when commitments are made. The overly naïve or optimistic therapist may choose to avoid that part of the discussion for fear that it will bring an unnecessarily negative tone to the work. However, this neglect of identification of potential barriers leaves the client unprepared for such obstacles when they inevitably do arise. The assessment of potential barriers makes for more realistic preparation and may also lead to the identification of other needed committed actions.

## Steps for Planning and Executing Committed Actions

- Identify relevant values

- Designate a SMART goal or behavior that embodies the value

- Anticipate potential barriers

- Link barriers with specific ACT strategies that can be used to overcome the barriers

- Commit to taking action

- Review and reflect on the outcome of the committed action once completed (what was learned, what was new, feelings that arose after engaging in a personally valuable action

- If the action was not successfully accomplished, determine whether there was a values disconnect, whether the goal needs to be reframed or adjusted, or if there are additional barriers to committed action that need to be planned for and overcome

# Using Language to Facilitate Committed Action

Therapists often ask clients to write down or say out loud their commitments as a way of having them take ownership of the planned action. However, it is important to recognize the distinction between words and actions. Making verbal commitments can have important social and motivational functions and consequences as the client strives to maintain coherence by following through with a publicly stated goal (Villatte, Villatte, & Hayes, 2015). However, the act of making a commitment can also be based on pliance or rule-following in a way that reduces the effectiveness of the commitment. Beyond simply having the client express an intention, there is much more that the therapist can contribute to the sticking power of the committed action process. Understanding the relationship between words and actions can help with executing more effective and consistent commitments.

One very useful model for understanding the role of language in creating meaning to support committed action comes from Villatte, Villatte, and Hayes (2015). Within this model, the authors explain that by using RFT principles, language processes can be used to elaborate relational networks related to meaning. These strengthened networks can then increase a client's ability to perform committed action even when there is no immediate source of satisfaction present for doing so. Through the process of values clarification and identification, the client is able to create and elaborate abstract symbolic relations with her committed actions that can both provide satisfaction in the present and guide action through to the future. Through the lens of RFT, Villatte and colleagues suggest that imbuing our committed actions with values helps us find intrinsic and inexhaustible sources of satisfaction for engaging in those behaviors, regardless of the immediate outcome. By doing this, the actions are transformed based on relational networks that have personal meaning to the individual, and the more personally meaningful the actions are to the client, the more likely she is to initiate and persist in the behavior.

Within this RFT-based approach to values and commitment, there is a specific focus on building hierarchical networks that link a desired overarching direction and specific actions with the immediate targets for behavioral commitments. Linking the behavior to the individual's values should be done 1) during goal setting, 2) at the time of the committed action, and 3) when debriefing how the committed action went afterward. This approach makes the process of engaging in the behavior more likely to be reinforcing without being dependent on a conditional outcome.

The skillful ACT therapist can use verbal behavior around values to help motivate and maintain action, even in the absence of immediate reinforcement. However, due to the power of language, cognitive fusion with the words that a client experiences to be "in her head" can also create significant barriers to following through with commitments. For example, fusion with self as content can reduce behavioral flexibility and prevent one from coming into contact with values-directed life experiences.

# The Essential Role of Values in Committed Action

Within functional contextualism, the effectiveness of a given committed action can be measured only against a person's values. In order for committed actions to be guided by a client's values, it is important to have a clear understanding of what is meant by values: verbally construed, global, desired life consequences for a given individual. By fully elucidating the client's relevant values, the therapist and client will be most effective together at setting appropriate and meaningful targets for commitment. Values provide the principle to be followed and the guiding direction, while taking committed action makes those values concrete. Using values exploration as part of the treatment planning process supports following through on goals, because the targets can then be framed in a hierarchical way with personally relevant reinforcers. This step is essential, because although some committed actions are desirable and simple enough for the client to initiate without much trouble, many other commitments bring up uncomfortable private events or do not provide any immediate source of reinforcement. Many obstacles to engaging in committed actions can be overcome by continually relating the chosen behaviors to the client's stated valued directions. Fortunately, ACT has several processes and techniques to directly address those obstacles in the service of effective action.

# Increasing the Likelihood of Successful Committed Action

In addition to addressing potential barriers to committed action, there are also steps that individuals can take in a proactive direction that can increase the likelihood of successful follow-through. As described throughout this book, it is important that the client set a specific and meaningful intention for action. A vague or general plan for moving forward is much less likely to succeed than a specific intention that is clearly articulated. Thus, saying the intention out loud, writing it down on a piece of paper, or putting it in an electronic to-do list can facilitate action. The client can also consider whether it might be helpful to enlist the support of other people who can shore up his resources if he is wavering on his intention. This may include coming up with a specific plan to ask someone for help or support, or simply communicating the intention to another person (not necessarily the therapist), in order to increase a sense of accountability. It is important that this not slip into pliance so that the client is following through on a commitment just for social approval, but more as a way of reminding the person that he has chosen something that is important to him. Individuals can also experiment with different ways of using memory aids to increase the likelihood that they follow through with committed actions. This may include basic steps like writing a sticky note and posting it somewhere that will be likely to serve as a reminder, or setting an alarm on the client's phone, or setting a photo that serves as a reminder of a key value as the digital wallpaper on the client's phone or computer.

When planning for implementing committed action, it can be very helpful to look into the future for inspiration and to reflect on times when the client has encountered obstacles to successful action in the past in order to increase the likelihood of success with the current process. However, no matter how useful those past lessons may be, in the end, committed action can happen only in the present moment. When possible, the therapist can look for opportunities to use the therapy session itself as the crucible to practice the needed skills to overcome barriers to effective action. In order to facilitate this, the therapist should develop a treatment plan in conjunction with the client that has specific, measurable outcomes. The therapist can then work with the client to use acceptance, defusion, perspective-taking, and mindfulness skills to increase the likelihood of the successful implementation of committed action that is in the service of a client's own values. There are a variety of barriers that can get in the way of a client engaging in committed action. Thus, a focused committed action process in ACT is most effective when supported by and combined with other core ACT processes that are specifically designed to address those barriers.

# Special Issues in Facilitating Committed Action

Even when the core processes of commitment and follow-through are understood at a conceptual level by the therapist and the client, unique situations will arise that will challenge the effectiveness of the committed action tools discussed in this text. Throughout therapy, it is important that the therapist underscore with the client that committed action skills are a way of living that will help her build a life of value, rather than simply being a set of circumscribed tools that were employed in response to a specific set of presenting problems. The therapist can promote generalization of learning by pointing out the application and relative success of committed actions across situations and contexts, which can help the client see that the skills are the same regardless of the content or size of the commitment required. It is essential for this generalization to new and future contexts that the client experience a sense of agency about the steps that she has taken. Even when external factors have an influence on progress, the client should still be encouraged to take responsibility for the choices she has made. For example, a client who takes medication alongside psychotherapy may sometimes attribute improvement to the medication rather than anything she has done. In such a case, the therapist would encourage the client to reflect on the fact that consistent compliance with pharmacotherapy requires daily committed action. Thus, even if there is an overt biological influence, the client still has made a difference in how that agent has worked for her. The therapist can then work on generalizing the committed action skills related to taking medication as prescribed to other valued behaviors that could be helpful to the client.

There may be other times when it is hard for either the therapist or the client to know how to go forward with committed action in the face of specific challenges. Skills for dealing with the times when either feels stuck were explored in chapters 6 and 7 and may bear frequent revisiting. One form that feeling stuck can take is the sense that a client may have that he has values that conflict with one another in some way (such as the ubiquitous "work-life balance" issue). At these times, the therapist can remind the client that we all have a variety of values that are important to us, and the relative importance of those values can wax and wane over time. Just because we prioritize one area at one moment doesn't mean that we refute the other values that may seem to be in conflict. It is perfectly natural to trade off in terms of which value takes precedence at a given moment.

This sort of conflict can be heightened in times of crisis. For example, if a client being treated for PTSD has had a death of someone close to her, the focus of therapy may shift for a period of time. Committed actions may temporarily turn more to self-care actions and a commitment to seeking support from others. However, it is important not to automatically allow crises or shifts in functioning (as with suicidality) to derail the work more than is truly necessary. Many times, the pressing issue can be addressed with sensitivity, while still staying focused on what the client can do to follow through on whatever needs to be done to garner the support and strength that the client needs to get through the crisis situation, and still moving forward with the treatment plan.

The final piece of committed action work to be planned in the therapeutic process arises in the context of therapy termination. If the therapist has been mindfully and overtly promoting the role of committed action throughout treatment, then there has been ample time to teach the process of commitment and follow-through. Thus, as the dyad approaches termination, there can be clear discussions about how to ensure that the client is able to continue to make progress with committed action after committed action even once therapy is over. It can often be useful to have the client write out her most important values, a way of remembering the steps of committed action that resonates for her, and a set of intermediate commitments that can carry her forward to progress in the months following termination.

# Pulling the ACT Core Processes Together: The Case of Mike

Mike is a 56-year-old man who struggled with substance use problems for much of his adult life and has now been sober for 14 months. One of the costs of his substance use was that he became estranged from his two children, who are now in their early 20s. Working with his therapist, he has identified that a value that is of very high importance to him is doing what he can to be an attentive father and reestablish a relationship with his children. Through an assessment of goals, actions, and barriers, he notes that several committed actions that he can take are calling his children on a regular basis, asking them to join him for a meal once a month, and asking about their current jobs and relationships so that he can get to know them better as young adults. Over the course of several discussions, these (and similar) actions are placed in a hierarchical network with connecting with his children. As this network is clarified and elaborated, the individual actions take on a deeper meaning.

For example, asking about his daughter's job (and really listening to the answer) is no longer just about making small talk, but is in the service of a higher purpose for him. Furthermore, even when he doesn't get a response, calling or texting his son is intrinsically reinforced, because it is in the service of his fatherly values. Thus, not every action needs to immediately provide a desired outcome. Even when a values-based action does not receive any immediate response or potentially goes slightly awry, Mike's therapist reminds him that he took action that was consistent with his most important value. Having this debriefing discussion strengthens similar responses in the future even if the current exemplar was not immediately gratifying. This comes in very handy, given the intermittently reinforcing nature of life! This approach also allows for alternatives—although the initial commitment he made was to asking his children to join him for a meal, if his daughter is out of town for several weeks, he can still take committed action toward a similar purpose by sending a card that will be waiting for her when she returns home. The form of the behavior is not important—it is the function of reaching out to maintain connection that matters. In fact, by generating as much variability in potential committed actions with the same functions as possible, the therapist can help ensure that Mike will never lack for something he can do in a given moment that is in the service of strengthening his father-child relationships.

In order to help make this point, the therapist can even gamify the goal-setting process in a given session. For example, the therapist could set a timer, and the therapist-client dyad could spend 60 seconds coming up with as many rapid-fire ideas as they can for behaviors consistent with his fathering values. They could then do this a second time, coming up with only behaviors that the children need not be aware of (for example, reading about topics of interest to his daughter, following his son's favorite football team, or writing down his favorite memories of their childhoods). They could then do this a third time, coming up with ridiculous or silly ideas that are still in line with this value. The goal of the exercise is not simply to identify concrete, practical committed actions that will definitely be undertaken. The goal is to teach the flexible and creative process of identifying values-consistent committed actions that can be executed at any time or in any circumstance. Goal setting does not always have to be serious and heavy—it can also be playful and generative. This work of repeated committed action incorporates all of the skills in the ACT treatment model:

*Acceptance*: In Mike's case, sometimes when he reaches out to his son, his son may not call him back. If the goal is Mike taking valued behaviors, then he can create intrinsic reinforcement for these actions by reminding himself that he has followed through with a commitment based on his values. This does not take away the sadness and disappointment he may feel if he doesn't hear from his son, but being willing to openly experience his sadness and disappointment makes it less likely that he will need to engage in avoidant and problematic behaviors.

*Defusion*: Mike may be fused with evaluations about how he has "ruined" his chances with his children, and likely will need to practice defusion around recognizing that these stories are just words, and he can still take positive, valued actions, even if he has made major mistakes in the past.

*Contact with the present moment*: When Mike is not actively practicing a mindful approach, he may find himself ruminating and lost in memories of times when he let his children down or when he could have done something differently. However, if he can catch himself doing this, then he can return to the present—the only moment in which he can take action—and see if there is something he can do in the here and now that is in line with his parenting values, rather than staying ineffectively fixated on the past.

*Self-as-context*: After half a year of consistently making the effort to connect with his adult children, Mike may even begin to receive invitations from them that he has not initiated himself. For example, he might be invited by his daughter to join the family for Thanksgiving dinner. However, if Mike is fused with a version of self-as-content in which he is "unwanted" and doesn't deserve a "normal" family experience, he may turn down the invitation or simply not show up on the day of the dinner, because attending the dinner does not fit with how he currently conceptualizes himself and his relationship with his family. However, if he is practicing self-as-context skills, he may be able to find a little more space for himself in which he has the flexibility to accept and follow through with the dinner invitation, even if it does not comport with the understanding he has developed over the past 10 years of how deeply (or shallowly) his children want him integrated into their lives. He can have the experience of feeling "unwanted," but he does not have to be defined by that label or that understanding of his relationship with his children.

*Values*: Mike's therapist works with him repeatedly to flesh out his description of his values around being a parent to his children. The values are described, elaborated, and returned to over and over. The therapist assists Mike in identifying multiple exemplars of valued action and contacting—in as much detail as possible—the emotions, bodily sensations, memories, and urges to act that are associated with these values to help make them as fully elaborated and powerful as possible.

# In Closing

Committed action work can be among the most vital and exciting parts of the therapy process. When commitments are made and subsequently achieved, and both client and therapist can see concrete progress in the client's life, it can be life affirming and highly reinforcing! However, it is also important to remember that slips and relapses are an almost inevitable part of any commitment process. Perfect, error-free execution of committed action is not the goal. The goal is to develop larger and more flexible patterns of values-directed behavior that move the client's life forward over time. The ACT therapist should not shy away from discussing the circuitous path of growth and progress with the client ahead of time, in order to inoculate against over-rotation to a direction that is not values-consistent after a given committed action is not achieved. If the purpose of a given committed action is only to achieve the direct extrinsic satisfaction of a behavior well-executed and well-received, then the client is likely to experience frequent aversive responses and disappointments. Thus, the effective therapist will appropriately challenge and prepare the client for a variety of potential outcomes, both to provide practical preparation and to reinforce values-consistent relational framing (Villatte et al., 2015).

Committed action in practice is much more than just identifying a list of goals and planned behaviors. In order to be successfully implemented, it requires all processes in the hexaflex, along with a strong therapeutic relationship. It also involves creating strong relational frames that link planned committed actions with overarching values that can provide ongoing intrinsic reinforcement. When applied and practiced consistently, committed action interventions can be the key to clients moving their lives forward, both now and in the future.

# References

Abramowitz, J. S., Tolin, D. F., & Street, G. P. (2001). Paradoxical effects of thought suppression: A meta-analysis of controlled studies. *Clinical Psychology Review, 21,* 683–703.

Agras, W. S., Walsh, T., Fairburn, C. G. Wilson, G. T., & Kraemer, H.C. (2000). A multicenter comparison of cognitive-behavioral therapy and interpersonal psychotherapy for bulimia nervosa. *Archives of General Psychiatry, 57*(5), 459–466.

American Psychological Association (2016). *Division 12 Society of Clinical Psychology Research-Supported Psychological Treatments.* http://www.div12.org/psychological -treatments/

American Psychological Association (December 2017). Behavioral and cognitive behavioral therapy for chronic low back pain. *Division 12 Society of Clinical Psychology Research-Supported Psychological Treatments.* https://www.div12.org/psy chological-treatments/treatments/behavioral-and-cognitive-behavioral -therapy-for-chronic-low-back-pain

Ariely, D. (2010). *Predictably irrational, revised and expanded edition: The hidden forces that shape our decisions.* NY: Harper Perennial.

Bach, P.A., & McCracken, S. (2002). Best practice guidelines for behavioral interventions. Developed for *Behavioral Health Recovery Management Project.* Bloomington, IL: Fayette Companies & Chestnut Health System.

Bach, P. A., & Moran, D. J. (2008). *ACT in practice: Case conceptualization in acceptance and commitment therapy.* Oakland, CA: New Harbinger.

Baer, R. A., Smith, G. T., Hopkins, J., Krietemeyer, J., & Toney, L. (2006). Using self-report assessment methods to explore facets of mindfulness. *Assessment, 13*(1), 27–45.

Bailey, A., Ciarrochi, J., & Hayes, L. (2012). *Get out of your mind and into your life for teens: A guide to living an extraordinary life.* Oakland, CA: New Harbinger.

Batten, S. V. (2011). *Essentials of acceptance and commitment therapy.* London: Sage.

Bijou, S. W. & Baer, D. M. (1961). *Child development: A systematic and empirical theory. Vol. 1.* Englewood Cliffs, NJ: Prentice-Hall.

Blackledge, J. T. (2015). *Cognitive defusion in practice: A clinician's guide to assessing, observing, and supporting change in your client*. Oakland, CA: New Harbinger.

Blackledge, J. T., & Moran, D. J. (2009). An introduction to relational frame theory for clinicians. *Kokoro no Rinsho, 28*(1), 87–97. (in Japanese).

Blackledge, J. T., Moran, D. J., & Ellis, A. (2009). Bridging the divide: Linking basic science to applied psychotherapeutic interventions—A relational frame theory account of cognitive disputations in rational emotive behavior therapy. *Journal of Cognitive and Rational Emotive Behavior Therapy, 27*, 232–248.

Borkovec, T. D., Abel, J. L., & Newman, H. (1995). Effects of psychotherapy on comorbid conditions in generalized anxiety disorder. *Journal of Consulting and Clinical Psychology, 63*, 479–483.

Brown, L. A., Gaudiano, B. A., & Miller, I. W. (2011). Investigating the similarities and differences between practitioners of second-and third-wave cognitive-behavioral therapies. *Behavior Modification, 35*(2), 187–200.

Capel, C. M. (2012). Mindlessness/mindfulness, classroom practices and quality of early childhood education: An auto-ethnographic and intrinsic case research. *International Journal of Quality & Reliability Management, 29*(6), 666–680.

Capriotti, M. R., Ely, L. J., Snorrason, I., & Woods, D. W. (2015). Acceptance-enhanced behavior therapy for excoriation (skin-picking) disorder in adults: A clinical case series. *Cognitive and Behavioral Practice, 22*(2), 230–239.

Chambless, D. L. & Hollon, S. D. (1998). Defining empirically supported therapies. *Journal of Consulting and Clinical Psychology, 66*(1), 7–18.

Ciarrochi, J., Harris, R., & Bailey, A. (2014). *The weight escape*. Australia: Penguin.

Coyne, L. W., McHugh, L., & Martinez, E. R. (2011). Acceptance and commitment therapy (ACT): Advances and applications with children, adolescents, and families. *Child and adolescent psychiatric clinics of North America, 20*(2), 379–399.

Dahl, J., Plumb, J., & Stewart, I., & Lundgren, T. (2009). *The art and science of valuing in psychotherapy: Helping clients discover, explore, and commit to valued action using acceptance and commitment therapy*. Oakland, CA: New Harbinger.

Deacon, B. J., Fawzy, T. I., Lickel, J. J., & Wolitzky-Taylor, K. B. (2011). Cognitive defusion versus cognitive restructuring in the treatment of negative self-referential thoughts: An investigation of process and outcomes. *Journal of Cognitive Psychotherapy, 25*(3), 218–232.

Eifert, G. H., & Heffner, M. (2003). The effects of acceptance versus control contexts on avoidance of panic-related symptoms. *Journal of Behavior Therapy and Experimental Psychiatry, 34*(3), 293–312.

Feske, U. & Chambless, D. L. (1995). Cognitive behavioral versus exposure only treatment for social phobia: A meta-analysis. *Behavior Therapy, 26*(4), 695–720.

Flessner, C. A., Busch, A. M., Heideman, P. W., & Woods, D. W. (2008). Acceptance-enhanced behavior therapy (AEBT) for trichotillomania and chronic skin picking: exploring the effects of component sequencing. *Behavior Modification, 32,* 579–594.

Follette, W.C., Naugle, A. E., & Linnerooth, P. J. N. (2000). Functional alternatives to traditional assessment and diagnosis. In M. J. Dougher (Ed.), *Clinical behavior analysis* (pp. 99–125). Reno, NV: Context Press.

Forman, E. M., Butryn, M. L., Hoffman, K. L., & Herbert, J. D. (2009). An open trial of an acceptance-based behavioral intervention for weight loss. *Cognitive and Behavioral Practice, 16*(2), 223–235.

Frank, R. I., & Davidson, J. (2014). *The transdiagnostic road map to case formulation and treatment planning: Practical guidance for clinical decision making.* Oakland, CA: New Harbinger.

Frank, E., Kupfer, D. J., Ehlers, C. L., Monk, T. H., Cornes, C., Carter, S., et al. (1994). Interpersonal and social rhythm therapy for bipolar disorder: Integrating interpersonal and behavioral approaches. *The Behavior Therapist, 17,* 143–149.

Frank, E., Kupfer, D. J., Thase, M. E., Mallinger, A. G., Swartz, H. A., Fagiolini, A. M., et al. (2005). Two-year outcomes for interpersonal and social rhythm therapy in individuals with bipolar I disorder. *Archives of General Psychiatry, 62,* 996–1004.

Frank, E., Swartz, H. A., & Kupfer, D. J. (2000). Interpersonal and social rhythm therapy: managing the chaos of bipolar disorder. *Biological Psychiatry, 48,* 593–604.

Frey, B. S. & Osterloh, M. (2002). *Successful management by motivation: Balancing intrinsic and extrinsic incentives.* New York, NY: Springer Publishing Company.

Harris, R. (2009). *ACT made simple: An easy-to-read primer on acceptance and commitment therapy.* Oakland, CA: New Harbinger.

Harvey, A., Watkins, E., Mansell, W., & Shafran, R. (2004). *Cognitive behavioral processes across psychological disorders: A transdiagnostic approach to research and treatment.* Oxford: Oxford University Press.

Hayes, S. C. (n.d.). Acceptance and Commitment Therapy (ACT). Retrieved November 4, 2016, from https://contextualscience.org/act

Hayes, S. C. (2006). ACT beginner workshop. *Workshop presented at the meeting of the Association for Contextual Behavioral Science World Congress II,* London, England.

Hayes, S. C. (1994). Content, context, and the types of psychological acceptance. In S. C. Hayes, N. S. Jacobson, V. M. Follette, & M. J. Dougher (Eds.), *Acceptance and change. Content and context in psychotherapy* (pp. 13–32). Reno, NV: Context Press.

Hayes, S. C. (2005). *Get out of your mind and into your life: The new acceptance and commitment therapy*. Oakland, CA: New Harbinger.

Hayes, S. C., Barnes-Holmes, D., & Roche, B. (2001). *Relational frame theory: A post-Skinnerian account of human language and cognition*. New York: Plenum.

Hayes, S. C., Barnes-Holmes, D., & Wilson, K. W. (2012). Contextual behavioral science: Creating a science more adequate to the challenge of the human condition. *Journal of Contextual Behavioral Science, 1*, 1–16.

Hayes, S. C., Kohlenberg, B. S., & Melancon, S. M. (1989). Avoiding and altering rule-control as a strategy of clinical intervention. In S. C. Hayes (Ed.), *Rule-governed behavior: Cognition, contingencies, and instructional control* (pp. 359–386). New York: Plenum Press.

Hayes, S. C., Luoma, J. B., Bond, F. W., Masuda, A., & Lillis, J. (2006). Acceptance and commitment therapy: Model, processes and outcomes. *Behaviour Research and Therapy, 44*(1), 1–25.

Hayes, S. C., Strosahl, K. D., & Wilson, K. G. (1999). *Acceptance and commitment therapy: An experiential approach to behavior change*. New York, NY: Guilford.

Hayes, S. C., Strosahl, K. D., & Wilson, K. G. (2012). *Acceptance and commitment therapy: The process and practice of mindful change* (2nd edition). New York, NY: Guilford.

Hayes, S. C., & Wilson, K. G. (1994). Acceptance and commitment therapy: Altering the verbal support for experiential avoidance. *The Behavior Analyst, 17*(2), 289.

Herbert, J. D., Gaudiano, B. A., Rheingold, A. A., Myers, V. H., Dalrymple, K., & Nolan, E. M. (2005). Social skills training augments the effectiveness of cognitive behavioral group therapy for social anxiety disorder. *Behavior Therapy, 36*(2), 125–138.

Hooper, N. & Larsson, A. (2015). *The research journey of acceptance and commitment therapy*. United Kingdom: Palgrave Macmillan.

Hopko, D. R., Ryba, M. M., McIndoo, C., & File, A. (2015). Behavioral Activation. *The Oxford Handbook of Cognitive and Behavioral Therapies, 229*.

Kashdan, T. B., Morina, N., & Priebe, S. (2009). Post-traumatic stress disorder, social anxiety disorder, and depression in survivors of the Kosovo War: Experiential avoidance as a contributor to distress and quality of life. *Journal of Anxiety Disorders, 23*(2), 185–196. doi:10.1016/j.janxdis.2008.06.006

Kazantzis, N., Whittington, C., & Dattilio, F. (2010). Meta–analysis of homework effects in cognitive and behavioral therapy: A replication and extension. *Clinical Psychology: Science and Practice, 17*(2), 144–156.

Kendell, R., & Jablensky, A. (2014). Distinguishing between the validity and utility of psychiatric diagnoses. *American Journal of Psychiatry*.

Kessler, R. C., Chiu, W. T., Demler, O. & Walters, E. E. (2005). Prevalence, severity, and comorbidity of 12-month *DSM-IV* disorders in the national comorbidity survey replication. *Archives of General Psychiatry, 62*, 617–627.

Killingsworth, M. A., & Gilbert, D. T. (2010). A wandering mind is an unhappy mind. *Science, 330*, 932.

Klerman, G. L., Weissman, M. M., Rounsaville, B. J., & Chevron, E. S. (1984) *Interpersonal psychotherapy of depression*. New York: Basic Books.

Langer, E. J. (1989). *Mindfulness*. Boston, MA: Addison-Wesley/Addison Wesley Longman.

Lejuez, C. W., Hopko, D. R., Acierno, R., Daughters, S. B., & Pagoto, S. L. (2011). Ten year revision of the brief behavioral activation treatment for depression: revised treatment manual. *Behavior Modification, 35*(2), 111–161.

Lindsley, O. R. (1991). From technical jargon to plain English for application. *Journal of Applied Behavior Analysis, 24*(3), 449–458.

Linehan, M. M. (1993). *Skills training manual for treating borderline personality disorder*. New York, NY: Guilford.

Locke, E.A. & Latham, G.P. (2006). New directions in goal-setting theory. *Current Directions in Psychological Science, 15*(5), 265–268.

Lundgren, T., Luoma, J. B., Dahl, J., Strosahl, K., & Melin, L. (2012). The Bull's-Eye Values Survey: A psychometric evaluation. *Cognitive and Behavioral Practice, 19*(4), 518–526.

Luoma, J. B., Hayes, S. C., & Walser, R. D. (2007). *Learning ACT: An acceptance & commitment therapy skills-training manual for therapists*. Oakland, CA: New Harbinger & Reno, NV: Context Press.

Malkoff-Schwartz, S., Frank, E., Anderson, B., Sherrill, J. T., Siegel, L., Patterson, D., & Kupfer, D. J. (1998). Stressful life events and social rhythm disruption in the onset of manic and depressive bipolar episodes. *Archives of General Psychiatry, 55*, 702–707.

Mansell, W., Harvey, A., Watkins, E., & Shafran, R. (2009). Conceptual foundations of the transdiagnostic approach to CBT. *Journal of Cognitive Psychotherapy, 23*, 6–19.

Markowitz, J. C., & Weissman, M. M. (2004). Interpersonal psychotherapy: Principles and applications. *World Psychiatry, 3*(3), 136–139.

Marlatt, G. A. (1994). Addiction, mindfulness, and acceptance. In S. C. Hayes, N. S., Jacobson, V. M. Follette, & M. J. Dougher (Eds.) *Acceptance and change: Content and context in psychotherapy* (pp. 175–197). Reno, NV: Context Press.

Martell, C. R., Dimidjian, S., & Herman-Dunn, R. (2013). *Behavioral activation for depression: A clinician's guide.* New York, NY: Guilford Press.

McCracken, L. M. (2013). Committed action: An application of the psychological flexibility model to activity patterns in chronic pain. *The Journal of Pain, 14*(8), 828–835.

McCracken, L. M., & Vowles, K. E. (2014). Acceptance and commitment therapy and mindfulness for chronic pain: model, process, and progress. *American Psychologist,* 69(2), 178.

McCracken, L. M., & Yang, S. Y. (2006). The role of values in a contextual cognitive-behavioral approach to chronic pain. *Pain, 123*(1), 137–145.

McLean, P. D., Whittal, M. L., Thordarson, D. S., Taylor, S., Söchting, I., Koch, W. J., Paterson, R., & Anderson, K. W. (2001). Cognitive versus behavior therapy in the group treatment of obsessive-compulsive disorder. *Journal of Consulting and Clinical Psychology,* 69(2), 205.

Michael, J. (1993). Establishing operations. *The Behavior Analyst, 16*(2), 191–206.

Miltenberger, R. (2012). *Behavior modification: Principles and procedures* (6th edition). Boston, MA: Cengage Learning.

Monk, T. H., Flaherty, J. F., Frank, E., Hoskinson, K., Kupfer, D. J. (1990). The Social rhythm metric: An instrument to quantify the daily rhythms of life. *Journal of Nervous and Mental Disease, 178,* 120–126.

Moran, D. J. (2015). Acceptance and commitment training in the workplace. *Current Opinions in Psychology, 2,* 26–31.

Moran, D. J. (2014). Balancing what's hot and what's not: Putting mindfulness in harmony with commitment. *Invited address at the Association for Contextual Behavioral Science conference.* Minneapolis, MN.

Moran, D. J. (2013). *Building safety commitment.* Illinois: Valued Living Books.

Moran, D. J. (2013b). How a leader speaks: Using commitment-based leadership to deliver feedback to employees. *Journal of Applied Radical Behavior Analysis, AARBA Conference Proceedings,* 9–16.

National Institute on Drug Abuse (2017). *National Institute on Drug Abuse archives: Treating cocaine addiction.* https://archives.drugabuse.gov/TXManuals/CBT/CBT4 .html

Nietzsche, F. (1895). *Twilight of the idols.* Indianapolis, IN: Hackett Publishing Company.

Nolen-Hoeksema, S., & Watkins, E. R. (2011). A heuristic for developing transdiagnostic models of psychopathology: Explaining multifinality and divergent trajectories. *Perspectives on Psychological Science, 6*, 589–609.

O'Neil, J. & Conzemius, A. (2006). *The power of SMART goals: Using goals to improve student learning.* NY: Solution Tree Press.

Ong, J. C., Manber, R., Segal, Z., Xia, Y., Shapiro, S. & Wyatt, J. K. (2014). A randomized controlled trial of mindfulness meditation for chronic insomnia. *Sleep, 37*(9), 1553–1563.

Öst, L. G., Havnen, A., Hansen, B., & Kvale, G. (2015). Cognitive behavioral treatments of obsessive–compulsive disorder. A systematic review and meta-analysis of studies published 1993–2014. *Clinical psychology review, 40*, 156–169.

Papa, A., Sewell, M. T., Garrison-Diehn, C., & Rummel, C. (2013). A randomized open trial assessing the feasibility of behavioral activation for pathological grief responding. *Behavior Therapy, 44*(4), 639–650.

Persons, J. B. (1986). The advantages of studying psychological phenomena rather than psychiatric diagnoses. *American Psychologist, 41*(11), 1252.

Roemer, L., & Orsillo, S. M. (2002). Expanding our conceptualization of and treatment for generalized anxiety disorder: Integrating mindfulness/acceptance–based approaches with existing cognitive–behavioral models. *Clinical Psychology: Science and Practice, 9*(1), 54–68.

Roemer, L., & Orsillo, S. M. (2012) Anxiety Disorders: Acceptance, compassion and Wisdom. In C. K. Germer & R. D. Siegel (Eds.). *Wisdom and compassion in psychotherapy: Deepening mindfulness in clinical practice* (pp. 234–248). New York, NY: Guilford Press.

Sartre, J. P. (1963). *Essays in Aesthetics*, translated by Wade Baskin. New York, NY: The Citadel Press.

Smalley, S. L., Loo, S. K., Hale, T. S., Shrestha, A., McGough, J., Flook, L., & Reise, S. (2009). Mindfulness and attention deficit hyperactivity disorder. *Journal of Clinical Psychology, 65*(10), 1087–1098.

Stewart, I., & Roche, B. (2013). Relational frame theory: An overview. In S. Dymond, & B. Roche (Eds.), *Advances in relational frame theory: Research and application* (pp. 51–71). Oakland, CA: New Harbinger.

Stoddard, J. A., & Afari, N. (2014). *The big book of ACT metaphors: A practitioner's guide to experiential exercises and metaphors in acceptance and commitment therapy.* Oakland, CA: New Harbinger.

Törneke, N. (2010). *Learning RFT: An introduction to relational frame theory and its clinical application.* Oakland, CA: New Harbinger.

Törneke, N., Luciano, C., & Valdivia Salas, S. (2008). Rule-governed behavior and psychological problems. *International Journal of Psychology and Psychological Therapy, 8*(2), 141–156.

Turner, J. S., & Leach, D. J. (2012). Behavioural activation therapy: philosophy, concepts, and techniques. *Behaviour Change, 29*(2), 77–96.

Twohig, M. P., Hayes, S. C., Plumb, J. C., Pruitt, L. D., Collins, A. B., Hazlett-Stevens, H., & Woidneck, M. R. (2010). A randomized clinical trial of Acceptance and Commitment Therapy vs. Progressive Relaxation Training for obsessive compulsive disorder. *Journal of Consulting and Clinical Psychology, 78*(5), 705–716. http://doi.org/10.1037/a0020508

van Os, J. Delespaul, P., Wigman, J., Myin-Germeys, I., & Wichers, M. (2013). Beyond DSM and ICD: Introducing "precision diagnosis" for psychiatry using momentary assessment technology. *World Psychiatry, 12*(2), 113–117.

Villatte, J. L., Vilardaga, R., Villatte, M., Vilardaga, J. C. P., Atkins, D. C., & Hayes, S. C. (2016). Acceptance and Commitment Therapy modules: Differential impact on treatment processes and outcomes. *Behaviour Research and Therapy, 77*, 52–61.

Villatte, M., Villatte, J. L., & Hayes, S. C. (2015). *Mastering the clinical conversation: Language as intervention.* New York, NY: Guilford.

Wenzlaff, R. M., & Wegner, D. M. (2000). Thought suppression. *Annual Review of Psychology, 51*(1), 59–91.

Westrup, D. (2014). *Advanced acceptance and commitment therapy: The experienced practitioner's guide to optimizing delivery.* Oakland, CA: New Harbinger.

Wilson, K. G., & DuFrene, T. (2009). *Mindfulness for two: An acceptance and commitment therapy approach to mindfulness in psychotherapy.* Oakland, CA: New Harbinger.

Woods, D. W., & Twohig, M. P. (2008). *Trichotillomania: An ACT-enhanced behavior therapy approach therapist guide.* Oxford, United Kingdom: Oxford University Press.

World Health Organization (2014). *Mental health: a state of well-being.* http://www.who.int/features/factfiles/mental_health/en/

Zettle, R. D., & Hayes, S. C. (1986). Dysfunctional control by client verbal behavior: The context of reason giving. *The Analysis of Verbal Behavior, 4*, 30–38.

**Daniel J. Moran, PhD, BCBA-D,** is founder and director of the MidAmerican Psychological Institute, and founder of Pickslyde Consulting. He coauthored *ACT in Practice* with Patricia Bach, as well as other contextual behavioral science publications. Moran has appeared on The Learning Channel, Animal Planet, and FOX News discussing obsessive-compulsive disorder (OCD) and hoarding. He is also a recognized acceptance and commitment therapy (ACT) trainer, board-certified behavior analyst, and past president and fellow of the Association for Contextual Behavioral Science (ACBS).

**Patricia A. Bach, PhD,** is clinical assistant professor at the University of Central Florida. She completed her PhD at the University of Nevada, and has been providing psychotherapy, supervision, and training in ACT for more than fifteen years. Bach is a past president of the ACBS, and has coauthored a book on ACT case conceptualization.

**Sonja Batten, PhD,** is a clinical psychologist with a specialization in traumatic stress, who has worked in policy, clinical, and research leadership positions in the public and private sector. She is currently a senior associate at Booz Allen Hamilton in Washington, DC. Batten is a recognized ACT trainer, past president and fellow of ACBS, and author of *Essentials of Acceptance and Commitment Therapy.*

# Index

# D

# MORE BOOKS *from*
# NEW HARBINGER PUBLICATIONS

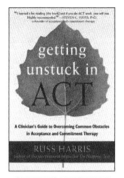

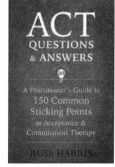
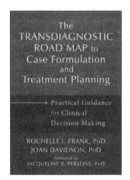